Asia's Banking CEOs

The Future of Finance in Asia

Asia's Banking CEOs

The Future of Finance in Asia

Peter Hoflich

THE ASIAN BANKER®

STRATEGIC BUSINESS INTELLIGENCE FOR THE FINANCIAL SERVICES COMMUNITY

John Wiley & Sons (Asia) Pte. Ltd.

Copyright © 2008 John Wiley & Sons (Asia) Pte. Ltd.
Published in 2008 by John Wiley & Sons (Asia) Pte. Ltd.
2 Clementi Loop, #02-01, Singapore 129809

This publication is designed to provide accurate and authoritative information in regard to the subject matter covered. It is sold with the understanding that the publisher is not engaged in rendering professional services. If professional advice or other expert assistance is required, the services of a competent professional person should be sought.

Other Wiley Editorial Offices

John Wiley & Sons, 111 River Street, Hoboken, NJ 07030, USA
John Wiley & Sons, The Atrium Southern Gate, Chichester P019 8SQ, England
John Wiley & Sons (Canada), Ltd., 5353 Dundas Street West, Suite 400, Toronto, Ontario M9B 6H8, Canada
John Wiley & Sons Australia Ltd., 42 McDougall Street, Milton, Queensland 4064, Australia
Wiley-VCH, Boschstrasse 12, D-69469 Weinheim, Germany

Library of Congress Cataloging-in-Publication Data

ISBN 978-0-470-82359-0

Typeset in 11/13 point, Minion by diacriTech, India.
Printed in Singapore by Markono Print Media Pte. Ltd.
10 9 8 7 6 5 4 3 2 1

CONTENTS

ACKNOWLEDGMENTS

There are many people to thank for getting this project under way, but none more than Emmanuel Daniel, president and editor-in-chief at The Asian Banker, for having so much confidence in me and putting me into a program of profiling senior bankers. His vision in founding a unique company that addresses a very real need for business information for the financial services industry in Asia is impressive, and the wealth of understanding he has about the field is as inspirational as his raft of ideas. He also conducted most of the interviews that these profiles are based on.

There are also the many senior executives willing to tell me their stories, both included in this book and not, that I wish to thank, along with their support staff, who answered phones and emails, sent maps, and dealt with confused taxi drivers. And I can't forget Nick and his crew at John Wiley & Sons for their persistence in getting the project up and moving. Thanks, guys.

I also have to thank my family for their patience in dealing with the long hours I needed to spend in front of the computer, as well as listening patiently to the occasional anecdotes about banking (which they really don't understand). Last, the team at The Asian Banker also deserve my gratitude for their spirit and camaraderie.

FOREWORD

One of the best business books I have read in many years. It accurately describes our recent history in banking, especially in the fast-moving consumer banking world. It is also a book about strategy, management and innovation, but, more difficult, it is a unique gallery of portraits of leaders who made Asian financial services what it is today, with managers who taught us many lessons and whose clarity of analysis, efficiency in action and contributions to the industry and society will continue to influence all of us and help us building the future of banking in our region.

I first read the manuscript like a history book, enjoying its easy style, its structure and format, its wealth of information and the various angles Peter Hoflich selected in his descriptions of the institutions and their leaders. Having studied most of these banks and knowing personally some of the characters, I could appreciate the accuracy of the descriptions and the pertinence of the analysis. I learned a lot, understood even more, and much better, I could also picture some of my friends telling their stories, all different in personality, style, and way of managing, accurately reflected in these interviews.

Re-reading it several times, I started underlining, making notes, going back to my own references, comparing, studying . . . and I enjoyed it even more.

Several friends helped me in this review. First, a "scholar," a bright young man who studied in the US, worked on strategies in a consulting firm, completed his studies at INSEAD in France and Singapore, and now a key executive in a leading bank in Asia. For him, these are some of the best "case studies" he has ever read, at par with the famous Harvard case studies on Citibank, a superb base for study, discussion and reflection. And that's what we did, a full afternoon, flipping through the profiles, comparing the strategic approaches, the searches for opportunities, and the qualities of implementation.

A human resources specialist helped me also. A lady who specialises in building "high performance teams" for financial institutions. We talked about the profiles, the leadership skills, the ability of these leaders to find people, to create action, and to mobilize their organisations. We also noted their passion, their humility, and most importantly, their resilience.

Finally, I went to two banker friends who also know some of the banks and their management teams. I wanted to go deeper in my search for information, understand what happened in these cases from their points of view. They quickly concurred with the facts described in the book, and both re-directed the conversations to their own banks. They were already using this book to reflect on their own opportunities, issues and action plans.

Bankers, that's what this book will make you do too!

This book is a must.

Reading it, you will discover banking in Asia.

Studying it, you will understand its development.

Reflecting on it you will be able to learn even more about yourself, about your opportunities, and your own way to demonstrate your leadership.

Thank you, Peter.

Philippe Paillart

Philippe Paillart, who resides in Singapore, is a board member or an advisor to financial institutions in Europe, the Middle East and Asia. He has also been on the boards of Diners Club (France), Citibank (Germany), Chartered Trust (UK), Ford Financials (US), Standard Chartered Bank (UK), Renaissance Credit (Russia), Link Financial (UK) and also Kwong On Bank (Hong Kong) Bank of the Philippine Islands (the Philippines), Standard Chartered Bank (Malaysia), and DBS (Singapore).

INTRODUCTION
TEN YEARS AFTER THE CRISIS

They are the fuel that ignites the engines of Asian growth, priming fires in the hearth of bustling new economies such as China, India, and Vietnam; they power the developed hubs of Hong Kong and Singapore, and they form the massively padded structure of the world's second-largest economy, Japan.

Banks in Asia are everywhere, and their branches sit on the corners of bustling city streets in every part of the world's largest continent—there seems to be no end to them. It's common to see three of them built next to each other along busy streets in Taipei, Bangkok, Manila, Shanghai, and Seoul. A visit to any city means familiarizing yourself with their logos and their colors, and observing the visible imprint they have on their cities and countries. Asian finance keeps a mighty machine, home to nearly four billion people, humming, and all eyes that look to Asia are in one way or another really looking at their banks.

A lot has changed in Asia during its decade of rebuilding, the ten years from 1997 to 2007, and naturally this also applies to banks. The crisis that dominated the last part of the second millennium left deep scars on many countries in Asia. But across the board, no other sector saw the type of consolidation that the banks did. Since they are such an important function of each economy, bad banks don't go away—they just become new banks.

The legacy of 1997 is a heavy one. The scars are the deepest in Thailand and Indonesia, where bankers still shudder when they think back to the dark days. In South Korea, bankers remember the period that they call the IMF Crisis. For them, the event marked the time when the doors to the country were blasted open and stayed that way. The financial services industry was privatized—some would say forcibly, some would say for the country's own benefit—and the world rushed in to buy up the country's banks. Bank ownership is now one of the most contentious issues in Asian banking, and Korea produces a good chunk of Asia's banking news. Since the crisis, Asia's banks have had their own dramas: they have been hit by SARS, credit card crises of one sort or another, even bizarre IT breakdowns.

Ironically, the two biggest and most interesting markets in Asia, China and India, have not yet been affected by any of these crises. Last time around, their banking industries had not developed enough to fall into the greed traps of bubble economies. In China, so far only one bank, Guangdong Development Bank, has fallen on such hard times by over-extending its businesses and running out of capital, and it had to be bailed out by a consortium of investors led by Citigroup.

But now, given the outrageous growth of China and India, the question is: how long can they keep up their momentum? It can't be forever. The year 2007 wasn't a repeat of 1997 for either of them, but how about 2008? Or 2009?

The question of runaway growth is particularly acute in China for those confident international institutions that have invested billions into the country's banks. Goldman Sachs, the bellwether of Wall Street, made its largest single investment in a Chinese bank, and it stands to earn billions—if it can survive the three year lock-in period. Many don't remember the whirlwind of debate in 2004 over whether China would suffer a "hard landing or soft landing;" the chatter has trickled out for lack of interest, but may resume after the Beijing Olympics of August 2008 when a post-games anticlimax sets in, possibly bringing a slowdown and a fresh round of bad loans.

There are 25 portraits of bank leaders in this book. And while each of them is different, all of these fifty-something men and women have some things in common: they have all padded the many long corridors of their institutions to the point that they know them inside out; all of them are passionate about their work; and (nearly) all of them have worked at more than one financial institution (in many cases the same financial institution—Citi).

And more than anything else, all of them also head pillars of their communities. As busy hives of lending, banks find the niches of the economy that need them to grow and fill them. And if they do it responsibly, then everyone is better off. If they are foolhardy and mismanage their growth, then sooner or later they will begin to hear a persistent whooshing sound as their balance sheet goes down the toilet.

Among them are a few entrepreneurs and dreamers, virtuosos who have mastered the skills of basic banking but hope for something new and unique. Others are minders, struggling with the various tasks that are part of tending their institutions while the economy floats them along. Yet others are still ambitious explorers, travelers who have found themselves near a fantastic opportunity and are willing to go wherever that might take them as long as they can steer.

Each leader, besides having a distinctive leadership style and goals, is also completely unique as a private individual. Saito Hiroshi, head of Mizuho Corporate Bank, which would be the ninth-largest in Asia if it was regarded as an individual bank, enjoys reading books about artists in his spare time; Syed Ali Raza, head of National Bank of Pakistan, the largest in that country, is a voracious reader of biographies and pulp fiction; Banthoon Lamsam is passionate about geomancy, the Chinese art of *feng shui*.

One of the strengths of The Asian Banker is the various programs it has to connect with the most senior people in financial institutions all over Asia. It engages with them to find out from the top down what makes these institutions hum. Getting to know a leader in the relaxed setting of his or her office is certainly different from seeing the same person on display at a results meeting, and this comes out in these profiles of some of Asia's most influential individuals. But besides getting to know the individuals, a bottom-up approach to learning the banks' numbers and their operational challenges is also vital; and somewhere in the middle we hope to reach the truth.

When Nick Wallwork of John Wiley & Sons approached me to write a book, my immediate thought was to propose what had been a dream project of mine for some time: a collection of profiles of the leaders that control Asia's top financial services institutions. I'd been writing short profiles of these people for years in the pages of *The Asian Banker Journal,* and was keen to expand them.

With the book format, I have been able to bring out some of the nuances of the characters that I am describing, as well as the banks they lead. I have also been able to put them more into a context of regional trends, and cross-reference them if their stories have relevant commonalities.

Of course, the danger of portraying business characters is between the time the manuscript is turned over and when the book reaches the stores some months later, a lot can happen, and some of the leaders may have moved on.

But hopefully, even if more than one of the bank leaders profiled is no longer at the reins, the book can still give a sense of what kind of a bank has been turned over to the successor. It can also perhaps give an idea of what that successor will have to *undo* to put his or her own stamp on the company. And of course, nobody can change a bank's footprint overnight, not to mention its niche, its character, or its flair.

Going into uncertain times, eyes are turning to Asia. Its conservative banks have been stable throughout the sub-prime crisis and resulting credit crunch that has affected banks in the U.S. and Europe and judged them so harshly; their exposure to "toxic" collateralized debt obligations has also been negligible. And for the global experts running the banks with so many decades of banking experience each, it may be possible to say that they've already seen it all and are looking ahead in great anticipation.

For many, Asia is a mystery, but there is no reason its banks should be.

Chapter 1
The Giants—Big and Bigger

A Giant's Giant

What have the eyes of Jiang Jianqing seen during his long rise to the top of China's largest bank?

Industrial and Commercial Bank of China Chairman Jiang Jianqing is responsible for so much more than the already mammoth task of seeing the bank through its preparations for what was the world's largest IPO.

To many, Industrial and Commercial Bank of China (ICBC) defies the imagination. The largest bank in the most populous nation on earth, it leads the country in nearly every count except for number of branches. That expensive honor is still held by the shambling Agricultural Bank of China (ABC) with its 31,000 outlets.

ICBC's initial public offering (IPO) of 22 percent of its shares in October 2006 was the largest the world had seen, and helped the bank raise nearly US$22 billion. By the end of the first day of trading, the bank was officially the world's fifth most-valuable bank, just behind JPMorgan Chase. At the outset, the listing was set to be one of the year's most ambitious projects. Through the course of the preparation it actually became even more ambitious; what had been intended as a Hong Kong-only listing eventually became the first major

Jiang Jianqing
Reproduced by permission of
TAB International

dual listing in Hong Kong and Shanghai. It was a fiendishly difficult exercise to pull off, and seven investment banks were needed to get the job done.

Confidence in the bank has been high since the listing: by July 2007, it had become the largest bank in the world by market capitalization, even though many other banks have larger asset bases—such as HSBC, Citi, and Bank of America. At current rates of asset growth, ICBC will soon be the largest bank by assets in the Asia Pacific region, passing Japan's lumbering mega-banks in 2011, with its main domestic competitor China Construction Bank (CCB) close behind. Watch out HSBC, Citi, and Bank of America.

A DRAGON AWAKENS

But the bank didn't always have the confidence of the marketplace, or even the Chinese government. With its four largest banks wallowing in non-performing loans (NPLs), and ICBC's level of bad loans at 19.1 percent at the end of 2004, the government chose CCB and Bank of China (BOC) for capital injections to spruce them up. In December 2003, those banks received US$22.5 billion each (in the case of BOC, US$3 billion of that was received in the form of 7.1 million ounces of gold) with the stipulation that they use the money to prepare for IPOs. In so doing, the plan was to instill the banks with greater transparency and force them to take the bitter pill of adopting international standards; similar actions for ICBC and ABC were left for later.

The much larger ICBC finally got a smaller capital injection of US$15 billion in April 2005, nearly a year and a half later. It then worked with China Huarong asset management company to resolve its NPLs, eventually bringing them down below 3.29 percent in mid-2007.

One year after the capital injection, in April 2006, it had three significant investors: Wall Street investment bank Goldman Sachs, German insurer Allianz, and financial services company American Express. Collectively, they had spent US$3.8 billion for an 8.5 percent stake in the lender, and clearly they saw something in the bank's incredible franchise, which includes more than 17,000 branches,

> **ICBC has 17,000 branches, 2.41 million corporate customers, and 170 million individual customers. The bank had 50 million online clients at the end of 2006, and adds millions more each year.**

2.41 million corporate customers, and 170 million individual customers. American Express has worked with the bank since 2004 issuing co-branded classic and gold cards.

The investment stands to pay off for these financiers. The boldest, Goldman Sachs, saw its US$2.5 billion investment for a 5.75 percent stake—its largest ever in a single institution—blossom to over US$6 billion in only the six months between the initial investment and the IPO. The stake continues to grow as the bank does. The catch is that the investors are locked in for three years. So while it is literally "money in the bank," time will tell if this is figuratively true as well.

They are called "strategic investments," but the question is: whose strategy? The largest bank in China, with funds and protection available from the central government, hardly needed further capital; from the start, the bank's chairman, Jiang Jianqing, was interested in these investments not for their capital but for their knowledge, experience, technology, friendship, goodwill, and branding. In some cases, this means US$3.5 billion dollars in goodwill, but it's all paying off. Diversification of ownership helps Jiang with corporate governance, as well as potential joint ventures and other projects. It is all part of the bank's movement from a domestic sluggard burdened by massive infrastructure to a global giant leveraging its massive distribution and the strength of scale with imported risk management and IT expertise.

One part of the puzzle is corporate internationalization and brand building, a topic of great interest for Jiang and also China's leaders; ICBC, like many of the other Chinese banks, has been on an internationalization trail through its interaction with its strategic investors, which followed through with the IPO, and the global journey has continued on after its listing. Clearly, the bank will continue to expand overseas as long as there are Chinese companies venturing abroad.

The roots of the bank's internationalization started early in the millennium in Hong Kong. ICBC has not had the same presence overseas as BOC, China's de-facto foreign exchange bank, which has a network of overseas branches and runs Hong Kong's second-largest bank, Bank of China (Hong Kong). But taking a page out of BOC's book, ICBC established a base in Hong Kong by buying the listed Union Bank of Hong Kong in 2000 and renaming it ICBC (Asia) in 2001; this was supplemented in 2003 with the purchase of the Hong Kong retail banking operations of Fortis Bank. In 2007, it bought a small bank in Macao, a safe bet and relatively close to home, before looking further and buying an even smaller bank in Indonesia.

Then, in late 2007, it spent US$5.5 billion, fully one quarter of China's annual outward investments, on a 20 percent stake in Standard Bank. As South Africa's largest bank, the deal wins ICBC access to the bank's 951 branches in 18 African countries—and 100 outside of the continent—and opens up the possibility of joint venture operations all around Africa. The deal represented the single largest ever private investment in the continent and by the end of 2007 the largest overseas investment by a Chinese bank. The bank continues to shop around, looking at small banks in Thailand and other Asian markets, and possibly resource-rich Australia as well.

ENTER JIANG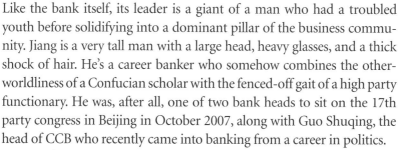

Like the bank itself, its leader is a giant of a man who had a troubled youth before solidifying into a dominant pillar of the business community. Jiang is a very tall man with a large head, heavy glasses, and a thick shock of hair. He's a career banker who somehow combines the other-worldliness of a Confucian scholar with the fenced-off gait of a high party functionary. He was, after all, one of two bank heads to sit on the 17th party congress in Beijing in October 2007, along with Guo Shuqing, the head of CCB who recently came into banking from a career in politics.

Now that nearly every senior Wall Street banker has passed through his reception area, the long-serving banker has an enviable list of connections that include Hank Paulson, now Secretary of the Treasury of the U.S., and Kenneth Chenault, CEO of American Express. With senior leaders, Jiang is an immaculate host who is the epitome of dignified formality. Paul Calello, now chief executive officer of Credit Suisse's global investment bank, met him on many occasions as the bank worked on ICBC's 2006 IPO, always conducting business properly through professional translators. It was only when they met informally in Switzerland and he was showing Jiang around that Calello found out that Jiang was a near-fluent English speaker.

Born in 1953 in Shanghai, Jiang came of age when the Cultural Revolution was in full swing. Like many of the senior bankers and business leaders of his generation, Jiang lost part of his youth to the country's wrangling with class struggle as he was sent to a village in rural Jiangxi for six years to work on a farm. Further experience as a contract worker in a coal mine in Henan province instilled in him a steely work ethic that he has kept with him for the rest of his career, and helped him to not just survive in politics but excel.

After leaving his work in the mines, Jiang started his career in the Jiangan banking office of the People's Bank of China in 1979, at that time the only commercial bank in China. He attended the Shanghai University of Finance and Economics in the evenings from 1981 to 1984 and graduated with a degree in finance and economics. Jiang joined ICBC when it was founded in 1984, working in the Shanghai branch.

He continued his studies at Shanghai's Jiao Tong University for a master's degree in database administration and received a Ph.D. in management in 1999. The school would later invite him back to be a guest professor.

Jiang rose to prominent positions at the bank before moving off to Shanghai City Cooperative Bank, which eventually became Bank of Shanghai, from 1995 to 1997 to serve as general manager. He returned to ICBC in 1997 as general manager of all of Shanghai for the bank. In 1999, the year he received his doctorate, he became the bank's vice chairman and executive vice president, before finally taking his current position as chairman and president of ICBC in February 2000. As a Shanghai native in banking in the 1990s, Jiang was in the right place at the right time when the country's leadership, under Shanghai-connected personalities such as Jiang Zemin and Zhu Rongji, looked favorably upon the coastal city.

When China signed its agreement with the World Trade Organization in 2001, a move that would eventually "level the playing field" for foreign banks in China (and Chinese banks outside of China), Jiang was optimistic about the changes. He used the five-year preparation period to focus on restructuring the bank's business operations and improving the bank's IT infrastructure. This included a focus on electronic banking, credit risk evaluation, and marketing outreach. He also got started right away on the long, arduous task of preparing the bank for its listing.

> **The bank had 50 million online clients at the end of 2006, and adds millions more each year.**

Clearly the bank needed many changes if it was going to make it. But Jiang kept his eye on banks such as HSBC and Citi for inspiration, knowing that these were the right institutions for a bank of ICBC's size to emulate. But with 580,000 employees and 38,000 outlets in 2000, which were the main contributors to the bank's bracing cost-to-income ratio of 63.6 percent, the bank needed drastic rationalizing to reach those global standards.

At the time, ICBC had clunky infrastructure and ran 21 provincial data centers. Jiang trimmed away the majority of branch locations that were less desirable, eventually coming up with 17,000 of the most profitable ones. The move was vital by 2002 when China's banks were "freed" to become more commercial. He also brought staff levels down to 360,000 by 2006, the same level as when the bank started in 1984 (but with 20 times the assets).

With his training in IT, Jiang made sure that the bank consolidated its many data centers. By the end of 2006, it reported a cost-to-income ratio of half of what it was in 2000. The data consolidation helped ICBC keep on top of customer service and roll out new businesses. As a result, its fee income quintupled in four years from 2000 to 2004. The bank also went from a loss of US$212 million in 1999 to profits of US$6.37 billion in 2006.

And so, even in the midst of restructuring ICBC for its eventual listing, the bank was passed over for recapitalization by the central government in favor of money for CCB and BOC. Jiang, with his cool demeanor and patient mien, did not take this preference out of context. It was important to note that everything comes with time, he said. ICBC was a more difficult bank to restructure and needed more work.

THE SURVIVOR

Restructuring such a massive organization was an incredibly arduous task, one that could certainly ruin a man's career just as easily as it could make it. The bank was also burdened by legacy NPLs that had grown out of an uncommercial era when the bank was a policy lender to industry. Jiang made sure that the bank got cracking on its credit risk systems, and managed to keep the level of NPLs on new loans from the early decade down to 1.8 percent; while legacy NPLs stood at over 20 percent, at least no new ones were adding to the problem.

But making changes to the company's infrastructure could not be done without looking at its people. Jiang had to focus on improving the bank's corporate culture to get it to match international standards for such things as bad-loan classification, as well as proper efficiency, quality, and management.

The bank is still not up to speed on its risk management, but in some ways this has proved fortuitous—when the temptation was there to buy collateralized debt obligations (CDOs) from the investment banks that the bank is close to, less sophisticated risk management capabilities kept ICBC away... and out of trouble. Citi, UBS, Morgan Stanley, Merrill Lynch, and Bear Stearns, international banks that Chinese banks sometimes admire, can only wish that they were so lucky: Jiang has survived both Prince and O'Neill of Citi and Merrill, retaining a seat at the top of China's banking world.

Jiang has also moved the bank away from the focus defined in its name as "industrial," and more toward another "I"—that of the individual. The bank started off early focusing on mortgage loans. It has also built a fine reputation for retail banking, raising the proportion of retail banking in its business focus from 9 percent in 1999 to over 20 percent in 2006. As the bank's retail banking franchise continues to grow, its exposure to the manufacturing sector keeps dropping.

In The Asian Banker's Excellence in Retail Financial Services program, held annually since 2002, ICBC has won either the Best Retail Bank in China overall award or the Best State-owned Retail Bank in China award every year. In 2007, it also won the Best Multi-Channel Banking award, recognizing its blend of branches, ATMs, and telephone and Internet banking as ways of reaching out to its clients, as well as its mobile phone and self-service banking center.

Jiang also invested in his online banking platform in 2003. As a result, he could reach out to millions more customers via the virtual channel. The bank had 50 million online clients at the end of 2006, and adds millions more each year.

Jiang knows that any bank can find a way to show profits in the short run, but he'd rather produce long-term, sustainable returns. Because of immature capital markets, money stays in the financial system in China, but ICBC is adjusting to the structure by selling financial products such as insurance, securities, and bonds. Jiang wants the bank to develop wealth management products to make better use of its funding book, since its deposits are still much greater than its loans.

And yet, despite the bank's high loan growth, the business potential is even greater as there are parts of the sector that are neglected and have a difficult time getting financing. Small and medium-sized enterprises (SMEs) typically pay interest rates that are 20 percent higher than those paid by large corporations because of the perceived risk in lending to them and also because they are poorly understood. Jiang is working on setting up an SME unit for his bank so that the playing field will be leveled. As big companies start to get more finance from capital markets, SMEs will become more important to Jiang. The bank has piloted offices to lend to SMEs in costal areas such as Zhejiang and Jiangsu provinces as well as Shanghai, which have helped the bank gain experience and train employees.

Working from the ground up for more than 20 years, the head of ICBC has built a thorough knowledge of the workings of his huge bank. Growing with China throughout the 1980s and 1990s, and especially during the country's breakneck economic expansion of the new century, has made Jiang into the perfect witness of the China growth story. Clearly Jiang's work in molding the bank into what it is today has been indispensable.

But preparing the bank for its current status is merely part one of the plan for the bank. ICBC's IPO and internationalization are now the first chapter of an amazing new story that will develop the bank into a formidable global player. With Jiang only in his fifties, and close to the political elite in China and many other countries, he is sure to still see much of this story run its course.

Scanning the Horizon

A decade of deflation can't keep a good bank down

It may be one of the biggest banks in Asia, but it's still got problems. Saito Hiroshi, president and CEO of Mizuho Corporate Bank, hopes to solve them by developing his wanderlust.

ALTHOUGH Mizuho Corporate Bank is a part of Mizuho Financial Group (Mizuho FG) alongside Mizuho Bank, Mizuho Trust and Banking, and Mizuho Securities, the corporate lender would be one of world's largest banks if it were to stand on its own. With assets of US$599 billion as of March 2007, Mizuho Corporate Bank would be Asia's seventh largest, falling between Bank of China and Norinchukin Bank according to The Asian Banker 300, a ranking of Asia's largest banks. It would also be Japan's third largest, larger than Norinchukin Bank, with US$577 billion, and Mizuho Bank, with US$566 billion. As it stands, Mizuho collectively is Asia's second-largest banking group.

This status probably won't last for long, though—Asian

Saito Hiroshi
Reproduced by permission of
Mizuho Corporate Bank

10

Banker Research forecasts that if trajectories continue at current levels, faltering asset levels in Japan and surging levels in China will mean that China's largest bank, Industrial and Commercial Bank of China (ICBC), will overtake Mizuho to become Asia's second-largest bank by 2009. Both ICBC and China Construction Bank will overtake Mitsubishi UFJ Financial Group (MUFG) and Mizuho FG by 2011 when the Japanese groups will become Asia's third and fourth largest banking groups respectively.

But while it is grounded in Asia's largest economy, Mizuho FG is not part of a very dynamic story as Japan comes out of a decade of deflation and low growth. With the levels of corporate loans only recently halting their steady decline, Mizuho Corporate Bank is likewise not in a particularly exciting business.

HIT THE GROUND FLAILING

Mizuho FG got off to a shaky start when it was formed early in the millennium. Like all of Japan's mega-banks, Mizuho FG was created in the harsh post-asset bubble environment of the late-1990s that forced nearly all of Japan's banks to seek government protection. The largest, known as the mega-banks, were forced to mega-merge and Mizuho FG was cobbled together from Industrial Bank of Japan (IBJ), Dai-Ichi Kangyo Bank (DKB), and Fuji Bank.

It was not a pretty sight, and the bank's tales of data integration nightmares are legendary. One particularly painful one occurred on April 1, 2002—the first day of the new financial year—when the consolidating banks went live too soon with their error-prone IT infrastructure. ATM transactions were debited but clients did not receive funds, or automatic debits were delayed and a massive volume of unprocessed transactions began to accumulate. There were also 30,000 cases of double debiting of transactions.

But structuring the organization to create a unit strictly focused on corporate banking does have certain benefits, among them its tighter staff and branch structure as well as isolating a business that benefits from diversification between Japanese business and overseas operations. In this way, Mizuho Corporate Bank has had a relatively

> **Our structure has more transparency than a single-bank entity, because by having a two-bank system, both banks have to disclose all the segmentation, all the details related to that.**

easier time than its retail banking partner Mizuho Bank, which is almost completely Japan-based, and also bound to the expensive and fiddly domestic branch banking business for retail and SME clients. Mizuho Bank was also the most affected by the early IT integration troubles.

Mizuho Corporate Bank is still by far the largest contributor to the group's bottom line. As of March 2007, it showed net income of US$2.7 billion compared with US$1.7 billion from Mizuho Bank, US$58 million from Mizuho Trust and Banking, and US$235 million from Mizuho Securities. This means that Mizuho Corporate Bank's net income is 51.3 percent of the contribution of the four businesses, with Mizuho Bank underperforming at 32.9 percent, despite relative proximity in asset size.

In the financial year that ended March 2007 the story was similar, but with a twist. While Mizuho Bank booked only US$2 billion in ordinary profits to Mizuho Corporate Bank's US$3.4 billion, extraordinary losses of US$4.4 billion at Mizuho Corporate Bank—largely the result of subprime-related debt—gave it a loss of US$820 million, while steady-as-she-goes Mizuho Bank showed net income of US$1.8 billion.

While he can claim just over half of the net income from his division, with the other three making up the rest, Mizuho Corporate Bank President and CEO Saito Hiroshi is not keen to gloat. The bulky, silver-haired man looks more like a politician than a banker, and his heavy glasses give him the air of a professional poker player as well. But like all Japanese businesses, Mizuho's senior management culture tends to close ranks in favor of harmony and consensus over outright competition and personal one-upmanship. The bank is doing well, although its success is actually quite relative: analysts remain unimpressed by the bank's overall profitability, and its very low 0.52 percent return on assets isn't blowing anyone away.

"At the very beginning when Mizuho Financial Group started, our intention was 50/50 [business mix between the two banks]," explained

Saito. "However, until financial year 2004 and 2005, the Corporate Bank led the group, meaning that the Corporate Bank constituted 70 percent to 80 percent, and the remainder was Mizuho Bank."

Mizuho Bank had struggled with various systemic problems at that time, and also went through various consolidations of its branch offices, he said. The current business mix is 60/40, but the group has a goal of bringing it up to 50/50.

"But that 50/50 does not mean the income of Mizuho Corporate Bank will go down," he said. "Rather it has more to do with Mizuho Bank catching up and then further expanding the two portfolios."

THE ORIGINAL INVESTMENT BANKER

Born in 1944, Saito graduated in 1966 from the elite Tokyo University, the training ground of nearly all of Japan's political and industrial leaders. He entered IBJ, Japan's original investment bank, the same year, rising through the ranks to become the head of the corporate banking unit in 1999. He has been the CEO of Mizuho Corporate Bank since 2002, occupying an office in the former IBJ building.

In another bank, Saito would be a business division head and not a CEO. But the decision was made early on to have the unusual parallel structure of a corporate and investment bank almost completely separate from the retail bank. The holding company that's structured above him is, after all, not much more than a shell. It has 258 employees and is presided over by group CEO Maeda Terunobu, who keeps an eye on all sides of the equation.

"The capital allocation by risk is done by the Mizuho holding company by looking at the entire situation of how the revenue could sway," explained Maeda. "They try and allocate the risk assets to where they foresee will have better revenue. This is something done by the holding company so that they are always keeping track of the ROA [return on assets] as well as the return as a group-wide effort, and this is a commitment to our shareholders."

According to Mizuho's website, the holding company plans and develops the group's business strategies and promotes synergies between the group companies. It also reinforces risk management, regulatory compliance, and internal audit systems. It also publishes a snazzy annual report.

As a planner of group business strategies, Mizuho has been more progressive than its mega-rivals; it has shown a great deal of vision in producing a well-branded expansion plan called Channel To Discovery and in forging international tie-ups. It has engaged in businesses with Wells Fargo Bank, Wachovia Corporation, and the Bank of New York (now Bank of New York Mellon Corporation). It was also the first Japanese bank to invest in a Korean banking group, Shinhan Financial Group, and it has formed a business agreement with Korea Development Bank. In December 2006, it became the first Japanese banking group to receive financial holding company status in the U.S. In China it made an investment in China CITIC Bank, and hit another milestone by becoming the first Japanese bank to be locally incorporated. All of these tie-ups are managed by Mizuho Corporate Bank directly, and Saito clearly spends a lot of time scanning the horizon.

The group has also been particularly good at keeping its nose clean as its competitors have run afoul of regulators. Citigroup and UFJ's brushes with Japan's Financial Services Agency (FSA) in 2004 are legendary, MUFG has been investigated by regulators in the U.S. and Japan, while Sumitomo Mitsui Financial Group (SMFG) has been warned in the U.S. and Japan as well. Even strong local players like Shinsei Bank have not been immune to administrative actions from Japan's tough regulator. Clearly, the 17 pages Mizuho devotes to internal controls systems in its annual report are an indicator of forward thinking in this regard, and the transparency of the bank's corporate structure also seems to be paying off.

"Mizuho is the only group that has two systems, one corporate and one retail," said Saito, explaining the difference between the two banks and the reason for the unusual structure. "At the beginning, many people criticized us for taking such a structure."

Mizuho Corporate Bank deals with customers such as large companies, financial institutions, or international businesses. Mizuho Bank is targeting consumers as well as small to medium-sized businesses.

"Even if it is a one-bank system, those banks actually have segments; they'll segment customers into two, or five or six internally," Saito said.

"But in our case, we have segmented that from a legal standpoint so that we will have more agility in our business models."

Saito sees the structure as more transparent, especially from the investor and analyst standpoint.

> From the human resources standpoint, having the three banks together means there are more very good and talented individuals in place.

Individual reporting means that it will be easier to identify which group businesses are doing well and which ones aren't, even if it is indelicate to discuss it. One look at the Mizuho annual report does show a breakdown buried in the bottom pages, with group results emphasized clearly at the top.

"Our structure has more transparency than a single-bank entity, because by having a two-bank system, both banks have to disclose all the segmentation, all the details related to that," says Saito. "For example, if we lend money to a major company, it will have a high credit standing and therefore the margin could be low. The reason why we have such high earnings at Mizuho Corporate Bank is because we're not just lending money to those major companies, we also provide them with investment banking type services, and this is fee income [for Mizuho Corporate Bank]. At the same time, we take more risk, especially in the market-related business, so that we will be able to get more income from that."

THE GALLOPING TROIKA

Saito is satisfied with the wider international reach that he has now that the three banks have come together. He notes that while his former bank, IBJ, was a corporate bank in Japan with corporate and investment banking activities overseas, it did not have branches in India, Vietnam, the Philippines, and Taipei before the merger. The bank has also been able to maximize the staff of three banks and retain the strongest from each. The group shed 8,000 workers in its first three post-merger years.

"From the human resources standpoint, having the three banks together means there are more very good and talented individuals in place, especially when it comes to international business," he said. "So we take the good parts of IBJ and at the same time we merge the good aspects of Fuji and DKB with IBJ. By doing so, we are moving towards an ideal."

If Saito focuses on the struggling Japanese market, his bank will only stagnate, especially with cash-rich corporations looking less and less to banks for their financing. Saito's main focus is on globalizing his business, and he sees this strategy as the only way forward with Japan at the tail end of over a decade of deflation. He is also following his clients, which more and more are turning toward China and other horizons.

"Many of the Japanese companies, especially the large companies in the corporate sector, are increasingly being globalized. This is accelerating," he said. "They are not only influenced by the 2 percent GDP growth in Japan, but they're also doing global business in countries with GDP growth averaging 4–5 percent, as well as China or India where the growth rate is eight to nine percent. Those are actually influencing the corporate sector as a whole."

So far Mizuho is well underway in carving a name for itself overseas. It was third in 2006 on the league tables for global mandated project finance deals according to Thomson Financial. In Asia Pacific, the bank is expanding into areas such as shipping finance, real estate non-recourse finance, and invoice discount finance, as well as investment banking. It has entered the league tables for such businesses as syndicated loans and club deals in the first half of 2007, where according to Hong Kong's Basis Point Publishing it was ranked tenth; it was eighth for syndicated loans and club deals in China and was particularly strong in Taiwanese non-NT$ deals, where it hit number two in the league tables.

In Europe the bank has a similarly strong presence among the Japanese banks, and in Europe, the Middle East, and Africa in 2006, according to Thomson Financial, the bank placed tenth as a mandated lead arranger of syndicated loans and fifth as an arranger or co-arranger of leveraged loans. In project finance, it placed fourth as a mandated lead arranger according to Loanware, just above MUFG.

In the Americas, the bank has focused on project finance, where it was third in the league tables in 2006 according to Project Finance International, behind Credit Suisse and Goldman Sachs. In February 2007, the bank became a financial advisor to the US$5.25 billion Panama Canal Expansion project. In March 2007, it signed a business cooperation agreement with Banorte, the first for a Japanese bank with a Mexican bank, while also forming an alternative investments business in New York in April 2007.

Saito plans to bring its percentage of international business to 40 percent by 2010 from about 22 percent in 2007. He is setting high targets for himself, especially since his bank is already ahead of his competitors. "Even 22 percent is the highest among Japanese banks," he said.

OVER THERE

Saito's overseas operations are roughly evenly divided between Asia, the U.S., and Europe. But Asia is clearly where he wants to see his growth, and when he achieves his 40 percent, his targets will be that a quarter will be in Asia, a quarter will be from ASEAN, and a quarter each for the U.S. and Europe.

"What would be in demand by Japanese companies when launching abroad is the M&A of the local companies in that particular country," explains Saito. "By acquiring the local entities, they would be able to minimize the time for launching business and at the same time expand more quickly."

Another lucrative area will be financial support for the sales activities of Japanese companies launching business abroad, he said.

> **The loan-related business will not increase; it may decrease, but will not increase.**

"Our financial support would be the factoring business or cash management services needed by those companies that are actively doing sales activities in those countries," he said. "Our branch offices are limited in number, but we've already started doing it. We partner with the local bank in providing this type of service."

The bank will also establish infrastructure in emerging economies such as India.

"In order for Japanese companies to launch businesses in these countries, they need the infrastructure to be ready, so we invest and partner with the local company, or in some cases ministries and governments, to help them to establish this infrastructure," he said.

For the long term, Saito wants the bank to become less reliant on lending and net interest income, which is a sick business in Japan. He hopes that in the mid term he will see lending income that takes credit risk represent 40 percent of his business. Another 20 percent should come from the markets business, with a focus on treasury-related activities that face market risk; for this portion of his business he hopes that half will be in the bond-related businesses and the other half in trading where there is no risk and the bank earns pure fees. The remaining 40 percent will be a broad base of various fee incomes, including cash management, foreign exchange, money transfers, and investment banking-related fees for M&As, structured finance, or project finance.

"The loan-related business will not increase; it may decrease, but will not increase," said Saito. "The market-related area, the treasury-related area, if we lean too much on that we will be exposed to major risks."

Saito wants to increase his investment banking and advisory services to 30 percent or 40 percent of the business.

Saito is clearly concerned about the type of liabilities that his companions in Mizuho Securities got trapped by in mid-2007 when the unit's exposure to subprime-linked CDOs led it to book US$245 million in net losses in the first six months of the 2007 financial year ending March 2008. With the unit facing a potential US$1.2 billion in losses, it had to take a US$1.4 billion injection from the group, via the issuance of new shares to Mizuho Corporate Bank, in order to get back on course. This is especially important for the unit, which is trying to keep a merger with Shinko Securities on track. The merger is part of Mizuho FG's, and Mizuho Corporate Bank's, aspirations to be an investment banking player overseas—the merged entity will be Japan's fourth-largest securities house.

To get his investment-banking business on track and to pull him away from risky businesses such as treasury, Saito wants the bank to do more in securities transactions and underwriting. The foundation of a financial holding company in New York will be a benefit to developing this business. He also is pushing a more global platform with a stronger team. To get there he will need to find the right talent, although getting international-minded people in Japan is difficult.

Saito claims that Mizuho is already a very international organization, with nearly 50 percent of the corporate bank's staff non-Japanese.

"The human resources system of a company needs to adjust to the market to be competitive," said Saito. "The greatest advantage of Mizuho is our huge customer base. Therefore, if a person works at a certain bank with the same skill, and if they come to our bank, they would be able to show a great performance leveraging off that huge customer base."

Mizuho Corporate Bank deals with 70 percent of the large companies in Japan and is the main bank for 40 percent of those companies, according to Saito. But there is no doubt that, of Japan's other two mega-banks, the larger MUFG will have somewhat more than that and the smaller SMFG somewhat less.

WHY BUY?

Despite the immensity of his need to expand overseas, Saito is clear that the bank will grow organically. It is seemingly not in the charter of Japanese bankers to acquire overseas banks any more the way that they tried—and failed—in the 1990s. That role is shifting to the Chinese and Korean banks, which have already shown themselves much bolder in recent years by buying banks in Africa and Southeast Asia. Saito is more inclined to take small stakes, and in early 2008 Mizuho Corporate Bank became just one more of the Asian-based investors in Merrill Lynch with a US$1.2 billion investment.

"If you look at the needs of the Japanese companies in Asia, we will be able to fulfill their needs by having the branch offices of our corporate bank or branch offices of our subsidiary Mizuho Securities," Saito said.

Building an overseas retail banking proposition is, after all, something that only a few global players have attempted. While HSBC and Citi have proven successful, Bank of America and ABN AMRO tried and failed. JPMorgan Chase didn't even try, despite its strong retail banking presence in the U.S.

"In our case, we are more like UBS or Deutsche Bank in that we centralize more on the corporate banking when it comes to overseas business," Saito said.

Saito's focus is squarely on the expanding markets of Asia. While India and China are both important for him, he is still much more focused on China than on India because "there are 33,000 Japanese firms currently doing business in China. On the other hand, 300 are present in India."

The bank has six branches in China, and now that it has incorporated locally, it will see the approval process for opening up branch offices expedited while *renminbi*-related transactions can begin immediately at any branch, giving the bank a ride on the China wave.

India will have a vastly different focus. Infrastructure improvements are needed before Japanese companies will move there in large numbers, Saito said. This includes upgrading ports, airports, and roads.

The number of Japanese companies in India may soon increase to 500 or 600 from 300, he said. But predictions of 10,000 are unrealistic, according to Saito. The bank is cooperating with the Japanese Bank for International Cooperation to develop infrastructure in India.

"In doing so, we will be able to support the Japanese companies launching business in India," he said.

Mizuho Corporate Bank's way forward in the U.S. will require going through all of the steps one by one, almost mechanically, conservatively, and methodically. The bank has repaid the public funds that the government used to bail its component banks out at the onset of the post-bubble troubles. It has grown its tier-one capital to 6 percent, while putting its anti-money-laundering structure firmly in place to the level that would satisfy U.S. authorities.

"Two years ago, the three mega-banks were instructed by the Federal Reserve Bank to have a very clear structure in place for anti-money laundering, and we have actually done that ourselves," said Saito. The fact that his two other mega-bank competitors have both been cited for failing to provide adequate anti-money-laundering facilities clearly gives his bank a head start on Wall Street.

"Up until now, without the financial holding company license, the subsidiary was able to handle U.S. government bonds only, however, not when it comes to the company's corporate bonds," he said. "But with this license in place, we will now be able to do the corporate bond underwriting together. This is going to be a major opportunity for us."

Big in Japan may be one thing, but big in the U.S. is something all Japanese companies have aspired to ever since Mitsubishi Estate bought Rockefeller Center in 1989. Mizuho seems to have done a few things right with its distinctive advantages relative to its main Japanese rivals: holding company status in the U.S., local incorporation in China, a relatively clean record with regulators, a well-branded expansion strategy, and agreements with banks all over Asia.

But without an acquisition strategy, finding talent will still be a major battle. A stiff corporate culture could also create problems. To say that there are only a few truly internationalized Japanese companies would be a major understatement, and Mizuho has a lot of cultural baggage to unload, not just from the merger but also from the country's strong corporate culture. Whether Mizuho Corporate Bank will be the Japanese company that can make itself as international as Citi or GE remains to be seen.

But with his optimism, and the bank's strong operational standpoint, Saito will have a lot going for him if he can build some momentum on the businesses that he's launched overseas. He may have beaten his local rivals to the punch on some points, but MUFG and SMFG are major players in Japan and their strategies will be similar to Saito's. The channel to discovery is, after all, a long and arduous road to follow. Japanese banks have waited over a decade for their chance to build a name overseas. Hopefully, this time the road will be smoother than last time around.

Pedal to the Metal in Slow Motion

Who can stop the tide from turning?

Kookmin Bank CEO Kang Chung-won may have improved the bank tremendously, but can he help the bank face the tremendous challenges on the horizon?

KOREA's largest retail bank, Kookmin Bank, which means "the people's bank," has long been the most visible fixture of the country's banking scene. More than 75 percent of its business is retail banking, meaning that it has the largest branch network and also the strongest national brand name. It was the country's largest lender by assets until it was overtaken in 2007 by government-owned corporate lender Woori, but remains the country's largest by far in terms of market capitalization.

But despite its current position comfortably at the top of the financial services game, the new millennium has been more tumultuous for the country's largest bank

Kang Chung-won
Reproduced by permission of
Kookmin Bank

than for most others. And considering the impact that the 1997 Asian financial crisis had on Korea's banks, that's really saying something.

The 1990s were, in fact, relatively trouble-free times for Kookmin; the bank escaped the worst of the financial crisis since its large retail banking portfolio kept it out of the hazardous speculative corporate lending that other banks engaged in with their corporate partners. Kookmin worked with the government to take in struggling lenders, such as Daedong Bank in 1998 with its 49 branches. It acquired Korea Long Term Credit Bank, which made it Korea's largest bank.

Kookmin also took in Goldman Sachs as an investor, starting off a trend that would eventually give the bank more than 80 percent foreign ownership. This is clearly a contentious issue for a bank that has its Korean identity plastered all over it, but is now commonly accepted in the industry. Throughout the first decade of the twentieth century, the presence of foreign stakeholders has become a common point for all Korean privately-held banks after the hard times of 1997 forced them to open their doors to outside capital. There has been no turning back.

Kookmin began merger talks in 2000 with Housing and Commercial Bank of Korea (Housing Bank), led by the daring and progressive Kim Jung-tae. He is the former head of Dongwon Securities who revitalized the brokerage and began to apply the same magic to Housing Bank, turning it into Korea's third-largest and most profitable bank. Backed by foreign shareholders such as ING and Goldman Sachs, Kim was chosen to lead the new bank when the merger went through, even though he had come from the smaller partner, a contentious issue in patriarchal Korea.

In Korea's hierarchical society, Kim's entry into management as well as his brusque management style rubbed some the wrong way, and his stormy leadership of the merged bank continued for three years after the April 2001 merger. He was eventually toppled in late 2004 because of legal concerns over his share options. At that time Kookmin was by far Korea's largest bank by assets, more than four times larger than its nearest competitor, Shinhan Financial Group (Shinhan).

A NEW OLD FACE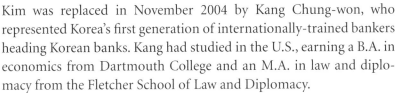

Kim was replaced in November 2004 by Kang Chung-won, who represented Korea's first generation of internationally-trained bankers heading Korean banks. Kang had studied in the U.S., earning a B.A. in economics from Dartmouth College and an M.A. in law and diplomacy from the Fletcher School of Law and Diplomacy.

The son of a banker working at Korea Exchange Bank overseas, Kang began his career at Citibank. He was then invited to join Bankers Trust in Korea by K.S. Lee, who later became the North Asia regional head of the bank. The invitation was part of Lee's dream of bringing smart young Koreans back to their native soil to grow businesses in their home country. Lee impressed Kang so much with his passion that Kang put his stake into something new and worked to turn a small operation into something respectable. Kang eventually rose to be the chief country officer for Bankers Trust in Korea, staying on in the position after its acquisition by Deutsche Bank in 1998.

Combining youthful looks and an energetic smile with the grizzled demeanor of a chain smoker, Kang is a complex study in contrasts. In June of 2000, he left international banking and became chief executive officer of the struggling Seoul Bank, which had been nationalized when it faced collapse after 1997. Kang spent several years stemming the bleeding in the bank before handling acquisition talks. With HSBC and other banks interested in buying Seoul Bank, the government's stake finally went to Hana Bank in 2002. In November of that year, Kang found himself without a job as his work at Seoul Bank had run its course.

In the wilderness for over a year, Kang was a natural choice for leadership of Kookmin in 2004. With his international experience and connections, as well as his experience fixing up Seoul Bank (and the resulting peek into that part of competitor Hana Bank's enlarged operations), Kang had quickly graduated to the profile of a top banker. He was the type of outsider that the bank needed to carve out a cancer that was growing inside the country's largest bank.

Kookmin Bank was still suffering cultural issues around the integration of Kookmin and Housing Bank. There were also other inefficiencies that were preventing Kookmin from being as profitable as it should be, and as much as Kim had helped build the bank to the best of his abilities, the strong-willed, highly focused Kang had also proven his magic touch with Seoul Bank and was going to give Kookmin a crack.

"As the second CEO of the merged bank, I suppose they decided to bring someone from outside, rather than from the inside," said Kang, remembering the early days. "So I tried to address the legacy problem of the bank, which was that there was a merger of two relatively large, equal-sized banks. I knew that this bank had not found the necessary people with experience within the first three years of the merger, so I knew that it is one of my first priority items. I also knew that I needed to bring in the professionals. There wasn't enough expertise at the bank at the top level to deal with the various specific functional issues that required to be dealt with for a bank of this size."

> **I also knew that I needed to bring in the professionals. Professionals that could add value to the bank.**

Within two weeks of his arrival, Kang brought in seven people from outside, many of them ex-Citi or ex-Deutsche like himself. But instead of removing long-standing executives who knew the bank well, Kang diplomatically expanded top-level positions from nine to 15 and put outsiders into seven of those positions. While he did take some resignations, the eight positions for Kookmin staff were taken up by a mix of incumbents and strong candidates from within the bank who were promoted to the top level. Clearly Kang had to put a lot of thought into who he was going to choose to work with him as it would mean not just the bank's success but also his own survival. His gambit paid off as his three-year contract was renewed in November 2007.

But the restructuring went deeper than just the senior level leadership. "I consolidated the credit functions that were dispersed among different business groups," Kang said. "Retail credit belonged to retail marketing, corporate credit was part of corporate banking, so I consolidated the credit functions into a chief credit officer. I separated the credit functions from business groups and consolidated them on the CCO, who also joined from outside."

Kang felt that managing a one thousand-branch network involving a portfolio of more than 80 trillion won (US$85 billion) was too much for one person and so he divided the retail banking group into three and split the geographical responsibilities into two "so each EVP (executive vice president) handles about 500 branches, about a 40 trillion won (US$42.5 billion) portfolio, and about 6,000–7,000 people under each group," he said. The marketing and product functions were taken over by a third EVP.

Splitting the retail banking function is a somewhat unusual move, but not totally unique. Citi made the same move in 2005 after the retirement of Marge Magner, who had been the head of the global giant's entire retail banking empire, clearly too much for one person to handle as well.

But not every change has been radical. One of the people who stayed over from the entire process has been Donald MacKenzie, a Canadian banker who has been Kookmin's chief risk officer for many years, and has recently been appointed chief finance officer after the retirement of Kang associate Kap Shin.

TAKING A STANCE

Having been a leader in several institutions, Kang has had the opportunity to develop his team-building skills, and as an outsider coming into a troubled institution he drew on a long list of contacts formed over many years.

"People are absolutely key," Kang explained. "My chief credit officer formerly was my chief credit officer at Seoul Bank, so I have full confidence in him for managing the credit side of the business. He was also the chief rating officer in a local rating agency in the late 1980s, so he knows Korean corporates very well."

With most of the bank's retail loans collateralized, only 5–10 percent of the bank's loans needed to pass through a credit scoring system when Kang joined the bank. That quickly rose beyond 15 percent in his first months behind the wheel, and he is now enforcing a comprehensive credit policy so that all of his loans pass through the credit scoring system.

The business and technology structure that Kang walked into was inefficient, and he even rolled up his sleeves and dug his hands into Kookmin's IT systems when he joined the bank. He studied

> **I recognized the importance of the retail banking base of this bank as its key strength.**

systems that were being developed, as well as systems that had been put in place but weren't really being used effectively, and explained their relevance and function to his staff.

"Most people didn't see the relevance of the systems, because they hadn't lived with such systems in the past, so I was able to pick up quite a few of them, refine, develop more," he said.

That the systems were there made his work pulling Kookmin together easier than it had been with Seoul Bank, but also provided a fantastic challenge in that they were part of a substantially larger bank.

The bank's inefficiencies ran deeper than just its IT, and it wasn't properly leveraging its greatest competitive advantage; Kookmin had serious problems in its massive retail banking franchise, a unit that makes up over three-quarters of its business. The pragmatic Kang made it a priority to put his mark on the unit.

"I recognized the importance of the retail banking base of this bank as its key strength," Kang said. "The problem with retail banking is the system of managing that very valuable large portfolio and customer base is still underdeveloped. We started with the credit side first, then we started a customer satisfaction campaign, because the customer satisfaction ranking of this bank in 2003, 2004 [was low]. We ranked as the lowest customer satisfaction bank two years in a row."

Clearly the market leader won't be the market leader for long if its clients are unhappy with it, and Kang made sure he was going to do something different from his predecessor to protect the brand. The customer satisfaction campaign paid off quickly for the bank, and within three months of starting it they were beginning to see strong improvements. In December 2006, the bank was ranked top among banks in the National Customer Satisfaction Index by Korea Productivity Center.

"There's tremendous potential, but this franchise hadn't been really cared for, nurtured, in its very basic banking principles so to speak," Kang said.

Although the bank is improving in this regard, that it is the country's largest retail bank means that brand protection is even more important to it than to other banks. Improvements in one part of the business are probably not quite enough to satisfy the ambitious strategist in Kang, and he is keen to be a decisive driver of the massive Kookmin machine.

"I think I'm mostly on the accelerator," said Kang. "I do push quite a bit. There's a lot to be done."

Ultimately, Kang had inherited a sophisticated institution that had in place so many of the structures he needed to create a world-class bank. In the parts of the business where he really needed to make changes he wasn't afraid to push hard.

> **I mostly have my foot on the accelerator, not the brake. I do push quite a bit. There's a lot to be done.**

Kang needed to be sure that the staff understood that Kookmin was a new organization, that internal control systems and procedures had to be respected, and that the bank needed to be risk sensitive to prevent mistakes and to protect the bank's reputation with clients. He worked with his human resources group to initiate an early retirement program that initially let 2,000 full-time employees go. He also began training for the remaining 24,000 full- and part-time or contract employees to help the bank build a common culture as the new Kookmin. This included the senior managers, the employees, the union staff, and even the security guards. Kang may have his foot on the accelerator, but his hand's not very far from the emergency brake either. Preserving the bank's reputation is clearly just as important to him as establishing global best practices. In many cases they are the same thing.

GROWTH THROUGH CHANGE

Kang has faced his biggest challenges working on the bank's culture at large. This is most acutely represented by his position with the unions.

"When I came in [in November 2004], there were three separate unions at this bank: one representing the former Kookmin side, one representing the former Housing and Commercial, and one representing the former credit card company," he said. "So it was a split culture then. And the labor unions also consolidated in January of 2005. We only have one labor union, but underneath, the legacy policies are still active. I have monthly meetings with the union leaders."

Kang has also been focusing on more strategic areas. The bank is large and has the profitability that comes with its scale and relatively conservative lending strategy. In Kang's first two full years at the helm, the bank grew its assets 1.5 times and saw its profits slightly more than double. By comparison, it has lost its lead in asset size to fantastically aggressive organizations such as Woori Financial Group.

Woori grew its assets 7.6 times but increased its profit by only 6.4 times. Shinhan, which acquired the country's largest credit card player LG Card during this time, saw assets grow 5.7 times and profit 4.3 times. In terms of profitability indicators like ROE and ROA, Kookmin and Shinhan have both been doing very well, while the government-owned Woori Financial Group has slumped somewhat in its profitability.

But it is Kookmin that has surged the most in terms of ROA, traveling from a measly 0.9 percent at the end of 2004 to 1.3 percent at the end of 2006 while the others saw their ROA remain relatively flat. And of the top three banks, Kookmin has the highest capital adequacy ratio: over 14 percent.

Kang knows that, despite the bank's size and profitability, he needs to look for something else as the tide is turning against the Korean banks. They are suffering from a similar malady to the one the Japanese banks have: their corporations are cash rich, and when they need funding they are turning less frequently to banks than to other sources of funding, such as capital markets; whatever margins are left are thinning in a highly competitive space.

High profits of recent years have often come from the return of money set aside for provisioning against bad loans as the banks have brought down their NPLs. Once provisioning bottoms out they will have to rely on their actual business cases to show concrete growth. Retail banking, Kookmin's ace in the hole, hasn't proven as safe a fallback as it should. The government has put a lid on some types of mortgage lending, hoping to avoid the real estate bubble in Seoul's most desirable neighborhoods from ballooning out of control. And on top of everything else, banks' funds are being disintermediated, sapped by other avenues such as insurance or securities as clients seek higher returns and more efficient use of their funds.

It is for this reason that banks on the peninsula have been seeking financial holding company status so that they can acquire insurance and securities units and bring them under the same umbrella, and Kookmin is considering seeking this status as well. It is also acquiring the businesses it will put under that umbrella, albeit somewhat clumsily. In 2007, Kookmin was engaged in a complex acquisition campaign for a brokerage where it walked away from the table and then came back. It finally bought Hannuri Investment and Securities in late 2007 for US$307 million, beating out a bid by Standard Chartered Bank.

GROWTH THROUGH ACQUISITION

A bigger acquisition has been on Kang's mind for even longer, one that has proven frustratingly elusive. In 2006, Kang outbid Hana Financial Group (Hana) and Singapore's DBS Bank and Temasek Holdings, for private equity player Lone Star Holdings' 51 percent stake in Korea Exchange Bank (KEB). KEB is the country's premier trade finance institution, with 18 branches overseas and 324 in Korea.

Kang had initially said in 2005 that he was not interested in buying KEB, preferring to focus on resolving the bank's outstanding structural and organizational issues, rather than integrating such a large bank into his operations. However, it is more likely that he was being coy, sitting back to watch the bidding process and make a strategic move, rather than join the game too soon. Clearly, the bank offers a full range of business lines that Kookmin, as a predominantly retail bank, either doesn't have or is weak in. It would help to fill in the structural areas that Kang *didn't* have when he walked into the bank. It also would help it regain the status of Korea's largest bank without aggressively competing for asset growth. It would maintain Kookmin's dominance both in Korea and also outside the country as the government seeks among its banks a "regional champion" to represent Korea around Asia. But managing a merger of that size would be no easy task for Kang, who has little experience in the area compared with his rivals in the bid, such as Hana Financial Group's Kim Seung-yu, the company's chairman, who has been overseeing mergers at his company for nearly 30 years.

With his easy, fluent English, Kang is already an effective communicator to both his Korean and foreign stakeholders. The bank is starting to spread its wings regionally now that hyper-competitive Korea is starting to prove too crowded. Kookmin is, after all, one of the first Korean banks to make a significant investment in a bank overseas. This was in the form of a consortium investment with Temasek Holdings for a 56 percent stake in Bank Internasional Indonesia. Kookmin represented one third of the consortium before the stake was sold to Maybank, Malaysia's largest lender.

But the KEB story has been a nightmare for Kang and everybody else involved. Unfortunately for Kang and Lone Star, instead of being a relatively straight forward transaction between a seller and a series of competitive bidders, KEB and Lone Star were pulled into a political whirlwind. Lone Star came under investigation over possible manipulation in 2003 when the fund first bought KEB, and the issue of the bank's ownership went into limbo (although the bank itself continued to function as usual). The case lingered so long that the Kookmin offer on KEB expired, and Lone Star pulled out of the agreement. It later conducted talks with HSBC, which desperately wants to buy a bank in Korea to counter acquisitions by regional rivals Citi and Standard Chartered Bank, but the legal and political entanglement is a stalemate that may not be solved any time soon.

When it is resolved, it will have been many years since Kookmin won the bid to buy more than half of the bank from Lone Star, which adds up to a lifetime of waste for a frustrated Kang. But with a new pro-business president elected in December 2007, there is an entirely new political environment for KEB and Lone Star—and for Korea's banks in general, since banking on the peninsula cannot be extricated from national politics.

The debate is now over allowing conglomerates—Korea's *chaebol*—more right to invest in the financial services sector to help Korean interests retain ownership of Korea's banks, even if it is a step backward in terms of corporate governance. Allowing corporate ownership in banks is a contentious issue and leaves greater possibilities of abuse of the financial system by big business that can have possibly disastrous side-effects (witness the effects in Korea of the 1997 Asian financial crisis). The aggressive Woori is already being fingered in shady dealings with corporate accounts that may have held slush funds, and the movement is troubled from the start. And what this all bodes for Kookmin's aspirations to buy KEB is still uncertain— the game is far from being played out. A more purely Korean-owned bank might still be the one groomed to become the touted "regional champion" bank, in which case it may not be Kookmin after all, but Woori Financial Group, which is due to be privatized in 2008. Again, the tide is turning.

THE NEXT STEPS

But even with the derailing of his ambition to grow dramatically through the acquisition of KEB, the bank his father worked at as an overseas-based senior executive, Kang still has other plans to grow his business organically.

One of them is the fund management business. "The way it relates to this bank is distribution of fund management products, in which we are already quite strong," explained Kang. "We already have about 24 percent market share in bancassurance, and we have over 40 percent market share in the sale of investment products. Through strengthening the credit management process, customer satisfaction, CRM, and product management, we'll truly be a very dominant player across retail banking; but on the customer segmentation side we'll be strongest in mass retail."

Kang doesn't want to take on local or foreign banks just yet in the wealth management business, but with strong foundations and new acquisition pieces filling out the puzzle, he aims to gradually develop the offerings to segments through mass retail, mass affluent, and eventually into high net areas where the bank currently concedes turf to strong wealth management players like Shinhan and Hana.

This strategy will keep Kang from butting heads in the space for some time still. Foreign banks often see the Korean market as under-served with wealth management and hope to become players there.

> **You do need to grow, but I think you can grow either in terms of assets or in terms of revenue.**

When they come in to cherry pick customers, they work from the top down, where they will be going head-to-head with these players, not Kookmin.

Kang has not been an aggressive lender. Instead he has focused on asset quality and trying to inject a measure of sanity in a market that has been expanding its asset base aggressively. He is possibly biding his time until the opportunity for KEB presents itself again in one form or another. Instead, Kang has increased fees, from 24 percent of his revenue at the end of 2004 to beyond one-third of total income.

"I don't particularly think increasing the asset side has much mean-ing," Kang said. "You do need to grow, but I think you can grow either in terms of assets or in terms of revenue."

Most of the bank's fees come from its retail banking outfit, as its cor-porate banking asset size is a quarter of its total asset size. Here Kang is again selective about his lending and is growing the bank with quality. After the SK Global scandal of 2003, the bank got rid of most of its large corporate portfolio. But since 2005 Kang has been trying to rebuild this by courting very creditworthy large companies as well as larger SMEs. Kang is focusing on transaction banking, in particular cash manage-ment, which will boost his fee income and enlarge his customer base. This includes re-engaging with some of the old customers Kookmin had neglected in the past, and also focusing on new customers.

Kang is also continually boosting his product capabilities in cor-porate banking, and in the past he has plundered Deutsche Bank, Crédit Lyonnais, and others to get his derivatives, foreign exchange, and equity and capital markets people. He has also kick-started the bank's treasury function with a new head of treasury up from the very limited function it had when he arrived.

Checking Kang is his board, which needs to keep an eye on how man-agement is drawing together the many varied parts of the business.

"We have quite a demanding board, and I think that's very healthy, and the outside board members really have very diverse backgrounds," says Kang. "I think that it's also a very productive profile for this very large bank that has to address the needs of a very diverse customer base, from mass-retail to private banking to large corporate to small office home office (SOHO) businesses, so they keep us busy, and we try to do the best we can."

Kang, with his restless mind, is in an interesting spot. His international experience pushes the bank operationally so that it can run more efficiently under a unified corporate culture; he stays his hand when managing asset growth, but he also keeps an eye on strategic leaps. Being a very large player in such a complex environment requires intense concentration, and with the country's financial services industry at a crossroads this makes his position even more fascinating. Even if it looks like Kang has taken his foot off of the accelerator somewhat, the scene is deceptive. The huge engine is roaring, and at any moment could shoot ahead again—no lumbering giant, but a nimble global player.

Chapter 2
Visionaries—Changing the Rules

The Giant-in-Waiting

Are questions about India's growth story all rhetorical?

> *Although he helped found HDFC Bank in 1994, managing director Aditya Puri is still astounded by the change he's seen in his country through the years.*

INDIA is the buzzword of the decade, often coupled with its BRIC partner China—as in "China and…" But things were not always this way; 20 years ago the term "new generation of Indian banks" might have seemed like a curious term for outsiders not certain where exactly the country was headed. Nonetheless, these new banks are among the most exciting in India. Chief among them is HDFC, seemingly joined at the hip with ICICI Bank—as in "HDFC and…"

Set up in 1994, the bank was initially backed by the Housing Development Finance Corporation Limited, a privately owned housing finance company established in 1977.

Like many Indian companies, HDFC Bank has a strong and charismatic leader at its helm. The bank has been run since it started by Aditya Puri, who was born in Punjab and raised in Poona in the hills above Mumbai. He earned a bachelor's degree in commerce from Punjab University, Chandigarh, before receiving

Aditya Puri
Reproduced by permission of
TAB International

a chartered accountancy degree from the Institute of Chartered Accountants of India. After graduation, he went to work for Citibank, where he stayed for 20 years, and in the last ten he was country head for India, Sri Lanka, Nepal, and Bangladesh for institutional banking.

Eventually he moved to Citibank in Malaysia and rose to the position of country head of Citibank in Malaysia. It was the chairman of HDFC at the time, Deepak S. Parekh, who lured him in 1996 to start up the new bank, which Puri launched with six employees in an abandoned textile mill in Mumbai. He has been with the company as its managing director—the bank's highest position as it does not have a CEO—ever since it started, the only leader its employees have ever known.

But much has changed in that time. The bank now has more than 750 branches and is present in more than 320 cities in India. Over this time, Puri has seen the Indian banking scene grow, develop, and charge ahead, taking HDFC Bank with it. From a time of sleepy, cautious growth, the sector has thrown off its shackles and exploded with wild asset expansion that is funding the many growth industries that are making India thrive. But more recently, banks have been bucking the trend of natural growth and are trying to fight at all costs for new assets, willing to sacrifice their margins in order to get ahead.

Puri, at the top of a premier Indian bank, finds himself in a good position, although his view of the situation around him may make him want to cling on for dear life.

"When you're looking at an economy like India's which is growing somewhere between 7.5 percent and 10 percent and it's undergoing a change in its GDP composition and in income, its age profile, you are basically seeing an economy that will grow its consumer demand," he said. "If consumer demand grows, so will the demand for financial services. Demand is not the issue."

Of course, Puri cannot simply jump into the business, as he'd be jumping in blind; India does not yet have a credit bureau with enough depth to keep a former Citibanker happy, and banks in India need to find the appropriate pricing. The challenge for managing a period of explosive growth is that the banks have not had enough business cycles to test this, and Puri knows this better than anybody. He's aware of the operating risk and technology risk inherent in growing beyond certain limits in market share and percentage growth rate.

"When you grow beyond that, you really don't know whether risks are going to come or if risks are inherent," he said. "The issue then is what do you do? Do you go after everybody and say, 'I will just go for market share?' And if you get too large a market share in any product, you are likely to get an adverse selection, which will come back to you at some point of time."

Puri fears that irrational practices will make delinquency a problem, especially as absolute bad loans will grow disproportionately faster than the entire loan book, creeping up on banks. And then there is the headache of collecting on delinquent loans.

"You can only do so much for recovery because in a poor country, most laws as well as institutions will always favor the consumer and that's a fact of life," he said.

But the bank's managing director has made a choice, and he knows what type of business he wants to be, for which returns, and at what risk.

"In this scenario, we clearly have said that market share at the cost of what we call 'viable returns'—to take care of our needs for capital, to take care of delinquency, and to take care of return to investors, coupled with a fair competitive price to the consumer—is not what we want," he said.

CLOSE TO CUSTOMERS

With the bank's grassroots beginnings, Puri and HDFC retain an on-the-ground feel that comes with having built a bank from scratch. The knowledge of his customers is what Puri attributes a lot of his risk management abilities to.

"People like State Bank, ICICI, and us—we now really understand the Indian consumer," he explained. "We have learned across a very wide geography. We now have experience and understanding of the Indian consumers. We may not have a credit bureau; we may not have formalized statements; but we all developed credit tools whereby we can use aggregates to make a reasonably good assessment."

More than the complexities of consumer growth, which Puri looks at based on his understanding of his customers' profiles, histories, and geographies, the managing director of HDFC has India's integration with the global economy on his mind.

"We have a very robust capital market," he said, adding that "we still need a debt market with sufficient debt. People are working on it."

Puri is at his core an optimist, albeit a careful one, seeing neither large NPLs nor asset bubbles in either real estate or loans against shares. He also feels that risk assessment at Indian banks has improved so substantially, even in public sector banks, that there is no systemic risk.

> **We may not have a credit bureau; we may not have formalized statements; but we all developed credit tools whereby we can use aggregates to make a reasonably good assessment.**

Puri sees demand for credit growing in India at least until 2011, and probably even beyond as financial systems in the country mature. While moneylenders are still significant suppliers of credit to the market, banks and other finance companies will eventually be able to steal a certain percentage of their business away through greater efficiency and better pricing. Moneylenders' rates of interest can range from 10 percent to 50 percent. The government would support banks' efforts to bring more of India's active consumers out of the grey market. Significant initiatives are under way in Sri Lanka, the Philippines, and other similar developing economies as well.

"The boom is based on a shift from the unorganized to the organized sector," said Puri. "Car finance today is 95 percent in the organized sector. Housing finance is probably 98 percent in the organized sector. Two-wheeler finance is probably only 60 percent to 65 percent in the organized sector. Personal loans is probably only 40 percent in the organized sector."

The culture for bank credit in India only really began just after the turn of the century, around 2002, and many of the Indians who are taking a loan from banks are doing so for the first time. Puri feels that up to 80 percent of his customers are first-time borrowers.

Puri is harnessing the growth that is at his doorstep and managing it so that he keeps his delinquencies low despite the cycles. In credit cards it has crept up to what he feels are the "global standard" of around 7 percent. He's also eager to eventually make use of the country's new credit bureau and see credit histories act as a deterrent to potential defaulters.

Like an iceberg drifting past, Puri knows that a huge part of India's economy is untapped.

"We also must understand that when we're talking about the boom today, we are largely talking of the boom in metros and the semi-metros," he said. "The smaller towns and the regional markets or the sub-regional markets have not even been hit. Arguably, half to 65 percent of India's population live there. As we reform agriculture and we bring prosperity to a larger and larger section of the population, more and more of it will come into the organized financial services net."

Puri is also counting on government exposure and investment giving a boost to India's investment-based economy, and food inflation may mean a more robust agricultural system in India—and more wealth for farmers along with it.

FINANCIAL INCLUSION

With the regular business of pricing risk understood, expansion into other sectors is viable. To this end, Puri sees an urgent need to make credit available at reasonable prices to a larger section of the population that the banks have not reached yet. He feels that the government needs to push this as a development initiative. Banks are already being asked to service the need on a commercial basis to borrowers who have the ability to return the loans. More and more, Puri wants his new business to come from the untapped rural areas that house more than 700 million unbanked people.

"I can't be a large bank in India unless I develop products for this economy. I am moving to develop that irrespective of any regulatory statement," he said.

But "the unbanked" come in many forms, and Puri has strong opinions on financial inclusion, reaching out to the large parts of the Indian diaspora and local population who are not part of organized finance. Many of the people who don't have relationships with banks keep their money in gold and cling to traditional concepts of wealth and finance. This means aggressively taking banking as an idea out of the medium- and large-sized cities and into the towns and villages and also exploring new channels. Puri figures that the unbanked sector is 25–30 percent larger than the banked sector, and this is partly due to the fact that remote villages don't have access to financial services.

"How do we partake if there's going to be a change in the agricultural economy?" he said. "Where do we fit in? How do we use technology to go into remote areas in service? How do we use our architecture in such a way that we can service people on a low-cost basis?"

To reach new rural customers, the bank is considering different distribution channels such as the post office, cooperative banks, microfinance agencies, and moneylenders, he said, while also adding that "I don't know whether, at least in my time as MD, if we will ever develop enough distribution to take care of this vast country." The potential is vast, as is the amount of hard work needed.

These challenges will ease as villages get roads and mobile phones. The phenomenon is also tied to a wide variety of socio-economic incidents such as job migration. With new people living in cities, small and medium enterprises that serve these people grow. Ultimately, the money is fed back to the agricultural communities that the workers originally come from, transforming these places as well and injecting them with funds, some of which could end up with banks. Puri sees these developments directly through the bank's SME banking services, but the bank is obviously not yet present in all villages and doesn't see the end product of all wealth transfer—yet.

Puri has launched a product that is aimed at farmers. It is a microfinance credit card, launched together with Visa, that allows them to buy equipment for their farms, as well as some items for personal use.

"It's important as a card, but to me it's more important that for the first time I'm creating a banking habit in those farmers," said Puri. "When he takes a card, he will open an account, he will not put the money under the mattress; he will not carry sacks of money when he goes to town and be worried about it."

Puri is also looking at collateral management with insurance, where he will lend to a farmer against the farmer's warehouse receipt. Commodities exchanges are also looking to create exchanges where wholesale markets allow more balanced pricing mechanisms for farmers and also help farmers sell produce when the time and the price is right because financing for short-term needs is available.

Puri's products may make HDFC Bank seem like a microfinance operation, but he disagrees. "You will have to look at it segment-wise," he said. "Just like in an any other urban economy, there is a large farmer, a medium level farmer, an upper medium level farmer, and a very small farmer. For the medium and large farmers, unit size is not a problem. The problem with the small farmer is not just his unit size—the problem is his fundamental viability. That is what will take a little longer."

Puri is convinced that the groundwork has been laid and the market will begin to pick up soon.

"If infrastructure grows and there's proper pricing, if there's enough commodity then maybe these fellows can all get together, and the solution will come," he explained. "The fact that the organized finances are moving into the interior is a given. We have both the credit as well as the marketing tools to access it. Not because anybody has asked us but we feel that's where the growth is."

While microfinance and other rural banking initiatives have typically been high-cost operations due to the "high volume, low value" paradigm, Puri feels rural banking in India is different because of lower rentals and salaries. Even though the rural clients won't be shifting to mutual funds, without cutthroat competition from aggressive rivals there will be money for the banks that venture forth.

VILLAGE LIFE

Even now, HDFC Bank is close to India's rural populations.

"Almost 40-odd percent of our credit cards are sold outside the metros and semi-metros," Puri said. "There's a hub-and-spoke model that's going on. We have taken personal loans to about 150 to 200 cities. There is a misconception that you have to be in every village. If you go anywhere in the world, you have farms all over but your basic services are provided in the nearest small town."

Puri's ambitions are nearly limitless. Although he already has 750 branches, he aims to add 50 percent of that any year if he can get permission. The bank can afford it, since it has centralized processing and a branch is just a relay station to add deposits to the kitty and to add names to the database.

"I think this transformation will be the real transformation of India," he said. "I would love to see it. The government is talking about financial inclusion. You can't have two and three Indias. You can't have an India that is aping the lifestyle and the earning level of the West and another fellow doesn't have water to drink. You have a social obligation more than the social obligation in your own interest. It's not viable to have so much disparity. The country must come up with viable ways."

> You can't have two and three Indias. You can't have an India that is aping the lifestyle and the earning level of the West and another fellow doesn't have water to drink. You have a social obligation more than the social obligation in your own interest.

Perhaps one of the reasons that Puri is looking so idealistically to the countryside is the intense competition for asset growth that his competitors are engaging in. Puri is aghast at some of the insanity that he sees going on around him, particularly in price warfare. With so much undeveloped territory, and grassroots management techniques that may not sustain high margin pressure, there is no need yet for aggressive price competition with so much open territory ahead.

"Why should you have price warfare when there is no shortage in demand?" he said. "Presumably to either change the structure of the balance sheet or to have a higher market share. That could work in a declining interest rate environment. You follow that strategy in a rising interest rate environment and you're dead, however brilliant you may be and whatever your strategy may be. Every loan that you book today is in a loss tomorrow. And on top of that, if you book below market, you'll be paying for it."

Puri stays away from the riskiest segments, especially upper-end apartments and other expensive real estate where prices are going haywire, leaving those to banks like Citibank and others that he supposes have appropriate risk management procedures to take them on. Instead he sticks to middle market housing and doesn't view the segment as large enough to create troubles for the country.

"Some pockets have asset problems, no doubt," he said. "Are they large enough that if there was a drop of 20 percent to 25 percent—which I doubt, maybe 15 percent to 20 percent—will it create a systemic issue? The answer is no."

Despite his prudence, he sees HDFC Bank growing faster than other up-and-coming banks. Puri sees most of his bank's products in the top three in market share. Even in markets where they are not major players, he sees the bank growing well. "We may be a small player in two-wheelers, but have we lost our market position," he asks rhetorically, before answering: "No."

The bank took a big step in early 2008 in expanding with an agreement to acquire Centurion Bank of Punjab, which gave it 2.5 million more customers and moved it from India's ninth-largest bank to its sixth-largest. Its branch network swelled to 1,150 branches, temporarily giving it more branches than archrival ICICI Bank—which was in the midst of a one-year project to double its branch network from 700 to 1,400—although it won't

> **As long as we are in the top three, we don't feel the necessity to gain the number one position at the cost of margins**

beat it in assets by a far cry. But more than gaining customers and branches, HDFC Bank gets much needed human resources and talent, which are in increasingly short supply in India.

Puri passionately defends the bank's position as one of the main players in India, a position that just got boosted slightly with the acquisition of a smaller bank, reminding that the bank is a leader in cash management and derivatives.

"As long as we are in the top three, we don't feel the necessity to gain the number one position at the cost of margins," he said. "In every product that we know of, we're more likely to be a one or two. At maximum, say in cards, we were number three because we were the last entrant in cards."

And if non-consumer businesses are stripped out of the bank, he feels that his scale is comparable with that of India's biggest banks.

"If you strip out the non-consumer balance sheet of ICICI and then have a comparison, the difference is not that large," Puri said. "If you strip out the non-consumer balance sheet of State Bank of India and come to the consumer balance sheet, then you will not call me the middle child. I am not in certain markets. I'm not in project finance like ICICI and State Bank, which creates the asset size."

With the scale that the bank has achieved, much more is possible than for India's very small players; and yet Puri also doesn't feel the need to be as large as the State Bank of India with its 9,000 branches. As a former Citibanker, he suspects that beyond a certain size the economies of scale are reduced and just become an expense, so he runs a lean operation. He even books his loans through his parent corporation.

"We originate for HDFC, they book the loan," he said. "We've got an automatic securitization. If I were to take the HDFC balance sheet in consumer finance along with the HDFC Bank balance sheet, we, even in size, would be the number one consumer lender in the country today."

RUNNING THE BUSINESS

Puri's HDFC Bank is largely a retail banking player, with 57 percent of his business aimed squarely at consumers. Corporate banking is another 30 percent and the rest is treasury income. With high liquidity and uncertainty in interest and exchange rates, Puri keeps the treasury unit small as it's difficult to take positions and forecast a trend.

While lending income is naturally a strong part of Puri's business, 30 percent of his income comes from fees, something he calls a healthy growth area, one that doesn't need capital and isn't subject to volatility. The business has grown out of some long-term investments that the bank has been making, and being an Indian bank, that means Puri is buying into some of the technologies that are being born all around him.

"What we've also got now is a substantial expenditure in technology, cutting-edge technology which is only now starting to pay dividends,"

Puri said. "For instance, we completed setting up our data warehouse approximately two years back. Now we have developed analytical models on that data to allow us to do predictive marketing, which reduces the cost of our additional acquisition and also allows us to structure segmented offerings based on customer needs."

Although he is the head of the organization, Puri also has a fine understanding of its backbone. He is on top of his technology and likes digging around in it to find out what it can do. The bank has linked its branches with its analytics, and he claims staff have the ability to see a client's entire transaction history. The analytics also offer preferential pricing based on the customer's profile, and the whole suite gives Puri a great deal of marketing value, especially via his branch channel and his tele-sales and direct marketing divisions. With the power of analytics behind him, Puri has been an early starter in private banking and providing services to high-net-worth individuals.

"Here we are by far the market leader, because we started this much earlier," Puri said. "Based on technology, based on the channels, based on what we can do, we've been able to segment the customers, give them a better offering."

Puri is proud of his data warehouse, but the key to making it work for him is his analytics—and he is right in thinking that the data in his data warehouse is useless without an ability to understand it.

"Putting in analytics, a data warehouse without measuring it in with the sales channel is just a waste of money," he said. "That's why most customer relationship management (CRM) applications that are popularly known failed."

The bank sought to address the needs of its sales channels when setting up its data warehouse and analytics.

"We asked, 'What information do you want if our objective is to reduce our marketing cost, allow you to better service a particular segment of customer and offer them differentiated servicing, ensure that the right customer based on his profitability is using the right channel in terms of cost, and better penetration?' Based on their requirements is what the data warehouse and the analytics were set up," he said.

By building structures and acquiring the right customers via the right channels, Puri is able to save on marketing costs. The HDFC brand also helps, and the bank uses SMS information services to stay in close contact with its clients. It also uses technology for innovation, and the bank has created a "disposable credit card" that customers can use for Internet banking that is secured, and the bank can earn transaction fees while avoiding fraud.

Besides his recent acquisition of Centurion Bank of Punjab, Puri is following the well-worn international business expansion path of moving into the Middle East, the U.S., and parts of Europe. His two main businesses outside of India will be to cater to non-resident Indians, as well as the remittance market. The bank is also setting up business in Hong Kong, London, and Singapore. After that, he'll have to wait for Indian businesses to catch up to him in their own internationalization processes.

"SBI and ICICI are out there, yes, probably earlier than us," he said. "But the business model that they have is dependent upon how many Indian corporates become global.

> **We all came back to create a world-class Indian bank.**

General Motors is not going to use ICICI in London, it will use Citibank because that's its own country, whereas the [Tata Group] would. It's a question of how much internationalization it has started. Should it have been faster? Probably. Have we lost anything substantial? The answer is no. It's definitely on the cards."

In some of its businesses, HDFC Bank has been disadvantaged, starting many of its businesses from nothing after its foundation, compared with some of its rivals, which had advantages at their start. But Puri is pleased that he's been able to build most of his businesses to the top three in the country. His next challenge is to build a world-class Indian bank, something he feels he is already quite close to. But a great deal of what inspires him goes back to "the Spirit of 1996." Puri has a high sense of accomplishment in his many operations over the years since he's begun the incredible, lonely shift of bringing about the creation of HDFC Bank.

"We all came back to create a world-class Indian bank," Puri said. "I think to a large extent we have achieved that objective in terms of market positioning, in terms of the fight we give all the foreign banks, etc. I think the next step is to actually radically alter the financial landscape in a manner that we are able to make a difference to a larger section of society."

All of India is Puri's canvas, and with his artist's brush he's been painting a fascinating picture for over a decade. To open nearly 800 branches of his own in this period of time is quite an accomplishment, and says just as much of what Puri has in him as it does of what's to come. With India's growth story, HDFC Bank clearly has a full palette of colors to choose from, and a leader with a great sense of tone trying to fit into the rainbow that is India. From the cities to the plains, the villages and the hamlets, it is the private Indian financial institution that is more and more becoming branded to a strong history, especially with tumultuous changes coming to its agriculture-based economy. It will be especially exciting for Aditya Puri.

The Northern Advance

Business savvy in southern China

As its second president, Ma Weihua has built China Merchants Bank into one of China's strongest banks.

WHILE it's "only" the sixth-biggest bank in the country with US$171 billion in assets as of September 2007, China Merchants Bank (CMB) has one of China's most powerful brands. The well-performing bank had been one of the first to pay serious attention to retail banking at the beginning of the millennium, with particular strength in cards and Internet banking. It regularly tops The Asian Banker's Excellence in Retail Financial Services survey of Asian banks for the China section.

In 2006 and 2007, it was ranked not only the best joint stock retail bank in China but the best overall bank in China, also winning several product awards. In The Asian Banker 300 list of Asia's biggest banks it comes in at number 25, but in terms of the strength ranking by five performance variables, the bank is tops in China, and it is ranked the thirteenth strongest bank in all of Asia Pacific. CMB was listed in Shenzhen in March 2002 and in Shanghai the following month.

One of the most unique features of the bank is that it is the only bank among China's biggest banks to *not* take a foreign equity investor in preparation for its Hong Kong IPO, which happened in September 2006. With its support from the large China Merchants Group, the bank may have had less need to look elsewhere for support. While the country's poorly run state banks needed their foreign investors to lend them a halo effect to help their listings along, CMB did fine without.

The bank listed at US$1.09 a share, helping the bank raise US$2.4 billion; by the end of the following year, the share price had gone up nearly four times.

Insiders at the bank are more prone to talking about CMB buying other banks than being bought into by anyone else, and they feel very protected in their fortress. In late 2007, CMB became the first new bank in more than two decades to get approval to open a branch in the U.S. In June 2008 it paid US$2.5 billion to buy 53.12 percent of Hong Kong's Wing Lung Bank, Hong Kong's twelfth-largest bank by assets. The first major purchase of a Hong Kong lender since Singapore's DBS bought Dao Heng Bank in 2001, it is the fifth Chinese banking group to buy into the Hong Kong market.

TWO SHORT DECADES AGO...

Founded in Shenzhen in 1987, the bank has been led since 1999 by Ma Weihua, a salty northerner who graduated from the School of Economics at Jilin University before serving in the government of Liaoning and Anhui provinces in the industrial northeast. He began working in the central bank, the People's Bank of China (PBoC), in 1988 as the secretary of the governor. He eventually became the central bank's senior man in Hainan province before taking the position at CMB in January 1999 as the bank's second president.

Once at the bank, Ma worked on launching the bank's successful "All-in-one" Internet service in 2001 that built on the bank's "All-in-one" card bundle of 1995, and then China's first international credit card in 2002.

"China Merchants Bank is actually the earliest bank in China to attach great importance to the retail banking business," said Ma. "It is common sense: when small and medium sized banks start their business, they start wholesale banking business because they don't have the advantage of a network. We benefited from technology and product innovation to make up for our shortcomings in the network."

Ma considers the bank to be roughly at the same level as his peers in terms of wholesale banking, and the bank's assets are indeed merely half of the fifth-biggest bank in the country, and at least a fifth the size or less than any of the big four banks. But he knew that he would have to give the bank a specialty of its own, and he saw an opportunity with the individual—and China is well-known for having lots of them.

"We realized that if we want to outshine our peers, we have to explore something that the others have ignored or have not thought of," said Ma. "I was first inspired by the Internet development. The initial form of retail banking in China was solely focusing on deposit saving. Banks can use the Internet as a platform to provide a wide range of financial products. The Internet provides a unique opportunity to compete with well-branched state banks."

> **We realized that if we want to outshine our peers, we have to explore something that the others have ignored or have not thought of.**

When the bank began its initial push into retail banking it had a difficult time gathering deposits. But through a solid IT foundation established by his predecessor, Ma found himself with interconnected platforms that could launch an "all-in-one" card that combined a debit card and an ATM card. The bank branded it with a plethora of bundled services to which it kept adding over time. So far it has not been matched by other banks. The product provided an opportunity for the bank to attract deposits, and it was heavily promoted across the provinces where the bank had operations.

For Ma, the Internet is the greatest enabler. "Our advantage remains in Internet," said Ma. "Compared with the big state banks or well-established banks such as Citibank or HSBC, we may spend some time to catch up with them [in other businesses]. But for the Internet, we are at the same starting line and we may even outpace them."

With over 100 million Chinese online, it's clear that plugged-in China represents a huge, relatively mature market for CMB to tap. Ma, who has been invited overseas to Taiwan, Hong Kong, and the U.S. to speak on the opportunities offered by the Internet, feels that it provides more for banks than just online banking. Rather, it's a foundation for all of the bank's businesses, and the level of development of the channel determines the maturity of a bank's retail banking.

> **The bank stood out among its peers in early 2007 by being the first in China to turn profitable in cards.**

Ma sees Internet banking as a complement to branches, and as a "mortar and mouse" model. About 70 percent of his retail banking clients access the bank through the Internet, while more than 50 percent of his corporate clients access the bank on the Web. But the bank doesn't have many clients who rely exclusively on the Internet, preferring to combine it with visits to branches.

With the credit card as the bank's other strong point, Ma is happy with the success the bank has enjoyed in payments.

"We can say we are successful in our credit card business, which is also beyond our expectation," said Ma. "Within less than three years, we started from nothing to become the number one credit card issuer. What's more, the average spending of our card is also number one. We also created the most favorable credit card brand. A lot of celebrities called us and complained they lost face because they didn't own a CMB card. For them, the CMB card is a way to show off their status."

The bank stood out among its peers in early 2007 by being the first in China to turn profitable in cards. With competition so high for market share in these early days of the credit card, and with so many sophisticated products already being offered, the race is on to win loyalty from China's most desirable consumers. Time is of the essence here: China's banks have developed a market for credit cards in just five years, while Western markets took 40 years to do so. Now that Ma's credit cards business is up and really running at a profit, he's going to work on converting even more of his 40 million debit card holders into credit card users. He will find potential high-end card customers from the debit card customer base and with direct sales teams to promote the business. Although foreign banks are good at cards, the fact that they have only recently been allowed to get into the cards market on their own means that they will become serious competitors in only a few years time, perhaps as early as 2010, he said.

Chinese banks, particularly the very large ones, are only recently recovering from a problem of high NPLs. There is also always the danger that bad loans on the credit cards—which are always higher than on

other loans—will come up, especially if the economy doesn't grow
as fast in the years after the Olympics as it did in the years leading up
to it. Ma says the bank has a tight
grip on risk management in cards.

> **We dreamed of building our own national brand. We decided to build our own credit card brand.**

"We are quite careful in issuing our credit cards," he said. "In the first one or two years, we were doing research on how to do risk management. It's only after we understood the fundamental rules when we accelerated the speed of issuance."

Having built up the brand and reputation for service, Ma is better able to be choosy about his customers, and often works through the HR department of large companies to get cards into the hands of salaried workers.

Ma knew that from the point of investment he'd need to wait five to eight years to see any money, but with increasing standards of living in China and changing consumer appetites it's come in a little quicker than expected. Along the way, he also made sure to protect his investment by sheltering his brand.

"We dreamed of building our own national brand and we rejected a proposal from a prestigious foreign bank to cooperate in the credit card business, and we decided to build our own credit card brand," Ma said. "At that time, it was a quite controversial decision, and time proved it to be right."

BRING THEM ON

As foreign banks begin setting up in China, they will need to focus on building their branding with individuals since they have already been doing business with Chinese companies for quite some time. The avenue of entry, as it always is when foreign banks go overseas, will be through the credit card.

But Ma sees a competitive advantage in his bank's customer base and understanding of local culture. He will also be helped by government rulings that say that if foreign banks want to issue cards in China they will need to build local credit card processing centers. This means that foreign banks will not just have the additional expense of building and staffing the centers, but they will also not be able to leverage the economies of scale provided by their regional data centers in Singapore and elsewhere. This will mean that there will be serious meetings in headquarters overseas, but once a decision is made to enter it will up the stakes for all of China's banks by bringing with it an even deadlier resolve to succeed.

Naturally, local banks will be greater competitors for Ma, and that pressure will really begin to make itself felt as soon as they also begin to show profits. So far, Ma has made use of foreign bankers, such as Taiwanese and Singaporeans to run his credit card operations. But as the bank trains people, they will also begin drifting off to other banks when the labor market becomes white hot along with the economy.

The competition is so close behind him.

"The more technology is developed, the faster innovation is copied," said Ma. "We need to innovate continually. That's the core competency of our bank. Such power comes from our senior managers' decisions and the drive and passion of our employees."

But despite his complaints, Ma and senior managers in the bank are so completely confident in their capabilities that they repeatedly say that the bank isn't seeking to improve its operations through help from foreign banks and other investors.

"It is not necessary that every bank should take the same route of inviting foreign partners and overseas listing," he said.

Instead of relinquishing ownership in exchange for expertise, the bank is hiring the expertise away from other banks. Ma will still be diplomatic and add a caveat that he's open to the cooperation model, but so far he has not used it in his bank.

"We have many foreign banks approaching us for buying our stakes or setting up joint ventures," he said of banks from the U.S., Europe, Hong Kong, Taiwan, and the rest of Asia. "How we select them will be based on the needs of our development strategy."

While the bank has forged ahead in the Internet and in cards, it needs more time to develop its wealth management business. As people get their passbook and then graduate to their first credit cards, wealth management will be a natural progression.

Being located in Shenzhen also helps. The Pearl River Delta was the first area to be opened to capitalism by Deng Xiaoping in 1979—billboards all over Shenzhen commemorate the act that spurred China's economic revolution—and

> **All banks should be transformed into real commercially viable institutions rather than semi-government agencies.**

the area has China's "old money." Proximity to Hong Kong and its international markets and influence is also beneficial to the bank in terms of providing an aspirational culture of wealth, success, and prosperity.

From its base in southern China, far from Beijing and Shanghai, CMB has the sense of being "the little bank that could." With its thought leadership toward innovation channels, its diversity into other product lines such as retail banking, and in its profitability, the bank is in some way leading the transformation of the Chinese banking industry.

IT'S THE ECONOMY, COMRADE

Ma claims that the bank does not pursue scale the way small to mid-sized banks in China do. He claims that it focuses on quality rather than quantity, similar to some medium-sized banks around Asia, such as HDFC bank in India, or even large-scale banks, such as Kookmin in Korea.

While the bank used to look at large companies, the focus is now more on mid-sized companies that are of a high quality. Ma says he's more concerned about economic profits over book profits, and intensive marketing over extensive marketing.

Over a short period, cultural change has occurred in so many parts of the organization, and Ma cites as examples a move from passive pricing to active pricing, and from risk control to real risk management. Even client culture has changed. Sales people used to spend time drinking with clients and entertaining them in night clubs. This strategy doesn't work as well any more and clients would prefer to see the bank offer them win-win products, Ma said.

But a pervasive change still eludes the country at large.

"The first imperative is the reform of the governance structure," said Ma. "All banks should be transformed into real commercially viable institutions rather than semi-government agencies. This also includes the management teams, which should be professional managers rather than government officers." Other things that the banks lack are an understanding of the right performance measures and incentive systems, he said.

CMB's size puts it in an unusual position in China. It is successful and well run and leads the pack of joint stock banks in the country, but it is still very much a mid-sized bank in China. Despite the difficult restructuring work that the large state banks are still undergoing, they are miles ahead of CMB in asset size. CMB will need to go a long way to catch up to even the smallest of them just by virtue of their incredible scale. It also has its own maturing to do as it diversifies. Gradually it is trying to push into the businesses of underwriting bonds to take advantage of overseas opportunities and to find a business that is less capital-intensive. To get into the business, Ma has groomed staff from within as well as hiring from outside.

"As long as we keep on the right track, the underwriting business will develop very fast," said Ma. "But as we are still at the initial stage, we would like to take a very prudent view to first explore the regulations."

Ma is trying to develop wholesale and retail banking at the same time, but with different business priorities.

"Wholesale is the foundation of retail business," he said. If we discard wholesale, we can't survive today. But if we discard retail, we can't survive tomorrow."

With his wily business sense, Ma's bank is forging ahead and growing wildly along with China's economy. Nestled in among the bustling manufacturing centers of the south, as well as important industrial centers all around China, the bank has developed dominance in important niches.

With a healthy brand, CMB is also steadily carving out its fair mindshare of its home market. It is not likely that much will be heard from the bank outside of China, the way blockbuster banks like Industrial and Commercial Bank of China is building itself into a regional or global player. But with a steely focus, Ma is making plenty of headway into building one of the smartest banks in the world's busiest emerging market.

A Decade of Change

Whatever doesn't kill me
makes me stronger

Having survived 1997, Kasikornbank has embraced change in fundamental ways, led by its straight-talking CEO Banthoon Lamsam.

Few bankers encapsulate modern Thai banking history the way the CEO of Kasikornbank does. Born in 1953 into the ethnically Chinese Lamsam family eight years after the bank was founded by patriarch Choti Lamsam, Banthoon Lamsam is the fourth Lamsam to lead the group. The first in his family to go off to the U.S. for his studies, where he hoped to train to become a doctor, he earned degrees from top schools such as Princeton and Harvard Business School.

Lamsam returned in 1977 to work in the international banking division of the bank. At the time, Kasikornbank was led by his uncle Banyong, who had succeeded Bancha Lamsam, the man who had led the bank for 30 years and presided over the kingdom's shift from an agriculture-based economy to an

Banthoon Lamsam
Reproduced by permission of Kasikornbank

57

industrial one. Over the course of his long career, Bancha Lamsam built it into Thailand's third-largest bank by assets (a title it has only recently lost to Siam Commercial Bank [SCB]).

Kasikornbank, which changed its name from Thai Farmers Bank in 2003, is well known as a "Chinese bank" in Thailand. It is one of several lenders founded by members of the Chinese community, the large ones being Bangkok Bank (Thailand's largest), and Bank of Ayudhya (BAY; its fifth largest).

It is also considered the seventh-largest ethnically Chinese bank outside China, Taiwan, and Hong Kong. It is perhaps Thailand's most broadly diversified universal banking group, with its hands in nearly every pie in financial services. It is particularly strong in SME lending, and to some extent retail banking, besides the usual core function of corporate lending.

> **The economy is going sideways and so banks have to adjust accordingly to make sure that we ride the waves. It's always like this.**

It has also engaged in snazzy, urban branding with the letter "K"—KBank, K-BizNet, K-Cyber-Banking—that it couldn't do when it had the pastoral Thai Farmers moniker. In Thailand, Kasikornbank obviously hopes to own the letter "K" the way Apple owns the letter "i."

When he took over the bank in 1992, Banthoon Lamsam did not have many years in the top seat before it was nearly swept away by the 1997 Asian financial crisis, which devastated Thailand first before spreading to Indonesia, South Korea, and other parts of Asia. It hit Kasikornbank hard, as it did all of the bank's peers.

The impact of the crisis was so pervasive in Thailand that evidence of the bad loans originated by the bank, and others, can to this day still be seen around Bangkok in the form of half-complete concrete monstrosities that nobody will ever finish paying off, much less provide money to tear down. But next to these battle scars, fresh projects are budding, and both can be seen from Lamsam's office in the Kasikornbank tower built on the banks of the Chao Phraya River close to the Bank of Aduyhya building but secluded from other bank headquarters in the city's financial district.

A brusque man with a keen eye, Lamsam has vivid memories of what life was like in the pressure cooker of 1997 when the struggle to survive made managing time a supreme challenge. Having learned not to waste time, Lamsam makes it a habit to get to the point, and he is considered by many a straight talker. When thinking back to the easy days leading up to the crisis he almost snickers at the type of foolhardy culture banks had at the time, and he resolves confidently that there won't be a repeat ten years later.

"The economy is slowing down naturally, and in a slowing economy it's difficult to do business," he said, referring to the rise in NPLs and stalling bank profits linked to poor consumer sentiment after the military coup of September 2006. "There's the issue of making sure we don't overstep the boundary of credit management and end up with more than necessary NPLs down the road. We've seen this before—the economy is going sideways and so banks have to adjust accordingly to make sure that we ride the waves. It's always like this."

But besides the problems of Thailand, the global unease about credit must be chilling for Lamsam, who remembers clearly the mistakes that banks across the entire industry made in 1996, as lenders went overboard. When many of them disappeared, it was a clear sign to the survivors that better credit controls were needed, and Lamsam for his part, has heeded the warning. Indeed, Kasikornbank is credited with having been swifter than most at the time in actively embracing restructuring and getting its act together to deliver sophisticated modern banking services in order to avoid being wiped out.

"So, we're comfortable that we have a better credit control platform [now]," said Lamsam. "But it's difficult with the competition, because if your competitors take the customers away from you in a price war by doubling credit lines, then the whole system is at risk."

Lamsam is confident that his systems can handle the changing situation, and in the first quarter of 2007, his bank was already showing better profitability than some of his peers.

BREAD AND BUTTER

"Lending is a dynamic process," Lamsam said. "You don't say, 'this is the right model, we're going to stick with this forever.' The real model is flexibility. You adjust your model according to the cycle of the economy; you adjust it according to the viability of that particular industry that the customer is in, and adjust the model according to a particular customer. It changes from month to month. That's the real competitiveness—to be able to read and adjust to the lending markets. That's the only way you can control risk, and at the same time you re-engineer your processes so that the cost is not overwhelming."

A tense, precarious position for the banks to be in, perhaps, as the economy slows and the temptation is to sacrifice margins for the sake of growth. The Bank of Thailand still doesn't have the teeth it needs to be a strong, independent regulator—that is in a bill working its way through parliament. But until it does, or until Thailand gets a Financial Services Commission of its own to balance the political appointments of the governorship of the Bank of Thailand, the banks may still be in a world of their own. Lamsam himself admits that publicly listed banks, like his now is, still need to issue annual targets… and meet them!

"You are pressured to perform according to the targets you've announced," he said. "The easiest way to do that is to over-lend in terms of granting too much credit for business use—over-lend and not properly manage the credit risk you are undertaking. Even if you do it wrong, you don't see the [bad] results overnight, that's the sticky thing about the lending markets. It will be two or three years down the road, and it will be somebody else who has to come in and solve the problems if the results are bad."

Lamsam sees targets stretched for all the banks in Thailand, and the result will be a relaxation of credit vigilance, reduced prices, and looser lending conditions; it is the latter, in his experience, that is the killer.

"That's the most subtle kind of deterioration," he said. "You don't see that until the crash comes. Then you find out, 'oh, we can't come after this loan, we have to be slow because the conditions have been so loose.' And that's what happened. We've gone through this one cycle before, and we've seen that on the horizon. It doesn't mean that it's going to happen in exactly the same way, but you can see it on the horizon."

Nonetheless, Lamsam is certain that it's going to be different this time. He laughs when he remembers that "back in 1996 and 1997 [people] said, 'when you enter the curve, speed up!'" Lamsam falls back on his board of directors whose message is that they won't go for lending at any cost. It's the mantra of most banks around the

region—to disdain quantity for
quality—but how much Lamsam
can follow through on this remains
to be seen.

> **The only thing that is
> family dominated here
> is my name. It's the only
> thing that's left!**

The reliance on the board of
directors is a clear sign that the
bank is a much different creature now than it was when the asset bubble burst over ten years ago. The family bank has become a publicly-
held bank, moving to five percent ownership by the Lamsam family
in 2007 from 25 percent in 1997. In fact, the change in the situation is
so severe that Lamsam himself jokes that "the only thing that is family dominated here is my name [laughs]. It's the only thing that's left!
The shareholding has been depleted, and the board of directors is very
independent. It's a very intense board." The bank and its investor relations team generally get high marks for transparency.

GRAND UNIFICATION THEORY

Change has been regular throughout the tumultuous decade, but simply giving the bank over to the public hasn't been enough to satisfy
Lamsam's craving to build a modern bank that can compete with anyone. Lamsam is currently in the middle of an ambitious plan to stitch
together all of the pieces of the financial services jigsaw that sit under
the Kasikornbank Group and integrate them into the bank to create a
universal bank.

Ironically, this has only been possible since the banks were crippled
in the crisis years. Before 1997, when the banks were more fully con-
trolled by families, the government kept them from gaining too much
influence and restricted the financial activities they could become
involved in. After 1997, when so many of them fell, the government
had to allow them to engage in a broader range of businesses simply to
prevent them from going under. This was especially important when
they started to come up against more and more foreign competitors
that had entered the market buying distressed assets to leverage into
new operations. Over the years, Kasikornbank Group has been assem-
bling business units to cover any type of banking service.

Back in 1996 and 1997 [people] said, 'when you enter the curve, speed up!'

"We can do any business within financial circles that we have licenses for, and we have all the licenses," said Lamsam.

But making efficient use of these licenses is not as easy as it would appear as the units, bolted onto the organization over the years, are run like silos and need to be integrated. It is a challenge that Lamsam still thinks a great deal about as he sets about bringing down costs and boosting efficiency as his competitors close in on him. To pull it off, he'll need to work on changing the culture and get staff to think outside of their silos.

"People think 'I'm in charge of home loans, I'm going to grab at home loans,'" Lamsam said. "Somebody else is in charge of credit cards, and he is going to go after credit cards—that's the normal mentality."

As he turns the company from a collective of separate businesses that chase their own customers into a customer-centric model branded under the letter "K," where each business is aware of each client within the group, he'll also need to think about new organizational structures and get some help from some good IT. Ultimately, he's aiming to sell the full, appropriate range of Kasikornbank products to as many clients as possible.

"If we are successful in executing this strategy, which is not easy, then we will be able to cater to a customer's total needs without the customer having to go outside the Kasikornbank Group for anything as far as financial services are concerned," he said.

HARSH REALITIES

The concept sounds like a dream come true. But Lamsam is very grounded in reality and under no illusions, nor is he trying to sell his dreams to anyone else.

"It's a nice concept—it's very difficult to execute," he said. "You know why? Because people in the bank, they look at the world from their own unit's point of view, they look at the world from their unit's *product's* point of view. It's a silo; it's automatically and naturally a silo."

The job of breaking apart his silos and integrating his units to a common cause will not be easy, and he'll use a multipronged strategy. But like other reformers, Lamsam is aware that his greatest task will be to change the culture within his bank, and to communicate with his staff.

"To break that silo is the most difficult part of this strategy," he said. "It takes a good IT system to integrate information, and it takes a lot of talking and a lot of training so that people are more capable of understanding the bank's products so that they're able to talk to the bank's customers as the representative of Kasikornbank Group, regardless of where the customer touches Kasikornbank Group."

With his competitors also embracing financial sophistication by breaking into new areas to make more robust, stable, diversified business models, Lamsam knows he has to come up with something good to win the trust and loyalty of his clients or regain ground lost in the retail banking space to SCB. He's envisioned a road map, and he's keeping an eye on structuring the bank with a customer-centric point of view. His goal is to find a way to get around the limitations in his IT systems and make it possible for staff to see a customer's entire relationship with the bank, as well as a mapping of the same customer's *potential* business with the bank.

As a straight talker, Lamsam doesn't understate the vastness of the task before him, or even the commoditized nature of the industry that he's been an intractable part of for so long. As part of his mission to protect the bank, the battle of culture and IT that he's fighting could eventually make his bank a well-rounded institution that is able to work efficiently and effectively. Maybe.

"Innovations on paper don't mean anything, and in the end, financial services are just repackaging information flow," he said. "So the sooner you can do that, the more innovative you become to the markets, and that's the key to being competitive. Each financial services product is by nature a commodity. Nobody's going to beat anybody on a killer application home loan. By definition, it's not true—a home loan is a home loan. You differentiate yourself by having a better total package, presentation, and delivery."

Of course, there are "killer products" out there, but they are so extremely niche that they belong to specialized investment banks, not a bank that once marketed itself to Thai farmers.

But if his bank is not there yet, at least none of the other banks are there either. It's a long-term plan, and everybody's future is at stake as the banks stare down the barrel of modernization.

"I think all the banks are undergoing some process of restructuring in their thinking if they want to survive," said Lamsam. "And we swear by our customer-centric KBank concept, and we're working along that line."

With his long career in banking, Lamsam understands his art intuitively, and a short conversation with him covers a great deal of ground. He speaks of finance in the way that a professor or academic or even a management consultant would, with business concepts reproduced intact, verbatim. He can talk about his operations in a way that few other CEOs can, and he appears to know the machinery down to the smallest bolt. Clearly he knows what he's got under the hood and is very hands-on in the operation.

Looking at all of the segments the bank services, Lamsam sees customers that go from individuals in the mass retail segment all the way up to huge conglomerates like Siam Cement.

"We focus on seven segments, it goes beyond retail banking," he said. "Retail, by definition, it covers the mass, the high net worth, the medium income, and then you go up to SME, lower SME—which is something we are recognized as being a pioneer in. We are not specifically emphasizing anything; we emphasize every segment as necessary to achieve a fair share of the market, a fair share of the customer wallet, and as a whole, support the whole economy."

BARBARIANS AT THE GATES?

A strain to this model will be the recent emergence of more foreign investors on the scene in Thailand. Citibank, Standard Chartered Bank, and HSBC are present in the country, and in 2007, Canada's Bank of Nova Scotia made an equity investment in Thanachart Bank. Of particular note in Thailand now is GE Money, with its 31 percent share in BAY.

GE is helping the Thai bank improve its processes, its risk management, and diversify its businesses. Where the bank had been weak in retail banking, for instance, the American conglomerate will strengthen operations. It has already rolled out

> **The ultimate objective of banking is to not have the customers feel as though they have to come to the bank.**

innovative cell phone-enabled money transfers that allow the recipients to pick up their cash at ATMs as well as a series of back office cost-saving operations.

But Lamsam is not worried yet about his new competitors—he just laughs. "Foreign banks in Thailand have not proven they will run away with our business," he said. His reaction is very different to that of the grave head of SCB Vichit Suraphongchai, who is wary of the power of their deep pockets.

Lamsam's stance is one of pure confidence in his position as a heavily entrenched local player.

"The financial services business in Thailand, a lot of it is still lending," he said. "And with lending, you have to take a risk. So you can't run away with market share because then you run into the risk issue. The foreign banks, they have risk management regimes in place, they can't just announce they will take away all the customers. It's not selling cars or selling TVs—with lending, you take the risk. So that's one reason why no foreign banks have run away with all the asset size."

But foreign banks will at least sharpen the game of competition, to which Lamsam, confident that he'll eventually make headway in his restructuring plan, would say "bring them on."

Of course, he does see GE as a tougher competitor than most, but even with the U.S. giant, he's not overly concerned.

"They will bring in new management, but the limitations will be that they still have to access the Thai labor markets, and the HR issue is the real matter in the financial services industry," he said. "There are not enough good people to go around, especially in the financial services, because that's where all the best engineering graduates are working. And without capable people, you cannot compete."

NOT AN AVID SHOPPER

Mergers and acquisitions are the furthest thing from Lamsam's mind. And with financial services so very fragmented in every market all over the world, Thailand is certainly no different. Yet even as the smaller banks consider merging to gain scale, Lamsam sees it as too great a cost.

"Mergers and acquisitions is something that people pay lip service to, but nobody really does," said Lamsam. "Why? Because they cannot rationalize the costs."

Clearly, the time to buy cheaply has passed. In 1997, no Thai bank was in a position to take on new investments from their dangerous sink or swim positions, which made foreigners the net beneficiaries of the situation.

Lamsam's view is different from that of SCB's Suraphongchai, who feels Thai banks need to consolidate in order to survive in the long term; more significantly, Lamsam's view is the opposite of BAY CEO K.K. Tan, a former Standard Chartered Bank executive, who finds acquisition the most sensible way of growing.

But so far, Thai banks haven't had a good track record of successful mergers, and they are still a relatively rare phenomenon in the kingdom.

"You look at TMB Bank, with the merger of three banks, they get the worst of all worlds," Lamsam said referring to the deal that brought together Thai Military Bank, DBS Thai Danu, and Industrial Finance Corporation of Thailand to form TMB, which has been bleeding capital. "It didn't work like the Western model where you combine three, and you come out as five, no. You combine three, you come up with the cost of five and end up with the efficiency of two. So that's the real example for everyone to see, that it's not easy to achieve cost rationalization in the first place, and two, they're not achieving any competitiveness. Somebody's strength added to somebody's strength. That's all hot air by investment bankers. They're not competitive."

Lamsam is clearly happy with the capabilities he has under his belt. In fact, it may be more than he can handle at the moment. He would only be interested in buying failed companies at a steep discount where the pricing is attractive and the costs and integration become more manageable. His goals are obviously different from the foreign banks that are buying into Thailand, such as Scotiabank, which is buying into Thanachart Bank after 20 years as a foreign bank in Thailand.

"For Scotiabank, they want a foothold. I don't need a foothold," he said.

To stay ahead of his competitors, and to improve his bank's reputation as a hip, modern bank in the face of sophisticated foreign entrants, Lamsam has pushed innovation. Kasikornbank has built a reputation as a bank that is not afraid to try new things. The bank is introducing inventive services such as a pawn shop and an insect exterminator service. But the innovations are not always meant to bring in dividends and are just as much about marketing and curiosity. Lamsam is philosophical about the closure of one of the bank's much talked-about programs: coffee shop banking.

"We did an experiment with coffee banking, it didn't turn out to be as successful as we hoped," he said. "Two things—one is that there was not an effective business capture model implemented at the time. It was just window dressing. Also, the reason was that we wanted that space back; we need it for other financial services. So, we now, as a group, the leasing company, the security company, use that very precious space."

Certainly, many banks now have tried to ride on the back of coffee shop culture, blending the mood of sophisticated relaxation with the more negative moods often associated with bank branches—financial insecurity, boredom, frustration—to get clients to feel that banks are places where they can spend time comfortably. Banks in Japan and Singapore have tried the same thing.

"The ultimate objective of banking is to not have the customers feel as though they have to come to the bank," he said. Unfortunately, not many of the patrons of the coffee shops ever became clients; they were just there to get a cup of coffee. Other clients liked to keep their banking separate from their time relaxing with friends and thinking about less serious matters than mortgages and investments.

"Coffee is not high in our priorities," Lamsam said. "It was an interesting experiment, it didn't turn out the way we thought it would. And as a good, flexible business, you have to adjust."

Lamsam is already looking for his next innovation, one that will make sense to the bank, especially lesser-seen back office innovations that can add process- and cost efficiencies.

With all of the reinventing of the system, and the tweaking of the client approach, Lamsam's experimentation may seem random to some. But he has a keen sense of the patterns that are affecting his bank. He has studied them abroad and knows what he needs to do in his country when the time is right. He also knows his customers. They are still keen to come into the branches; they don't want to do their banking in remote channels. With the substantive penetration of Internet banking still nearly a generation away, owing to low Internet penetration in Thailand, Lamsam is keeping close to where his clients are.

Lamsam's experiments are not cheap, but he can rationalize their costs nonetheless, and certainly they'd be lower than an acquisition would be. As Thailand's fourth-largest bank, he's still relatively comfortable in his position, and confident of his ability to invest in his business.

With a multi-year project on his hands to build a Citibank of Thailand under a customer-centric universal banking model, Lamsam has his work cut out for him. With inorganic growth by acquisition the furthest thing from his mind, he's clearly anxious to get the show on the road. Confident that he can handle a temporary economic slowdown as Thailand's fragile democracy resets itself, Thailand's wily survivor is still optimistic about the economic prospects of his bank helping bit by bit to develop the country that he loves.

Chapter 3
The Upstarts—Messing With the Formula

Dance to the Music

Keeping your ears open and listening to the market

> *Chairperson Tessie Sy's ability to nurture Banco de Oro of the Philippines into one of the country's largest banks is a real banking coup.*

THE year 2007 was a big one for the Philippines, when the biggest event in the country's financial services sector occurred: the merger of Banco de Oro and Equitable PCI Bank to create Banco de Oro EPCI Bank (BDO-EPCI). The event infused the sleepy community with a great energy and set new industry benchmarks. BDO-EPCI dislodged Bank of the Philippine Islands (BPI) as the second-largest bank in the Philippines by assets and became one of the country's new retail banking giants by marrying the strong capital base of Banco de Oro with Equitable PCI's branch presence and retail banking capabilities.

Consumer lending will be the driver of growth in the Philippines in 2008, fuelled by remittances from overseas workers, which account for 20 percent to 40 percent of the growth of various parts of that business. The overseas remittance business expanded 18 percent year on year in the first half of 2007, and experts call for the market to hit US$15 billion in 2008. The fact that

Tessie Sy
Reproduced by permission of
TAB International

70

corporations have other sources of funding and will increasingly be cutting their proportionate exposure to bank loans is also a factor of this tilt.

Banco de Oro had always been considered a well-run bank, and it was linked to Henry Sy's giant Shoemart empire, which includes shopping malls, retail outlets, real estate ventures, and other businesses. But its acquisition trail up until 2006 had created a bank that catered to small and medium-sized businesses and corporations, and much less to consumers.

Philippine banks are weak in retail banking with only BPI showing any strength in the business among the large banks, doing more than 25 percent of its lending to consumers. BPI is followed distantly by the legacy Equitable PCI. With the merger, this will begin to change, especially after BDO-EPCI picked up the American Express portfolio in late 2007, and as the merging lenders capitalize on economies of scale. The merger has also encouraged other mergers among medium-sized players, and it's only a matter of time before larger players begin to feel the pressure to grow and achieve economies of scale of their own.

"The Philippine banking system's development is similar to how the British banking system evolved," said Nestor Tan, president of Banco de Oro. "You have branches that were, in a way, individual small banks. They were self-contained and scale was not really important. But as banks expanded, they moved more to the current model where you centralize a lot of things and let technology work for you. Size and scale then become an important factor in the competitiveness of banks."

The Philippines is still a very fragmented market with many small banks. It is also a very small market, with the combined assets of the country's top six banks in 2006 only equaling that of Taiwan's First Commercial Bank, the sixty-eighth largest in Asia Pacific according to The Asian Banker's ranking of the region's 300 largest banks. The combined assets of the mighty six are even smaller than Standard Chartered Bank in Hong Kong, the fourth-largest bank in a market of seven million people. The Philippines has more than 90 million people.

CHANGING TIMES

The country's financial services sector is finally waking up. This is greatly driven by an increasingly sophisticated business environment, as well as several global and regional trends that are shaking the industry to its core.

"Given what we have seen in 2005 and 2006, over the next three years, we foresee greater consolidation," said Amando Tetangco Jr., governor of the Philippine central bank Bangco Sentral ng Pilipinas. "We will see a banking landscape with around six big banks at the center, and this will be complemented by smaller banks serving market niches."

Tetangco attributed this consolidation to a more stringent regulatory framework and the adoption of international accounting standards. Competition will be fueled by foreign banks and foreign investors looking for partnerships with existing banks in the Philippines.

Leading the trend, of course, has been the aggressive rise of Banco de Oro in the Philippine financial services industry, led by Teresita "Tessie" Sy (pronounced *see*). The eldest child of the Philippines' richest man, Henry Sy, who built a retail and property empire out of his chain of shoe stores called Shoemart, Sy sits right at the heart of the Philippines business community. Together with her large, industrious family, Sy and her four brothers and sisters control a huge business empire under the SMI name.

A passionate woman, Sy is highly respected in the Philippines business community for her sharp mind and keen business sense, as well as fine modern sensibilities. The fact that the Banco de Oro and Equitable PCI merger is shocking the Philippines' financial services community is no surprise to anyone who knows Sy well.

Though no banker by training, Sy is one of the most influential figures in the Philippines due to her savvy deal-making prowess that has shaken up the sleepy financial services community. She has shown a passion for modernizing the clubby business and bringing it into the twenty-first century. Sy has also managed to turn one of the Philippines' smallest banks into one of the largest.

FINDING HER DESTINY

Sy began to get interested in the family's banking business, Banco de Oro, when she saw that there were units in the empire that weren't adding the synergies that they had potential for. Or perhaps she was just waking up to the fact that in the old world of the Philippines, a bank was a very desirable addition to a family's overall business.

"I come from another industry," said Sy, who had been heavily involved in the family's retail franchises. "I'd never been interested in a bank before, but since it was a family business I thought of looking into this investment. After being there for some time, I thought there were quite a lot of opportunities for financial services. Maybe I read a lot at that time and then I thought of expanding the organization, an organization of people who would see the same directions and opportunities in the bank."

Sy entered the bank in 1984 when she was 34 years old. At the time, the family corporation's investment in Banco de Oro was small compared to the money that it had tied up in the retail and shopping center businesses.

"I did spend some time in the bank but not as much," said Sy. "But, as you get to know a business, you get to see the opportunities."

By 1995, Sy was becoming restless in the mall and retail business that seemed to have developed its own momentum, and began re-examining the banking business. She saw opportunities for synergies between the bank and the other businesses that no one had thought much of before. The family tended to give development of these less priority than areas where there was faster growth.

"At that time, our business focus was not really consumer-oriented," Sy said. "We were looking at our suppliers and associates. Since we have been in the market for some time, we thought we could also offer them financial services."

However, it's clear to see that the bank was already deep in a tangent of business banking, and was not paying attention to the individuals who shopped in the company's cavernous malls.

"In 1995, we had a few malls and things had settled down," Sy said. "It has its own expansion strategy. Then, you notice this area with potential that has not been tapped. At 45, I saw more interesting things to do in the banks. I thought even though I may not be a banker, I'd like to take the challenge. At that time, I was confident that we could really grow the banking business. I don't know where the confidence came from. Maybe it was from doing something new for a change."

Sy said she focused on building a good organization because her background was not in finance.

"I thought, at that time, if I work with a good organization, I provide the right environment, and with the people's expertise, I can really go somewhere," Sy said.

> **If I work with a good organization, if I provide the right environment, with the people's expertise, I can really go somewhere.**

Banco de Oro was still a small bank in 1995, the 18th-largest in a very small market, according to Sy. She began to think of herself as a niche player that had expertise in business banking.

"It was more on the supply chain," Sy said. "We started with that. I remember I had to go out and really ask for business. That was a good experience. I didn't know much about banking but I was relying on relationships. We built it slowly and also at that time, we had to have good bottom lines, and with the group of people that I had, we hit anywhere as long as we can make some profit—whether it's in investment banking, treasury, or loans."

But there were psychological barriers that she had to overcome so that she could begin the journey from a niche player to the top of the heap. Among them was learning not to believe what other people said about her and her bank, a valuable lesson for navigating the sea of arrows that were eventually to be unleashed on her during her bid to bring Banco de Oro together with the much larger Equitable PCI Bank.

"Just like people were convinced by what they saw on TV, I was convinced by what I read," said Sy, who is an avid reader of business books. "I was always reading on certain banks. Of course, those banks were much bigger than us, but I thought that maybe one of these days, if we cannot be big, we can be a good niche player. I thought we could be a little bit more foreign in order to be different. I got quite a few people with foreign experience, commercial bankers. I thought they would tell me where to go."

AMMUNITION

Sy found an able lieutenant and confidante in Nestor Tan, who joined the bank in 1997 to be the bank's executive vice president, before rising to be its president in 1998. Tan worked for 15 years in banks such as Mellon Bank, Banker's Trust, and Barclays. The quiet, owlish Tan is an intense man with an analytical mind who has a reputation in the Philippines as being a very able manager and one of the country's most serious bankers.

"I told Nestor that we needed about three years to put the organization together," Sy said. "The Asian crisis also came in 1997. Most of the banks were saddled by a lot of bad loans. We were not because we were small then. We thought, 'we have a clean book, and we could move fast,' but the organization was not ready. I told Nestor at that time to slowly build the organization, reorganize ourselves, and work on the system so that in 2000 we can be more aggressive in the market. As 2000 came, we were in the market aggressively."

With Tan and "other people who would understand the same directions" on board, Sy had her team of commercial bankers to steer the ship. The modern course has been away from corporate lending, as traditional manufacturing jobs started moving to China and corporate borrowers began tapping the capital markets instead of banks for finance. Another growth area is project finance, particularly energy, infrastructure, and mining.

But an even more important customer area is the untapped one of the retail consumer.

"The banking system has to look for alternatives, and the most attractive one appears to be consumer lending," Tan said. "As consumers gain access to loans and other banking services, the economy experiences renewed demand for consumer items like houses, automobiles, and other consumables. That consumer demand is what we believe will spur our economic growth. However, you need scale to reach those consumer markets and to service them efficiently."

As Tan planned his operational strategies across all of the bank's businesses, Sy took a more overarching role in the organization. The bank prepared for listing from 2000 to 2003, and began its acquisition trail, gaining experience in the ins and outs of integrating new organizations, to the point where Sy boasts that "we can integrate a smaller bank completely in about three months."

The lessons have come in handy. In the decade from 1995 to 2005, Banco de Oro had grown from the eighteenth-largest to the fifth-largest bank in the country by assets, and graduated from a savings bank to a full service universal bank with all of the requisite licenses. Sy then turned her eye to Equitable PCI, taking a small investment and building it up to a major stake. When the industry learned of her intention to acquire the bank and possibly merge it with Banco de Oro, Sy earned a reputation as an upstart for trying to tackle a larger bank. Seasoned bankers and entrenched members of the investment community did not take a liking to this.

"Many people did not like the way I got [the shares]," she said. "Maybe because I was not really somebody, I'm really an outsider."

"To some extent, some of the industry players thought that Banco de Oro could just stay as a mom and pop operation," says Corazon P. Guidote, vice-president of investor relations at SM Investments (SMI), the Prime holding company of the Shoemart-linked retail chains, financial institutions, real estate developers and merchandisers. "So people got very surprised that all of a sudden it is a very aggressive buyer of other banks, aggressively buying a much bigger bank like Equitable PCI." At the end of 2005, the year that SMI got its first significant stake in Equitable PCI, Banco de Oro was valued at US$382 million in shareholder equity, while Equitable PCI was worth US$709 million.

PLAYING WITH THE BIG BOYS

The roots of the merger go back to the acquisition strategy that Banco de Oro launched in 2001 when it acquired the Philippine subsidiary of Hong Kong's Dao Heng Bank, which was in the process of being acquired by Singapore's DBS. In 2002, it added First e-Bank, in 2003, the Philippine subsidiary of Banco Santander Central Hispano, and in 2005, it bought 66 of the 67 branches in the Philippines of Singapore's United Overseas Bank.

In 2004, the bank tried to buy its first major block of shares of Equitable PCI Bank from the Social Security System (SSS) pension fund, but failed, leaving it with just the small 2.5 percent stake that it had built up. It was more successful in 2005 when it got the 24.76 percent share of Equitable PCI Bank founding Go family. With a large stake, Sy resigned from her chairmanship at Banco de Oro to take on a directorship at Equitable PCI. She was also the chairman of the executive committee at Equitable PCI. This marked the start of her work spanning both interests that only ended in 2007 when the merger was completed.

The years in between were marked by battles with personalities on the Equitable PCI board, SSS, and another pension fund investor in the bank called Government Service Insurance System over the strategic outlook for the bank. Sy battled to find a way to bring the two banks together and maximize synergies, with an eye also to grow the old Banco de Oro's asset books and improve the numbers for everyone's benefit.

Of course, with one major shareholder's unquestioning support—her father, Henry Sy—she still had a powerful ally. In the end, persistence paid off and one by one the shareholders came on board with her plan. The battle has been totally fought by Sy, a fierce combatant with a warrior's spirit.

> **Nothing comes to me easy. It's my personality. Why would people do things for me? I'm nobody, so I have to really go and do things and try to get the things that I want. I always work for it anyway.**

"Nothing comes to me easy," she said. "It's my personality. Why would people do things for me? I'm nobody so I have to really go and do things and try to get the things that I want. I always work for it anyway. So this is no difference except that this has been in a different size. The conflict has been played large in public."

The battle has taught the Philippines fighter many lessons about how to be a champion.

"You have to really persevere in whatever you're doing," said Sy. "It's not just going to happen the way you like it to happen. What I draw from there is the perseverance and that you will always be resilient."

DOMINOES?

Now that the merger has gone ahead, the real sparks are starting to fly, and nearly all of the country's banks will be affected by the high-level merger.

"There will be consolidation, there will be mergers, and that's because the realities of banking and financial services going forward will be tougher and tougher as we face the realities of Basel II, International Accounting Standards, and all of that," said Leonilo G. "Topper" Coronel, executive director of the Bankers Association of the Philippines. "Some of the biases, defenses of old families, and controlling stockholders have really softened quite significantly because they are facing the realities that either you have to put up your own capital and slug it out in a very different, very competitive playing field, or just open yourself to be a bigger fish in a bigger pond. Either you play in the NBA or you play in the local league."

> So this is no difference except that this has been in a different size. The conflict has been played large in public.

This doesn't mean small or medium-sized banks can't exist in this kind of environment, said Tetangco, "provided that you're well capitalized and well run, have built up a market niche. That's why we're seeing perhaps six big banks, complemented by smaller banks serving market niches."

The paradigm for the banks of the Philippines is shifting rapidly.

"If you want to be a universal bank," said Edwin Bautista, executive vice president at UnionBank of the Philippines, "it's either you go top five, or content yourself at being number 15 but be very profitable in the niches that you operate in," perhaps referring to Security Bank, a very attractive—albeit expensive—niche bank.

"There have been overtures," said Alberto Villarosa, CEO of Security Bank. "Basically we defined the market to still need a strong independent niche player, which is probably not aligned with a strong business interest. There are not many of us left in the niche. There's probably UnionBank of the Philippines and Rizal Commercial Banking

Corporation. All the others are with either the Shoemart Group, the Lucio Tan Group, the Metrobank Group, or the BPI Group."

Certainly the market is getting tighter, but not everyone has the "easy" option that Sy had of taking aim at Equitable PCI Bank.

"All of the banks will tell you that if there's an opportunity in the marketplace they would be open to it," said one senior banker who didn't wish to be named. "But it would be very hard for BPI to go on acquiring because they have a large chunk of the market, so it will probably be just a duplication of customers, so they have to be very careful of which bank to absorb."

Sy has pushed the industry hard, and as she enjoys the efficiencies of scale, she may still be looking around for a few more pieces of the puzzle. Meanwhile, some of her smaller competitors will be suffering a rude awakening.

> **It's not like the no-brainer business it was before where you can make your buck without so much of the sophistication and the skills you need to put in.**

"Some people might just say, 'Well, I give up, I'd probably better play in some other playing court rather than financial services, because it's really tough,'" Coronel said, referring to families that own banks along with other easier-to-manage businesses. "It's not like the no-brainer business it was before where you can make your buck without so much of the sophistication and the skills you need to put in, the organization, the training. It's a very different world out there now."

Having stirred up the pot, Sy is probably enjoying the new view she has on her newest passion, the Philippines' financial services sector. After all, her outlook on business also has a philosophical side. "Things here in the Philippines are unpredictable. You just have to dance," she said. While the music plays, dance.

Waking up the City that Never Sleeps

How to unlock part of US$14 trillion in consumer savings (part 1)

Japan's most ambitious foreign bank spent US$10 billion during its annus horribilis building up its local franchise. Sunil Kaul gets to sit behind the wheel.

ALTHOUGH any self-respecting bank will want to have at least *some* presence in Japan—or at least Tokyo—there is only one non-Japanese bank that is big in Japan in a really serious way. Citi has been present in the country since 1902, constantly facing off against massive Japanese banks. Until the emergence of three smaller banks owned by foreign private equity players and run by international bankers (often ex-Citibankers), it has been going it alone.

The bank made a brave foray into retail banking in the 1970s. It was an expensive venture that didn't break even for about ten years, but it introduced innovation to the country with such novelties as 24-hour ATMs, phone banking, and foreign exchange investment services and mutual funds. Japanese banks caught on

Sunil Kaul
Reproduced by permission of
Citibank Japan

eventually, but only now—with corporate lending stagnant—is the Japanese financial services industry really taking retail banking seriously. The massive group of Japanese savers is, after all, seen as a key source for building fee revenue in investment funds, insurance, and other businesses.

Of course, Citi is also infamous in Japan—and around the world—for an incident in 2004 when its separately-run private banking business lost its banking license and was forced to wind up its business in Japan. But the remaining Citi retail and corporate banking unit, with its own license intact, has carried on, despite suffering some initial "guilty by association" feedback that kept business quiet for a period.

It began laying plans to make up for lost time in 2006, and has now gone into rapid expansion mode. Citi was approved for local incorporation on July 1, 2007, and in the same year it acquired Nikko Cordial, the country's third-largest brokerage, which will become a wholly owned unit of the bank. It will also rapidly expand beyond the 30 branches it had in July 2007, with plans to have well over 40 by the end of 2008. With this it will match Shinsei Bank, the largest of the three "foreign" banks run by private equity firms… and in some ways its best imitator.

With its incorporation, Citi has brought in Sunil Kaul to be its new president under the bank's long-standing chairman Douglas Peterson, himself once described as former CEO Chuck Prince's "hand-picked troubleshooter in Japan." A cheerful man with a wide, friendly grin, Kaul is a career Citibanker who has bounced around the bank's various locations in Asia. Getting his start in India in 1985, Kaul worked in both corporate and consumer banking over the next 20 years, and he has been with Citi in the U.S., Japan, the Netherlands, and Singapore. During this time, he picked up skills in the bank's wealth management divisions, as well as in consumer and SME credit.

From 2002 to 2003, he did his first stint in Japan as the head of global transaction services in Citibank Japan's corporate banking division before going off to Singapore to head the Asia Pacific retail banking operations. Returning to Japan again in 2007 to take a position in the new locally listed institution, Kaul has found a totally new Citi.

Unfortunately, it is also a turbulent time for Citi globally, as the bank works in a new CEO and wrangles with its stock price. In late 2007, a falling stock price was a huge issue for what was once the world's largest bank by market capitalization, and Citi had to renegotiate the terms of its acquisition of Nikko Cordial because its stock price would not sit in the green zone.

The country unit may have picked a bad time to get ambitious for other reasons as well. While Japan had been identified under former CEO Chuck Prince as one of the key markets where Citi wanted to see a lot more growth, these plans could always give way to financing pressure as the bank goes through its current restructuring phase under new CEO Vikram Pandit.

> **We have built an extremely solid base in what we call the "mass affluent" segment.**

Nonetheless, Japan is still a rich market with untapped possibilities as Citi has already shown in its retail businesses. It is not the only global bank looking seriously at Japan—both HSBC and Standard Chartered Bank are trying to figure out how to break into the wealth management and other niche businesses, while private equity players like financial institutions-specialist Newbridge also circle the land looking for opportunities.

"Our key prerogative is to build our retail and corporate business," Kaul said. "On the retail side, we have built an extremely solid base in what we call the 'mass affluent' segment. We have done extremely well with that, and we want to accelerate that process."

The bank plans to invest in distribution to reach priority customers and double the number of branches in Japan, Kaul said.

ENGAGING CORPORATE JAPAN

"On the corporate side, we're looking to gain substantially from an increase in our customer base, so expanding our footprint is the second big thing," he said. "The third thing is obviously making sure that we use our partnership with Nikko in a way that adds value to the customer, whether it's on the corporate or consumer side. The fourth thing, which is always important and is not necessarily a specific business thing but a critical enabler, is to keep focus on how we conduct the business here and make sure that we abide by the letter and spirit of being a local company, which is what we've become now."

The bank has a massive spectrum of corporate banking solutions, but transaction banking and leveraged finance are its main strengths, Kaul said. He sees the bank helping Japanese companies raise finance overseas to fund acquisitions, which will increase as the Nikko Cordial transaction brings those clients closer to Citi.

"We are not bankers in the same way as a Mizuho or an SMBC (Sumitomo Mitsui Banking Corporation), but we operate across a spectrum of products with focus on those related to our core competence," he said.

Until the bank finalizes the Nikko Cordial acquisition, Kaul is not entirely sure how the broker will add synergies to his own corporate business, but the two companies have had a partnership for many years already in investment banking, and Kaul feels they work well together.

"Even before the recent Nikko Cordial transaction, we had a partnership with them called Nikko Citigroup that goes back many years," he said. "And that is an investment banking arm of the company. It was almost 50–50, and that's now obviously becoming even closer following the Nikko Cordial transaction."

But in one regard Citi is buying Nikko at just the right time, as regulations that prevent securities divisions of a bank from sharing client information with other parts of the bank are in the process of being changed to allow more client information to be shared.

Considering his years in Singapore spent away from Citibank Japan, Kaul has the benefit of some distance from the environment that poisoned the bank during the private bank fiasco of 2004. The experience has obviously resulted in some big changes in the bank since the time he left in 2003, and the bank exudes a *mea culpa* culture.

A BREAK WITH THE PAST

"From a lessons-learned perspective, first of all, it is very important to have a solid well-managed governance process in the organization," Kaul said. "We all need to ultimately recognize that we are working as part of the Citibank Japan organization. It's very, very critical. Number two is that we need to make sure that we regularly check the checks and balance system we have, and make sure that the compensation systems, the management systems, the goals, how we evaluate people, *et cetera*, are spread across a balanced set of variables that span the full spectrum of financial performance to control, compliance, etc. We learned a lot from this, and the ultimate thing is that we are in a business where trust matters."

The photo of Chuck Prince bowing in apology to regulators on October 25, 2004, three days after presenting regulators with a business improvement plan, was the snapshot seen around the banking world, and is surely a mark of shame for any career Citibanker. The fact that Japanese regulators stripped the bank of its private banking license anyway would be doubly severe, especially for those building a career there.

> **I keep saying to my staff, there is no declaring victory on this. It's a continuous process.**

"Citibank Japan made mistakes, and we acknowledge that and we believe we have fixed many of those issues," said Kaul. "And like I keep saying to my staff, there is no declaring victory on this. It's a continuous process. We need to remain vigilant and build on what we've done; and at the same time, all the things we've been able to do this year are hopefully a demonstration of the fact that some of the efforts we've put in are effective."

Clearly, the issue will haunt Kaul and his team for many more years, a constant reminder of the vigilance that they have sworn to, and Kaul is obviously certain that the bank will come out stronger from the process.

The plan to become more deeply embedded in Japan is not cheap for the company. Citigroup invested at least US$10 billion in the Japanese market in 2007 alone, which was a combination of localizing the bank's operations along with the Nikko Cordial transaction. Part of that was spent on the first phase of its branch-doubling exercise. Kaul will need to strike a balance so that his costs don't spiral out of control.

GOING RETAIL

"I don't think that there's a retail banking strategy for the mass affluent without branches," he said. "On the other hand, you don't need thousands. I think it's very important that we provide customers with multiple channels to interact because the same customer may come to your branch only two or three times per year; but it's exceedingly important to recognize that there's a sense of comfort, a sense of association, a sense of brand that goes with physical location. But do we need thousands? I don't think so."

In this sense, Kaul is pointing out one of the oddities of Japan—even Mitsubishi UFJ Financial Group, which runs Asia's largest bank, doesn't have 1,000 branches. Only the post office, which operates a bank as well, has thousands of branches—25,000 to be precise. The post office has a *real* branch network, and when it is privatized over the next five years it will become a serious competitor to Japan's financial institutions, Citi among them.

Despite the investment in the few branches that they do have, the investments pay off.

"Every branch we've opened here is [bringing in] substantially more than what I have seen in any branch we have opened anywhere else," Kaul said.

> **Every branch we've opened here is [bringing in] substantially more than what I have seen in any branch we have opened anywhere else.**

"In terms of the amount of customer assets you can collect in the first few weeks, in terms of the number of customers, the quality of those customers, the demographic impact, the income level of those customers, this is a very affluent market," Kaul said. "People keep talking about China and India and so on—they're extremely important markets that I've worked hard to cultivate in my previous assignment, but this is here and now. This is big."

Kaul is confident of the products that he will be bringing to his markets, and is keen to add Nikko's products to those that he sources from the industry. He said he expects a positive revenue trajectory that will come with the new branches.

"What is our business model? It's very straightforward," he said. "You find customers who are attracted to the type of product you have. You have the right set of solutions that appeal to them. Have a well-trained sales force. And if you can do that for 100, you can do that for 200, you can do that for 800. I have done this so many times. If you get the model right, if you can reach out to the right segment, if you have the right profiling and the right needs assessment processes, and if you have a well-trained sales person, it's just a question of the management or the volume."

Part of what Citi is doing in Japan is finding a way to mature with its clients and build a base of very Japanese offerings to provide for the very valuable customers that the bank already has. Kaul sees so much potential in his existing client base that he can substantially increase his business without even adding new clients. Clearly, the new clients that he gets from his new branches would then be the gravy.

"We wouldn't invest this kind of money unless we felt confident," he said.

A FISH OUT OF WATER?

Like other bankers in Japan, Kaul doesn't find Japan much of a place to practice the traditional art of banking.

"It's not as much of a lending market as you'd expect in Malaysia, India, or Korea for example," Kaul said. "But at the same time, there are needs and we are working on different ways to make sure that we meet those needs. It's more like Singapore and less like Malaysia."

Citibank needs to fine-tune itself to the many vagaries of such a unique market. This extends beyond corporate lending and funds into credit cards, where, despite the fact that the bank has built the country's best-known revolving business, Kaul can still note wryly that "some customers revolve, many don't."

Despite his experience across several businesses in several markets at one of the world's largest banks, Kaul approaches his work in Japan with an appropriately minimalistic view of the business, and he likes to keep it simple.

"My view is that we need to focus on the basics and do it right," he said. "We have affluent customers on the retail side, we have great corporates, we have wonderful solutions in cash and treasury management and security services and building our proposition around wealth management and so on. And it does make money."

Kaul insists that he is in Japan to build a business for the bank, not keep a ship in order, and he's keen to follow through on the company's aggressive plans in corporate

> **My view is that we need to focus on the basics and do it right.**

and consumer banking, which include strengthening the existing franchise. In the meantime, however, Kaul is wary of the heavy competition that he's going to face from the Japanese banks.

"They are big and well known," he said. "They're strong banks and very worthy competitors. On the other hand, we have some significant advantages for a sizable chunk of the Japanese customer segment, whether it's corporate or consumer, where we believe we can make a difference."

In terms of its global perspective and access to international best practices, Citi's main competitors in Japan will be the three private equity-led banks: Shinsei Bank, Tokyo Star Bank, and Aozora Bank. All three were failed banks that had been privatized and then bought from the government by private equity firms early in the decade. They have all been turned around by international management teams, and have been re-listed on the Tokyo Stock Exchange. They are all smart about building niches with small, focused branch networks in the Tokyo area.

But these three banks also suffer from lack of scale and could eventually be acquisition targets for an ambitious Citi with a little more money to spare. Still, with the big bank's recent problems, perhaps HSBC or Standard Chartered Bank are more likely buyers if none of the three are keen to merge with each other to gain scale.

With its international resources, Citi is in a better position to keep its costs low by leveraging global capabilities.

"We do leverage technology systems across a bunch of our products, and we leverage a service system outside of Japan.," Kaul said. It is part of the overall Citi strategy, sharing systems, resources, service structure, and technology."

The bank also shares talent, and lately it seems like a lot of heavy hitters have been flown in to get the bank rolling in a big way.

It may not be a moment too soon: more Western banks are starting to look at Japan seriously now, and Japan's gigantic mega banks are starting to wake from their long, asset bubble burst-induced hibernation. They are all stretching their wings and looking at the two areas that Kaul and Citi are going to focus on: retail and corporate banking. Japan's mega-banks are working on building overseas networks and incorporating in China the way Citi has; they are also working on building their retail banking offerings, in particular SMBC and Mizuho.

Citi Japan may also encounter trouble from its New York headquarters as the mighty beast reacts to a new leader and a new corporate culture. But for a resilient bank that has been around as long as Citi has, it should be able to hold on.

Sunil Kaul left Citibank Japan in June 2008 to work in private equity. Although he no longer works for Citibank Japan, the situations he describes in this chapter are still valid.

Going for the One

Slow and steady wins the race

> *UOB Buana's President Director Jimmy Laihad brought his bank to a local listing and oversaw the entrance of a significant outside investor.*

INDONESIA's banks have been through the ringer; as one of the countries hardest hit by the Asian financial crisis, Indonesia saw the number of banks in the country drop from more than 300 to less than 130. But even with this amount, there are still too many banks, and the regulator is trying to figure out how to reduce them.

Struggling along with the remaining banks is UOB Buana. Run as a family bank into the 1990s when it was still called Bank Buana, the directors decided to modernize the bank when they finally brought in a professional manager as its first non family-related senior manager. Jimmy Kurniawan Laihad, a somber and bespectacled banker with a book-lined office and the air of an intellectual, came from a background in international banking. He earlier worked at a joint venture bank that Bank Buana had formed with Mitsubishi Bank in Indonesia called Mitsubishi-Buana.

In 1996, he joined Bank Buana as a director before moving into the president director position in 1999 to run the bank. One of the first big projects he undertook as president director was to convince shareholders to have the bank publicly listed in 2000. He then helped bring in investors such as the International Finance Corporation (IFC), the private sector investment arm of the World Bank, which made its first post-Asian financial crisis investment in Indonesia in Bank Buana.

With the IFC showing confidence in the bank, more investors came in, including Singapore's United Overseas Bank (UOB). With an initial stake of 23 percent in late 2005, the family-run bank increased its stake to 61 percent just over a year later in December 2006, eventually changing the name to UOB Buana in 2007. The five founding owners of the bank have reduced their stake to 25 percent, and the rest of the bank is publicly held.

A BANK REBORN

Having been with the bank through its hardest times, Laihad has learned many important lessons from deep down within himself, as well as from far inside the character of the bank as well.

> If you want to survive, and not only survive but grow, we need a strong partner who can assist us in our business model and infrastructure platform. The banking business needs a lot of IT investment and capital expenditure.

"I became the president director in 1999, just after the Asian financial crisis," Laihad said. "It was a very challenging time. You live a day at a time. But Buana is known as a conservative, prudent bank, and during that period the prudent approach paid off. You have to see beyond your lifetime. This basically shows that, at Buana, we make decisions based on long-term goals, and it pays off."

A patient listener, Laihad measures his words carefully and speaks with the gravitas of a man who prefers to win his battles through careful preparation and planning than force of will. But if convincing shareholders to launch an IPO was a difficult task, convincing them to sell a stake to an outsider was even more so.

"That was not an easy decision, especially for the shareholders," said Laihad. "I convinced the shareholders that even though we are prudent, conservative, and doing very well as a bank in Indonesia, competition will become very tough three to five years down the road. If you want to survive, and not only survive but grow, we need a strong partner who can assist us in our business model and infrastructure platform. The banking business needs a lot of IT investment and capital expenditure."

The bank has seemingly learned

> **The most important consideration is whether the business is viable.**

that sitting on the sidelines as the banking sector grows around them, as had been the case in the late 1980s and the 1990s, was not the way to go, and some outside help was needed.

Besides the Singapore lender, some European banks came knocking, as well as some other Southeast Asian banks that wanted to skip the courtship process and jump into a quick marriage by becoming majority shareholders immediately. UOB, however, was patient enough to wait through a more traditionally protracted period of courtship to give Bank Buana enough space so that the two lenders could get to know each other better.

"By the end of the day, my shareholders decided that UOB is a very good match, because they know Indonesia, they know the operating environment in Indonesia," said Laihad. "But most importantly, they know the value of Bank Buana."

Among Singapore's banks, UOB is not the country's largest—that would be DBS—but smaller Singapore banks like UOB and OCBC have ironically been making better headway in building their overseas portfolios than the big bank across the street, perhaps because of this type of careful approach they take to wooing their overseas investments. And for the banks in crowded Singapore, scouring the region for business has become the key to growth.

UOB helped the 50-year-old bank build up its IT infrastructure and its product capabilities. They worked on improving processes in order to ensure efficiency, as well as centralizing operations. Compliance with the Basel II capital adequacy accord is another area where the bank has assisted, and Laihad is satisfied that there have been improvements.

Bank Buana had traditionally been known as a bank for Chinese SMEs, and the name change to UOB Buana will only emphasize that, as UOB in Singapore is known as the most Chinese of Singapore's three local banks since it is still run by the Wee family. To underscore its Chinese identity, UOB Buana's head office is in Jakarta's Chinatown district, although Laihad insists that the bank does not differentiate between Indonesian and Chinese clients.

"For me, the most important consideration is whether the business is viable," he said.

BIG MONEY IN SMALL BUSINESSES

Laihad notes that after the Asian financial crisis, all of the banks wanted to go into the SME businesses, but only in a conservative way, so everybody was fighting over the better businesses.

"There is a lot of potential for growth," Laihad said. "However, at the same time, there are certain criteria that SMEs should meet to obtain a bank loan—for example, submitting its financial statement. For SMEs outside Jakarta, this is quite a problem. For those SMEs, which are small in terms of the size of the business and operating with a limited range of products in markets in small cities, having their books audited would still be a challenge."

> In the future banks will be looking more at the SME market niche.

For banks borrowing under a certain amount, bookkeeping needs to be audited, meaning that many businesses fall into a grey area where they are too big for microfinance but too small for traditional SME loans, and a great deal of financial education is still required to bring these businesses online. In this sense, Laihad is meeting the same problems that professional bankers meet in their SME divisions all over the developing world, where there is no shortage of SMEs, but there is a dearth of small businesses that adhere to standardized accounting practices.

While the bank has been focused on SME clients, a profitable strategy that has given margins in the range of 7.2 percent, Laihad also wants to push the bank more into consumer banking and treasury operations in order to diversify its product capabilities. In both areas there will be some overlap with its existing base of SME clients.

"Since a lot of our customers have grown from small enterprises to medium-sized businesses, and medium-sized ones to large commercial entities, the need for treasury products will increase," said Laihad.

The need for personal products such as credit cards and wealth management products will grow for SME owners as well. SME banking forms 65 percent of the bank's business, while consumer banking is 20 percent, and large commercial business is roughly 15 percent.

"I think in the future banks will be looking more at the SME market niche, but the retail market will also be quite important, because banks see that when a country and its people are getting more affluent, the retail side will pick up," Laihad said. "If you look at the GDP of Indonesia, it is probably slightly higher now than it was in 1997/1998. So compared to the past, people can now afford to buy motorbikes, the next one will be white goods, and people have more easy access to credit now because of finance companies. So that is growing according to the growth of the country, but it will be gradual."

A HELPING HAND

Besides the more traditional products, the bank is adding sophisticated product lines. It has had credit cards since 2003, and with UOB on board, it is able to consider how to reposition itself in the market by adding new features such as the EMV chip for anti-fraud security.

> There is no change without pain. Yet, when the pain is gone, you will reap all the benefit.

"Consumer banking is relatively new to us, which is why we have taken advice from experienced bankers like Francis [Hsu, UOB's regional head of credit cards] on how we should launch it," said Laihad. "They have the experience, and they have all the expertise, so we do not have to reinvent. Actually, that is the incentive that we get from having UOB with us."

Laihad has asked UOB to look through the bank's processes to help them through the tough task of re-engineering them to enable shorter turnaround and processing time.

"Most of the banks now, one way or the other, are doing the process re-engineering," he said. "It is a tough time. However, my view is that during the tough times, it is actually a good time for you to look around and review your whole process. There is no change without pain. Yet, when the pain is gone, you will reap all the benefit."

Over the past several years, the bank has grown around 20 percent annually. But although it is not yet in the top ten of Indonesia's banks, UOB Buana is hoping to grow beyond the towns and cities to seize opportunities financing the country's surging commodities business. These opportunities exist especially in the state of Kalimantan on the ruggedly wild island of Borneo. Laihad visits the area regularly and sees massive barges carrying commodities up and down swollen rivers.

Laihad is encouraged by the noticeable growth that he observes from visit to visit, he said. With Indonesia enjoying a stable government, lower inflation, and a booming natural resources trade, Laihad may very well be in the right place at the right time. Rapid improvement in technical areas are now coming into the bank via UOB, and UOB Buana might finally be able to engage in the fast growth that it had been locked out of for too long when it was not under professional management. As a niche player, the bank is quickly maturing into a universal bank that is ready to engage in a wider spectrum of profitable activities. And with its building phase well underway, it is ready to engage in real growth.

Chapter 4
The Rebuilders—Starting Over, But Not From Scratch

Reviving the Golden Goose

Banks can change if they
apply themselves

The most important message Vichit Suraphongchai, head of Siam Commercial Bank, has about turning around a struggling bank: communication.

THAILAND. The Land of Smiles, home of the world's longest-reigning monarch… and birthplace of the devastating 1997 Asian financial crisis. While life has moved on in the country, fueled by a strong mix of manufacturing, agriculture, natural resources, and tourism, the scars of the crisis are still felt in the once-bitten-twice-shy conservatism shared by banks, regulators, government, and industry. In case anyone has forgotten what the devastation was like, reminders of the crisis still dot the cities and surrounding countryside in the form of concrete half-built structures that nobody has found the resources to tear down. These are skeletons of someone's ambitious dreams, now rusting in the wind.

All of these monstrosities, as well as the other overreaching disasters that were part of the event, were financed by banks, and long-time residents can point out "that one was financed by

Vichit Suraphongchai
Reproduced by permission of
Siam Commercial Bank

Bank of Ayudhya, that one was financed by Bangkok Bank, that one was financed by Siam Commercial Bank…" All of Thailand's bankers wince when they tell the story of those years, as it was the end of a cozy era for them and the start of a long drift back to a harsh reality that requires the proper definition of bad loans and compliance with global standards such as the Basel II capital adequacy accord.

The chairman of the executive committee of Siam Commercial Bank (SCB), Dr. Vichit Suraphongchai, sums up the results of those ambitions by explaining that "the money the banks had been making in the previous 20 years, within one or two years it had been wiped out. Everybody was in need of new capital."

Considered by some to be one of the sharpest minds in Thailand's financial services industry, Suraphongchai's youngish looks and keen smile clash somewhat with the owlish look of the scholar lent him by his round spectacles. He has an office on the thirty-second floor of

> There was a very important recommendation by the board: "don't feel that you are safe just because you have been able to raise that much money."

the bustling Siam Commercial Bank Center in Bangkok, a floor that he shares with a few of the bank's top executives. A banker with a 20-year history at Bangkok Bank, the country's largest, Suraphongchai rose to the top position in the bank from 1994 to 1996 before leaving for a government position in the Ministry of Transport and Communication.

Joining the bank in 1999, Suraphongchai was walking into a rapidly sinking ship—as he would have been at any Thai bank at that time. The bank had been able to secure 63 billion baht (US$1.2 billion) in emergency capital from the market to help it stay afloat, a sum that was matched by the government. But it didn't have a plan for how to turn that capital into something that could do more than just put the bank on life support for a few years. It needed to turn the money into something that could generate a new business model that would keep the bank going indefinitely.

"Once we got that capital, the board of directors realized that it would not last a long time if we didn't have change," Suraphongchai said. "At that time, there was a very important recommendation by the board: 'don't feel that you are safe just because you have been able to raise that much money.'"

CHANGE OR DIE

Suraphongchai was asked to become the chairman of the executive board at the end of 1999 and set about the difficult task of rebuilding a once-proud institution. The first thing he realized that the bank had to do was to break away from the model that had seemingly served the banks so well in previous decades of economic growth. Having concentrated on wholesale banking, an easy business with fat margins that gave banker's *large* salaries and plenty of time for golf, they were undiversified and ultimately over-exposed to a market crash.

Suraphongchai shows a good deal of disdain about the practices of the times.

> **The pie kept growing bigger and bigger—until 1997. And then** *bang!* **Gone!! The goose that laid the golden egg had died.**

"If you look back at the Thai banks, they have been making tons of money earlier, simply because of the key advantage of economic growth of an average of 9–10 percent for 20 years, it was the world's highest growth rate at that time," he said. "With that kind of growth, the biggest sector that had been growing of course was the wholesale market. The Thai banks had been making a lot of money by being wholesale banks. There was no need to look at retail banking, or small and medium enterprises [SME], because it seemed like small money, too many people involved and it was messy. Stick to a few big items, and that's already more money than you can spend."

Of course, all of the banks were doing the same, and enjoying the same fat margins as they rode the tide of economic growth.

"The pie kept growing bigger and bigger—until 1997. And then *bang!* Gone!!" Suraphongchai said. "The goose that laid the golden egg had died."

After 1997, with wholesale clients either out of business or struggling, there was no business for a wholesale bank. Siam Cement was saddled with US$4 billion in debt, and SCB certainly couldn't rely on its largest client for business. It needed to do something else for a living.

Knowing that the bank would only get one chance at life support, Suraphongchai led a movement to force the bank to start thinking differently and begin looking for a fresh, untapped customer base. The bank decided to move toward a universal banking model and to start with a focus on retail banking.

"But it's not easy to say, 'Hey, tomorrow we want to go into retail banking,' because things are not going to be like that," Suraphongchai said. "You've got to be prepared. The retail banking mindset and the wholesale banking mindset are totally different animals."

> **But it's not easy to say, "Hey, tomorrow we want to go into retail banking," because things are not going to be like that. You've got to be prepared.**

And so in those early years of his leadership, Suraphongchai set down a program for long-term change at the bank and gave it a simple name: he called it the Change Program. The program would guide the bank into new waters that could—through the sheer freshness of the business they were entering—provide new riches, although there would be fresh dangers as well. The program was conceptualized in three stages, starting with "foundation" from 2002 to 2004 before moving into "growth" from 2004 to 2006, and finally coming to "differentiation," where the bank is today. The bank has 15 "differentiation" projects that include a treasury business model, a cash card, Basel II compliance, a wealth management system, enterprise data warehousing, enterprise content management, and integrated sales and services.

"The Change Program was done in phases," Suraphongchai said. "The first phase was foundation building, everything about the infrastructure. If you're serious about retail banking, you have to make your retail customer come into the branch and feel that 'this is new, this is different.' One of the key parts of the project was the branches' physical redesign. In consumer banking, branding is really important."

The bank adopted royal purple as its branding color and standardized its logo so that it was consistent and easily recognizable.

> Unless you get the consensus and support from the rank and file, it's going to be a dream, and you can never realize it.

Suraphongchai was unafraid of engaging in the type of innovations he needed to set forth, and the bank went through the process of ripping apart the branches, removing the back office functions from each of the branches that used to take up 70 percent of the floor space, and centralizing those functions. This, in turn, allowed the bank to take its counters into the back of the shop and open up floor space and give customers some elbow room. Banks all around the region have gone through this process to varying degrees, but SCB approached the task with a vengeance, viciously hacking away at the concept of what a branch had been until then in Thailand and radically reinventing it, perhaps more than any other bank in the world.

BE TRANSPARENT

Suraphongchai, who had spent much of his career in the senior ranks, is clearly cut from strong leadership cloth, and reaching into his bag of tricks he knew that communication with employees is important in times of crisis. He needed to both keep his soldiers' morale up but also motivate them to put in the supreme effort that was needed to effect real change in a flabby institution that had been spoiled by too many soft years.

Going through this sort of radical change was not without its costs, and many of the bank's staff felt alienated by the bank's transformation. As a seasoned leader, Suraphongchai knew the importance of communicating the bank's new vision to the bank's entire staff in order to ensure success.

"Unless you get the consensus and support from the rank and file, it's going to be a dream, and you can never realize it," he said. "During the first two years, there was a lot of communication: meetings, workshops, forums, explaining and talking about these things. You could see the types of issues we were facing in the business. In the beginning, when we talked about change people asked, 'Why change?

I thought we're okay. Change what? What can we get from change? Are you sure you can do it?' There were many skeptics. And they did not know who this Vichit guy was; they did not know who this guy coming in to change the oldest, most prestigious bank was."

For Suraphongchai, the biggest challenge in the early days of change was trying to figure out how to proceed in his operations,

> In the beginning, when we talked about change people asked "Why change? I thought we're okay."

but it was also clear to him that communication was the key to success. He could crack his head to come up with a plan that would catapult the bank to the stars, but it was worthless if he couldn't implement it.

"You cannot underestimate the communication part," he said. "In the early phase [of the Change Program] our slogan was very clear: 'let's do it together.' We needed to get together to make it work, and once the foundation was there, the core banking, the IT bank platform, the physical platform, we moved into the second phase, which was business building."

Suraphongchai worked at building the bank's universal banking business, overseeing the bank's move through retail banking services, while also strengthening the asset management business, securities, and investment banking.

Retail banking is surely the area where the bank is due to outshine its competitors for the foreseeable future. It is not the largest bank in Thailand; it has only recently overtaken Kasikornbank to move into the position of third-largest bank by assets after the gargantuan Bangkok Bank and Krung Thai Bank. But it does have the most branches, the most ATMs, the most credit cards, and the lead in mortgages, as well as the new bancassurance industry. In effect, it *owns* the retail banking space in Thailand, with some strong competition from Kasikornbank and the up-and-coming Bank of Ayudhya (BAY). A short walk around the *sois* of Bangkok will testify that its spiffy branches stand out noticeably from the capital city's grimy shophouse exteriors, not to mention the other banks' branches.

Among the key agents of his retail strategy has been Kannikar Chalitaporn, since January 2007 the bank's president and previously

Suraphongchai's head of retail banking. Long recognized as one of Thailand's leading businesswomen, Chalitaporn had a long career at retail consumables giant Unilever. Overlooking a grueling regimen that saw her opening 150 new branches and kiosks in 2006—roughly a new outlet every two days—was not for the faint of heart. Chalitaporn is assertive, and at times gruff, but without a doubt she has the hot emotional quality that Suraphongchai valued specifically as a senior manager running a business that helped transform the bank.

BUBBLING EMOTIONS

"The word *passion* is very much missing in today's management talk," Suraphongchai said. "Passion must be found in the leaders. Once [staff] see that the leaders themselves are convinced and really want to do it, it has that contagious effect on the rank and file."

Suraphongchai admires the type of passion to win he sees in athletes of all stripes, and passion is obviously something that he himself has in abundance, although his emotions are also tinged with sadness that comes from his somewhat pessimistic view of the dirty world of business as he builds his future step by step, taking nothing for granted—a true pragmatist.

With her no-nonsense manner, Chalitaporn is clearly the type of person a bank fighting to redefine itself in the face of an uncertain future badly needed. Suraphongchai has found diamonds in the rough like her among the handful of non-bankers that have made up his senior management team throughout the years. Successful non-bankers have dotted Asia's most successful banks: there has been Yashiro Masamoto, the ex-oilman who built Citibank's retail operations in Japan before recreating Shinsei Bank; Mike DeNoma, a former Pepsi executive, who now runs Standard Chartered Bank's retail banking division; and Weber Lo, who now heads Citibank Hong Kong's retail banking operation after many years working for Proctor and Gamble.

"It's not so much that you need to know anything about banking or all the technicalities of the derivatives of the world," Suraphongchai said. "No, you've got to have passion in your heart. From there, you can actually change the culture. You change culture from the heart; you can't change culture from the head."

With passion on board, Suraphongchai could finally get something done.

"We embarked on this historical process of change within the bank, touching all aspects of the banking business: operations, risk management, treasury, retail banking, and wholesale," he said. "Another thing is that we want to build this operation to embrace change on a continual process. If you talk to the people about change, you're unlikely to find people saying 'why change' any more. They would say, 'okay, what can I do?'"

Since January 2007, Suraphongchai has brought the bank into yet another new phase, which saw a reshuffle of the bank's leadership that brought Chalitaporn into the role of president of the bank. With the fundamental aspects of the bank's reinvention established, the bank is ready to tweak the formula. Although bad loans are still high at 7.9 percent as of June 2007, having come up somewhat in the first half of the year, the bank has kept its NPL coverage between 80 percent and 90 percent.

Suraphongchai clearly feels that the bank is ready to pop the lid on other aspects of its universal banking formula.

"Although we have almost all the business platforms more or less in place, the level of operation, efficiency, can still be improved further in many areas," he said. "For example, two businesses that we think have the potential for growth for us is the SME business, the second one is hire purchase."

The bank clearly still has a lot of work to do in building out its full universal banking operations after so many years of focusing on retail banking. SME banking, which had previously been lumped under corporate banking, was a business that has traditionally gone to other players like Kasikornbank, and the bank is also finally re-examining its wholesale bank, the very unit that got the bank into bad financial waters in the first place.

With the never-satisfied, somewhat paranoid nature of a leader who knows there's always something that can be improved, Suraphongchai is also focusing on other areas such as securities and insurance, all businesses where the bank has some capability but not enough to satisfy its chairman. Some of its platforms aren't large enough for his satisfaction, and although the bank has diversified from its original model by building out retail banking, he wants to do the same with other businesses.

KEEP UP THE PACE

"We don't want to be big at the expense of SME," Suraphongchai said, meaning that there's no sense in being number one in retail and number 100 in other businesses. "Basically, we also want to be respectable. Hire purchase has to be a respectable cash management business. Maybe I can borrow the philosophy of Jack Welch of GE: any business we're in, we want to be number one or number two eventually. That's the direction. It's not so much the fact that we are greedy or very aggressive, I think this is the strategy that we use to devise our plans."

With its SME business, Suraphongchai knows that his bank had one of the smallest market shares in Thailand up until 2005, when it began to put more focus on the business. By 2007, he claimed that the bank had become the sixth-biggest in market share.

Clearly, Suraphongchai is making up for mistakes made a long lost time ago when the bank considered the market too risky, undesirable, and too fiddly. The bank had gone from large corporates over to the man on the street, perhaps for the marketing value, but ironically it had left out the business in the middle. Now SCB is working on building volume in that business as well, and for the time being he's satisfied that he's seeing the highest growth in the market, albeit from a small base.

To push these businesses forward, Suraphongchai is still fighting a culture in the bank that hides its shyest staff in the back office, leaving a small number of staff who are able to face customers.

"You'll find that a lot of staff in the local banks here, probably more than 60 percent, are not customer facing," he said. "They're back office paper-chasing types, and that limits your growth. If you don't meet your customers, how can you grow?"

While he has to fight a certain amount of baggage among his staff, Suraphongchai is fighting to instill a culture in the bank that is world class, and tries to keep his decision-making process lean and speedy. By avoiding bureaucracy and red tape, he tries to push decisions out as quickly as possible, always with an awareness that the rank and file is keeping an eye on him.

"Organizations need leadership that has the courage to make decisions," Suraphongchai said. "Sometimes you make good decisions, sometimes you make not-so-good decisions, but nonetheless they're going to see you're moving."

BARBARIANS AT THE GATES!

Suraphongchai, with his dark, pragmatic nature, seems generally pessimistic about the prospects Thailand faces in upcoming years, both in dealing with the aspirations of the central bank in pushing consolidation, and also in anticipating the increasing interest of outside players. In 2007, private equity player Newbridge Capital took a stake in Bank-Thai, Canada's Bank of Nova Scotia took a stake in Siam City Bank, and China's massive ICBC was vying for a stake for a small local bank. This is all on top of the fact that global consumer finance giant GE Money has its hooks in BAY, the county's sixth-largest lender. While BAY is not a large retail player, its new CEO K.K. Tan is a highly experienced retail banker, formerly in a regional role at Standard Chartered Bank, which is well known for its retail banking expertise in nearly 20 markets across Asia; GE Money, for its part, works mainly in the retail banking space, and together they are expected to give Thailand's retail banks a run for their money, which puts Suraphongchai in the hot seat.

With experience at the top of more than one Thai bank, Suraphongchai is a wily operator who has seen a lot. And while UOB and Standard Chartered Bank have come into the market by buying into small banks, and DBS suffered an aborted attempt to make headway into the decent-sized TMB Bank, he's watching GE Money and BAY carefully. Ultimately, he foresees his new competitor as needing to go through all of the changes that he has, and in some ways it will have even further to go.

"The culture part is something that I can't predict, but I assume that GE must have thought long and hard about that," he said. "For BAY, until now, the shares were majority owned by one family. How do you change the culture of a truly family-run bank? Here at SCB there's no family, although the major shareholder has to do with the crown, but that's not the same as a family-type bank. We are watching."

Besides retail, GE will be a competitor in the SME business as SCB works on developing it. Suraphongchai is wary of the new technology that GE Money, as the bank's largest investor, will bring to the bank, as well as processing power, risk management, and product diversification, in addition to an aggressive marketing machine. But on the human resources side, he sees that they will need more time to align their staff skills and hire the human resources needed to grow into his space. He has a bit of time before he needs to start worrying, but not much—one of his chief concerns is the deep pockets of his foreign rivals.

"Today, they will come in and buy a local bank, and money is no object," he said. "With [foreign banks'] dollars they bid for anything, it's mind-boggling. The market trades at ten dollars, they pay 15. If not, okay, they pay 20. Because of their balance sheet, they're able to offer a very high price. This is something that smaller, regional or local banks could never match. Not even close to it. That will be a real concern for us in the years to come; I'm not talking about next year. It's something to be mindful of."

Suraphongchai, as a sophisticated modern banker, is sure to consider acquisition as a means to grow, but here once again he is fighting culture; this time it is a broad belief among Thai businessmen that vying to be the biggest and the best is dishonorable, negative, and overly hostile, and ultimately makes an ambitious organization lose face. Banks that seek to grow by acquisition practically have to be presented with the excuse, 'I had to acquire the other bank, otherwise neither one of us would have survived' in order for them to grow inorganically. This puts them at a disadvantage next to non-Thai players, who are only too happy to grow by acquisition if presented with a good deal—K.K. Tan certainly won't be shy to buy—and opportunities *do* come along from time to time.

Suraphongchai, with the mind of an international businessman, despairs at the culture, and it's clear to him that Thai banks will need to come to terms with the modern culture of M&A if they want to compete with the new players entering the market; it clearly eats at the progressive Suraphongchai, perhaps betraying the battles he's having with his board on acquisition plans.

"For the foreign institutions, this is something that they've become very accustomed to, so they are more willing to make a bid than the Thais," he said. "The Thais think that whoever makes a bid will be viewed as greedy, as a bad guy. Nobody accused GE Money [when it invested in BAY] or Newbridge [with its purchase of BankThai] of being a bad guy. It's almost like a double standard—if they're foreigners, [Thais] understand it, but if it's the Thais [themselves]… they're seen as 'un-Thai.'"

GRIM OUTLOOK

The bank—and all Thailand's banks—also have other things to worry about such as the economic situation, not to mention the effects of the greater political game that is playing itself out in the country. And while margins were still good in 2007, since the bloodless coup of September 2006, the banks are dealing with a slowing economy as well as rising NPLs. This may turn around now that the December 2007 elections have given Thailand a civilian government again and the military steps away from politics, but nothing is guaranteed.

Suraphongchai takes macroeconomic issues in stride.

"I'm not too concerned about the interest margin—[I have] three plus, it's a good margin," he said. "To me that's not the most important issue. The most important issue is the slowing down of the economy."

With the military coup, uncertainty about political leadership, or the stability of the stop-and-start transition to a democratic system, not to mention the king's health, there are more important issues at hand. "This is an emerging market, not a mature market," Suraphongchai reminds. "What we need now is for the country to go forward; we need a certain level of growth. I would not feel happy if the economy grew 2–3 percent, and the margin was 4 percent.

I would rather see the economy grow at 5 percent, 6 percent, and the margin come down to 3.5. The long-term prospect of the country is to make sure you have enough growth to keep in line with the population."

Thai bankers are optimistic that the economy will grow at a faster pace, and they are calling for 5 percent growth in 2008 after the election. But a lot of this will also depend on how adversely the Thai economy is affected by a slowdown of the U.S. economy. U.S. job losses, low consumer sentiment, a housing slowdown, fewer imports, and other lingering problems in the world's largest economy are tightly linked to the world's exporting countries.

Of course, the concept of a strong, self-sustaining Asian economic hemisphere gaining independence by decoupling from the U.S. economy has been bandied about, and the following years may see a test of that; but whether or not it happens, at least the Asian sphere will continue to be part of the greater trend of globalization, and Thailand's banks need to be in tune with it like everybody else.

"In businesses today, with globalization, strategy is a must; the wrong strategy is going to hurt you a lot more," said Suraphongchai.

He notes the successes and failures of the large Japanese firms, which he looks to for inspiration.

"If you look at Sony's business manager, he's been very old fashioned and where did he find himself? Toyota introduced fuel economy, mid-sized: it was a huge success."

Again, Suraphongchai sees a major break from the past business practices—there will be no turning back.

"In the old days before globalization was at this scale, you could afford to make a few major mistakes," Suraphongchai said. "These days, it's much more difficult to survive if you've made some stupid mistakes in your strategy. I say, 'look, maybe the business model that we have been doing may be good for another five years, who knows, then we'll have to reinvent ourselves again.'"

Suraphongchai sees the cycles getting tighter and tighter, with the need to reinvent businesses getting closer to the timelines that are seen in manufacturing, and he feels that eventually banks will need to come up with killer applications such as the iPod, or pull off marketing coups as Intel did when it took a commoditized chip and gave it a brand value—and a life—of its own.

The push into running retail banking like retail sales, which had been a good strategy for the past five years, will have its limits as it gets closer and closer to the ground.

"We could be like 7-Eleven, but then our whole cost structure would have to change," said Suraphongchai, whose bank actually does run hundreds of convenience store-sized kiosks. "7-Eleven's operating costs are low because they hire high-school kids, cram all the products into a small place. Someone needs to think about that."

Time is ticking for Suraphongchai, his business plan, and for his bank.

"This cycle for SCB has worked out very well, but I'm thinking, 'what's next?'" he said. "That's how you survive the longest, by being very old then yet very new. At SCB, we're the oldest in a way, with an old heritage, and yet we are very young. We have to keep ourselves young—physically we get old."

Suraphongchai is clearly tired. Already nearly a decade into his second career running a major Thai bank, succession is on his mind. Ensuring that someone will be able to come along and continue the work he's started is crucial for the bank to stay on the right course through several more iterations before it becomes a universal bank for Thailand, or even onto another stage as a regional player.

"After me, someone will come in and open up new horizons," he said. "I can't be here forever! I *shouldn't* be here forever."

Giant Niches

And the leaders shall lead

> As the head of the largest bank in Pakistan, the 75-percent nationally owned National Bank of Pakistan, President/Chairman/CEO Syed Ali Raza is enjoying the wild ride of deregulation.

WHILE India and China get all of the headlines, one of the great economic rebirths in Asia has happened in Pakistan. With a government that was, until recently, relatively stable, and a partnership with the U.S. in the war on terrorism came a new lease on life for the country for many years at the start of the new millennium. The country had already started on the privatization of most of the state industries, including financial services, and Pakistan has also shown a more sincere welcome to foreign investors than most other countries in Asia. This is evidenced by the fact that Standard Chartered Bank could buy 81 percent of Union Bank of Pakistan in 2005, whereas being allowed to invest 10 percent in a bank in India is considered generous.

Pakistan's banks have come a long way. All was not well with the nation's banks in 2001, nor with its largest, National Bank of Pakistan (NBP). But just as President Pervez Musharraf looked overseas to source former Citibanker Shaukat Aziz to

Syed Ali Raza
Reproduced by permission of
TAB International

110

be his finance minister in 1999, Aziz in turn immediately looked for a prominent Pakistani banker working overseas to fill the role of the chairman and president of government-owned NBP. His eye fell on one: Syed Ali Raza.

Just as Aziz has been closely associated with influencing the rapid acceleration of Pakistan's economy, and even named Finance Minister of the Year in 2001 by organisations such as *EuroMoney* and *The Banker*, Raza has been instrumental in turning around the massive lending institution under his authority. The Asian Banker has also recognized this contribution, and chose Raza for the Achievement Award for Pakistan for leadership in financial services in 2007.

Born in Karachi in 1950 into a civil service family, Raza's father was noted literary figure Hashim Raza, also the first commissioner of Karachi. The family moved frequently, and Raza got used to the semi-nomadic lifestyle, heading off to London to study at the London School of Economics, graduating in 1971 with a degree in economics before doing post-graduate work at City University in London.

After graduating, his first job was as a relationship manager with Bank of America (BoA) in Pakistan, where he moved up to head of credit and marketing. He opened the bank's Islamabad branch in 1978, then headed the bank's Bahrain operations for nine months before becoming the general manager of the BoA-affiliated Bank of Yemen. There was another visit to London to head the credit division before returning to Pakistan as the first local-born country manager. After six years, this role was expanded to include 28 branches across the Middle East and North Africa. Raza wanted to pitch Pakistan as the location of the bank's regional hub, hoping to start a business trend. It did not catch on.

But in 1999, when Raza had 28 successful years at the company behind him, fate took a different turn and BoA's decision-makers in Charlotte, North Carolina, decided to sell operations in several Asian and Latin American countries, and this included Pakistan. Raza led negotiations that ended with the bank's local operations being sold to Union Bank (which is now a part of Standard Chartered Bank). Raza would have had a place with BoA in another part of the world, or perhaps even with Union Bank, but late in the year came Aziz's irresistible offer to lead the turnaround of the largest bank in the country. And the rest is history.

A NEW JOB

When he took over the bank in July 2000, it had a presence in 16 countries, 1,405 branches, and 15,000 employees. It was also hemorrhaging loans. Despite holding 22 percent of the deposits in the banking system, it was only turning them around to 3 percent of the system's operating income.

Raza had to work on fixing the bank's structure, bureaucracy, NPLs, excess branches, and staff, and on getting the balance sheet working efficiently. To get the complex organisation functioning more smoothly he stripped it of its multiple layers and created four heads in charge of business, customer service, portfolio management, and compliance. The new matrix organization moved the lender away from a bureaucratic formation to one that empowers its managers.

But despite being a tough internationally-trained manager who had never worked for a local institution, Raza claims to have been pleasantly surprised by the commitment of the employees and their willingness to change. Pakistan had started privatizing its banks in 1991, and that NBP had been partially privatized as well helped a bit.

"For all intents and purposes the government, with 75 percent [ownership], is simply a passive investor," he said. "There's absolutely no interference. We have a board consisting of people appointed by the government from the private sector. All decisions are made by the board and the management."

Being the largest bank in Pakistan means that the government would want to keep a part of the institution to maintain stability of such an important lender, but Raza insists that the future of the bank is not being guided.

"We're not really a nationalized bank in the sense that we were prior to the public flotation and prior to the government policy of completely privatizing the banking system," he said. "It's possible that going forward the government further divests its equity in

National Bank. When and how, that is not absolutely clear but it's entirely possible that down the road they'll divest another 20 percent."

Clearly, nothing will happen in a period of instability so it's even more difficult for him to say when they'll exercise the final divestment than it would be in normal times. Considering that the premium for Union Bank had been up to five times book value, the bank's negotiating position is quite enviable.

"As a single entity, it is by far the most valuable asset or entity in the country if you use the five times book value benchmark," he said.

Part of the pain early on meant letting go 3,000 employees and closing 205 branches to bring down the skyrocketing cost-to-income ratio, as well as bringing the struggling lender NDFC into the bank's structure so that it could have tighter control of it as well. Early on, the cuts were already starting to show results. In 2001, Raza's first full year leading the bank, pretax profit tripled to PKR 3 billion (US$52.2 million) from PKR 1 billion (US$17.44 million) the year earlier. From 2001 to 2006, the bank's net income has grown nearly 1,500 percent. In 2007, the bank's pre-tax profits grew 10 percent from the previous year.

Raza has also made the bank a larger part of the country's wholesale banking industry, taking a greater role in large syndications and corporate finance advisory work. But he's not stopping with corporate businesses, turning as well to agricultural financing—a business he came across financing Indian farmers in California in his early days at BoA—mortgages, debit cards, money market funds, and other consumer finance products.

No longer being a part of a large global corporation means less globetrotting, but he now spends his time traveling across the country talking to bank employees, often on mystery branch visits where people might wonder who he is and why he's poking around the office. Many of Raza's employees have found him a very accessible CEO, who's very sharp and focused. Garrulous and personable, he comes across as down-to-earth and humble, although his high requirements and formidable bursts of anger are sure to keep his staff in line as well.

BANKING FOR THE PEOPLE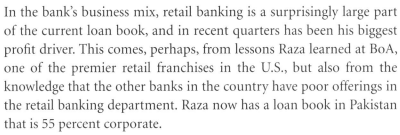

In the bank's business mix, retail banking is a surprisingly large part of the current loan book, and in recent quarters has been his biggest profit driver. This comes, perhaps, from lessons Raza learned at BoA, one of the premier retail franchises in the U.S., but also from the knowledge that the other banks in the country have poor offerings in the retail banking department. Raza now has a loan book in Pakistan that is 55 percent corporate.

"The balance is spread over retail, agriculture, small-and medium-enterprises, and so on," he said. "The retail business, from nearly zero percent of the business three to four years ago, now constitutes about 25 percent and corporate around 55 percent. The balance of 20 percent is basically agriculture and SMEs, or what we call commercial lending. We are on the market average in terms of retail lending *vis-à-vis* total lending."

Raza has been building up his retail banking business by finding niches where it can have some leverage and by creating products for salaried people, a relatively risk-free demographic in the country of 165 million. With his brand and distribution, the scale businesses that Pakistan has to offer are obviously in his grasp.

"We came up with what we call an advanced salary product, which no other bank had come up with," Raza said. "We didn't go into auto loans or personal loans because everyone was in that business. We created this product, we branded it, and it is the most successful retail product in the country today."

The product makes up 23 percent of all consumer loans in Pakistan, Raza said. It was initially designed for government employees and is now being adapted for the private sector.

"You don't really need credit scoring because here, if you're a government servant, this is based on an income estimation situation," Raza said. "We will give you a facility whereby your debt payments don't exceed 25 percent of your take-home salary. And then, we'll have an end on your service benefits so you have guaranteed repayment because the government obviously has to pay its employees' salaries. In the event that something unusual happens, then you have the end of service benefits.

We always ensure that our loan is less than the end of service benefits. In many ways it is the most risk-free loan that you can think of." More recently the bank has introduced a new loan aimed at small businesses, called Karobar, that is partly subsidized by the government and is helping entrepreneurs get started. Eight months after it started, the bank had lent out US$65 million. Raza aims for 15 times that by 2013.

Raza, more than most CEOs in the region, betrays a strong passion for retail banking, and it is clearly a major priority for his business, especially considering how under-penetrated the market is in Pakistan. Connection to government-employed individuals, or other government guarantees, is all a part of the business,

> We were a bank totally dependent on the government. If we hadn't moved into this commercial and private sector mode, this bank would have sunk.

although he does note that, "the government doesn't guarantee loans anymore. When the banks were nationalized, the government business was restricted to the nationalized banks, which was not really [just] National Bank, [but] which was Habib Bank, United Bank, Allied Bank, and so on. All those barriers have now gone. The government departments today put money in whichever bank they want, borrow from whichever bank they want, open letter of credit (L/Cs) from whichever bank they prefer depending on pricing," he said. Banking in Pakistan is slowly becoming less clubby.

LOOSENING UP

Ironically, these tough new deregulations have made Raza, a banker with extensive training in a huge global institution, more comfortable with his environment.

"When I took over the bank, the greatest apprehension I had when I looked at the balance sheet was that we were so dependent on the government," he said. "Ninety percent of our loans were either to the government or public sector. Eighty percent of our deposits were from government of public sector corporations, so we were a bank totally dependent on the government. If we hadn't moved into this commercial and private sector mode, this bank would have sunk." Current deposit and loan levels are now roughly opposite what they once were.

He explains his philosophy in retail banking by noting "the reason why financial institutions are successful is that it lies in their ability to find niches, where there is huge demand but banks have not created products to reach that demand."

Raza has called on his international experience to run a tighter ship. One of the most amazing things about the bank is its 34.5 percent cost-to-income ratio, which Raza describes as "embarrassing." Considering the bank's 12,000 branches, anything below 50 percent would be admirable.

> **When I joined the bank in 2000, our cost-income was 92 percent. In fact, that was one of the first things that we had to address.**

"When I joined the bank in 2000, our cost-income was 92 [percent]," Raza said. "In fact, that was one of the first things that we had to address."

Raza has been able to implement reforms, introduce modern, efficient procedures, and encourage staff to seek greater productivity, while also making the hard decision to cut into the register of redundant workers and unnecessary branches that he did.

Considering the bank's wide branch presence in Pakistan, it has ample opportunities to raise funds from deposits and dish out an equal amount in profits, ensuring an even distribution of funds with less drain from one area to another.

"For example, the biggest province in Pakistan is Punjab, so 50 percent of our deposits come from Punjab, and roughly 50 percent of our loans also go to Punjab," Raza said. "There might be a 5 or 10 percent variance here and there. This has not happened by design; this was just how it's happened."

Like Bank of Ceylon, the largest bank in Sri Lanka, which continues to conduct banking services in conflict-torn areas that are under control of the Tamil Tigers, NBP also still does business in disputed territories such as Azad Kashmir, where the bank generates "about PKR 10 billion (US$165 million) of deposits... [while] our loans there are less than PKR 2 billion (US$33 million)," Raza said. "What the Azad Kashmir government does for us is that it levies a tax, because it says, 'You're taking money from us and you're giving it somewhere else.' So they take the spread and they levy a tax, and the government is trying to resolve that problem now."

Part of developing the four regions has been stripping away the bureaucratic layers of the bank, which had hindered communication.

> We will be the only institution in the region to cover Central Asia, South Asia, and the Middle East. I think that is going to give us a huge competitive advantage. We're looking for niches; we can't open 20 offices in America, that won't help us.

"Prior to my coming we had a very bureaucratic structure of about six to seven layers; we've got rid of all of that now," he said. "So there is just one level between the branch and the head office, and we've divided the country into 29 regions to take away this region of centralization and bureaucratic decision making."

But Raza has more to oversee than just the domestic business. He has his international division, which has expanded to 21 countries and handles trade finance and the financial institutions business of global transactions, such as clearing. The bank is present in Pakistan's major trading partner nations. But Raza is the proudest of a unique position NBP has in its nearby geography, which puts it at the gateway to another world, poorly understood by those outside the region.

GEOGRAPHIC (DIS)ADVANTAGE

"Our most interesting franchise is Central Asia," he said. "We are present in every country in Central Asia, in the form of branches. The last one is Uzbekistan where we recently applied for a full branch license. We have a rep office there and hopefully we will also get a branch there."

NBP will be the only institution in the region to cover Central Asia, South Asia, and the Middle East, Raza said. It will open a branch in Saudi Arabia in 2008, and two more in Bangladesh to make four.

"I think that is going to give us a huge competitive advantage," he said. "We're looking for niches; we can't open 20 offices in America, that won't help us—it's a different market."

Raza clearly prides himself on being the most international of Pakistan's banks, and not just in its foreign presence but also in the clearing it does in U.S. dollars, euros, yen, and Hong Kong dollars.

"Pakistani banks aren't very international, so we serve as the international arm, that's from the clearing side," he said.

But the bank, as all Pakistani institutions, still faces immense international pressure for compliance, especially in light of fines for insufficient anti-money laundering (AML) capabilities and other regulatory difficulties given to various international banks from time to time.

There's "lots of pressure, especially in places like the U.S., because of Sarbanes-Oxley and so on," said Raza. "In eight years, Bank of China has been fined, State Bank of India has been fined, ABN AMRO has been fined, everyone is getting fined. We are there; we have a top set of policies for compliance. It's strictly full compliance to the laws and regulations of the countries that you operate in."

Raza is proud of the fact that Pakistani banks have been able to keep their noses clean on money laundering issues, although he did admit that the bank has had some trouble in Paris in a case that involved a spate of large global banks. He mentioned BNP Paribas, Crédit Lyonnais, American Express, and Barclays in the same incident.

Pakistani banks, after all, are practically considered guilty by suspicion of money laundering because of where the country lies in the world, and one false step would send them into no man's land in the eyes of investors and regulators.

"We know that for a Pakistani bank, if we get into a problem, it's much more dangerous than a German bank getting into a problem because the whole perception of Pakistan and the negative attitude, and so on, is automatically going to mean much more," he said. "We've never had a [know your customer] issue with compliance or a censor from the central bank."

This is a point of pride, perhaps, but clearly also something to be bitter about considering that Raza had once worked for a very different type of regional bank, BoA. The stigma that Pakistani banks carry in their reputation is especially hard to take for Raza when so many others are seen as getting away with it.

"Citibank have been fined in Japan, they've been fined in Mexico, all over the place. To them, it's a cost of doing business," he said. "To us, we can't afford that. We're under greater scrutiny."

Of course, things don't really look so great at Citibank these days either, as the cost of doing business has been taking a huge toll on the careers of the bank's senior management. But stray Citi executives can always walk across the street in Manhattan to find a new position; bankers in Karachi, Islamabad, Peshawar, Lahore, or Multan cannot do this as easily.

Things change, however, and Raza now finds his bank in a good position to become a regional player. As it builds its reputation and its capacity, Raza is also looking at taking the business to the next level. The Central Asian energy corridor runs through his neighborhood, stretching from Xinjiang through the "Stans" down to the Arabian Sea. It is a project that will fuel Central Asian and western Chinese development as well as the reconstruction of Afghanistan, where Raza boasts that NBP controls 70 percent of the country's banking activity from its two branches. The bank is also applying for a license to open a branch in India in the capital city that it expects to get by 2009.

"Pakistan has gone from a point, five years ago, when its location was considered to be a liability in the eye of the storm," Raza said. "It is now in the eye of the future because if there are any developments like, if India wants gas from Turkmenistan or Iran, it has to go through Pakistan."

Raza gets excited talking about the future of Pakistan and the chances that are being taken, both by the country and by the bank, as the region stands set to gain a much more important geopolitical position. From his view at the top of the largest bank in the country he can see for miles and miles, and it's obvious that he sees something big happening. Unfortunately, "big" is not always good, as has been the case with the intense turmoil around the 2008 elections.

SCANNING THE HORIZON

The bank is tying these grandiose projects in together with its global network. To launch massive infrastructure projects, Raza is seeking Saudi investment. NBP is building its relations in the kingdom, and as a government bank it fits the criteria for bank licenses, and the bank has become one of the seven new foreign banks in the kingdom. Unfortunately, despite good luck in Saudi Arabia, the bank hasn't fared as well in the UAE, where it has been denied licenses because the government is not giving new ones out.

Despite the optimism Raza has for the developing story in Central Asia, he has less to say about Islamic banking, which is unfolding so strongly in Malaysia, the Middle East, and other centers such as London. The pessimism very nearly borders on mistrust, an ironic situation in a country where Islam plays such a central role.

"The Islamic banking story is moving very slowly in Pakistan," he said. "The government decided five years ago that they would allow Islamic banks to open full-fledged operations, so three to four Islamic banks have opened. They're small and their market share is around 1 to 2 percent of the total market, which is not that big."

While his bank is newly licensed to open a window for Shariah-compliant products, Raza himself has no idea how big the market in Pakistan is going to be, and gives himself until 2009 to assess the situation. But there is still a story to be told in Pakistan, and with major investment expected in infrastructure in the country, Raza is expecting Islamic funds operated by large global banks to be coming in for at least another five years when the government taps all known sources of capital, extending it to Islamic banking or Islamic banks.

Besides the challenge of understanding Islamic finance in terms of products, Raza is also struggling with a goal to build a universal bank and fill some of the other holes in the bank's offerings, in particular in niches in the mass market that it has not explored. But challenges remain, especially at the lower end, the large section of Pakistan's population that is unbanked or under-banked.

"There is a lot of bankability in the poorer sectors provided you've got the right products, technology, and the right delivery system and we think that we have created that and we can improve on it going forward," he said. Raza has equipped many of his branches with systems to distribute the bank's Karobar loans to SMEs and entrepreneurs.

Raza has other, more practical measures to take advantage of his branch network and extensive sales teams. To increase the bank's fee revenues, he is pushing his bankers hard to improve the bank's level of cross-sell. He hopes to see the trend continue to the point that by 2010 the bank will be selling up to seven products to 30 percent of the bank's customers.

In terms of improving efficiency, Raza is making sure the bank is working on improving its IT systems, and in 2006 it turned to a new core banking system. But getting the bank on the right course was just as much a matter of getting the concept right, and the implementation dragged out over two and a half years.

"People say we wasted time, but I don't think we wasted time," he said. "If we had put in a core banking system at National Bank three years ago, even if it was crafted by the Almighty, it would have failed. You know why? Because the people were not ready to accept technology, our people were scared because of the effect that it would result in job losses, that it would result in their inefficiencies being exposed. We've spent three years in small wins in terms of upgrading."

> **If we had put in a core banking system at National Bank three years ago, even if it was crafted by the Almighty, it would have failed.**

But Raza sees the end result of the long implementation process as positive because his staff, many of whom once suffered from fear of progress, have finally developed an interest in the technology. Raza claims that the change of heart comes from knowing that instead of making them redundant, it is more likely to make their lives easier in the short run, and give them opportunities to advance their careers in the long run.

The technology needs to be quite versatile as the bank is already quite diversified and offers a variety of projects to be implemented, many of which Raza clearly considers very important.

PARTNERS

There is a joint venture mutual fund with Temasek Holdings that Raza describes as "the most successful mutual fund in the history of this country in the sense that when they launched a fund for PKR 1 billion (US$16.5 million), they got subscriptions for

PKR 4 billion (US$66 million)." The fund grew to PKR 38 billion (US$555 million) in 2008.

Raza has a variety of plans for the joint venture, one of which is folding it into the bank to start an asset management company. NBP also has some ownership in a bank it started in Saudi Arabia called Al Jazeera, which over the years the bank had slowly begun to divest. Raza resisted an offer to sell the remainder of his bank's stake in Al Jazeera during the post-9/11 period, when confidence in the country was low and a bid of US$10 million, that offered a steep premium, came in. Sticking to his guns has paid off as the stake is now worth several times that.

"Against all opposition, I decided not to sell it," Raza said. "I took the view that after what had happened, Arab money or Saudi money is going to come back in the tens and hundreds of billions. It's not going to go into the banking system because interest rates are very low, it's either going to go into real estate or the fledgling equity market. And as it turns out, time has proved me correct."

Raza may not want to buy more of a bank now that he has plans to open a branch in Saudi Arabia, but nonetheless he is aggressive with his expansion plans. He has a full war chest, and as soon as he sees something worth taking he'll evaluate the risks.

"I don't want to be a bank with a 17 percent capital adequacy ratio, because that means we're not using our balance sheet effectively, so everything is on the table right now," he said.

And while this raises the question about government pressure, Raza insists repeatedly that the government influence is absolutely zero, saying that he always works with the bank's best interests in mind.

Raza has several areas that he aims to build on, many of which the market is not quite ready for yet. Often they are mainstays of general banking, but demonstrate quite clearly the amount of catching up that Pakistan has to do in terms of developing financial services.

It also shows the advantages offered a large bank in a rapidly developing country, as well as opportunities to use technology to carve out profitable niches. But before it can do that, the bank will have to wait patiently until elements that function beyond its control, such as inflation and the sophistication of the legal system, improve to the level that certain banking services need to flourish.

"The one market that is not developed at all in Pakistan is the mortgage market, and it is the market with the most potential," he said. "It hasn't started yet, for a variety of reasons, a lot to do with the crazy increase in land prices and the cost of construction. Of course, it also has to do with the fact that land titles are not very easy; there has been a foreclosure law that is going well, but not as well as one would have expected."

Nonetheless, banks have the ability to react to the situation with products of their own. Thinking like an entrepreneur, Raza is keen to see the cup as half full and turn a disadvantage into an opportunity.

"It is my belief that this is such a serious issue, the housing issue, that banks will come up with products," Raza said. "I think REITs (real estate investment trusts) are the answer in my opinion and low-cost, middle-cost housing, which is still affordable in certain areas of the cities."

GETTING SOPHISTICATED

Investment banking is another area in its infancy in Pakistan. An experienced banker with a background at a global bank, albeit one that was weak in investment banking before it got out of the business in 2007, Raza is motivated to do more in the business.

"There have been a certain number of corporate bonds issued or term finance certificates, but there is no trading in these bonds," he said. "The rates are so high that everyone sits on them. Advisory business, M&A business... M&A is going to happen in Pakistan, but hasn't happened yet. There are no Chinese walls between commercial banks and investment banks, so banks can underwrite, and we do underwrite IPOs and so on. But investment banking business of the kind you're familiar with or that is done in Europe and America, that is on a very small scale."

Raza is constantly thinking about new ways to work the giant machine he has under his control, including introducing advanced banking capabilities.

"That's the reason I am so clean," said Raza. "I try to always think ahead and you could be wrong in terms of your forecast, but you have to make decisions today for the needs of tomorrow, and you've got to make a bet on what happens tomorrow. If you don't, then someone else will have taken on that initiative and left you back and we don't want that to happen to us."

Although he puts most of his life into his job, the affable, gregarious banker still reserves time for personal development, and claims to have seven books on the go at any one time. With an active mind unable to focus on one topic for an extended period of time, his thoughts jump from idea to idea and he reads on eclectic topics. He cites biographies, such as one of Elizabeth Taylor, books about cricket—one of his major passions—books on the revival of Shia, pulp fiction like *The Da Vinci Code*, popular titles like *The World Is Flat*, and books about contemporary politics.

Another passion of Raza's is getting to know how the wheels turn in the minds of his senior staff, and he almost makes a game out of lunching with his managers, encouraging them to relax, but also provoking them to think by having quiz sessions over lunch on a variety of topics.

Raza is beefing up his staff in a quest for talent that began by hiring MBAs from the best business schools, and he claims to be building up a management team of 400 people on contract from Citibank, BoA, Lehman Brothers, and others. He's also working on creating the next generation of leaders through a pan-generational 15-year program to eradicate the old way of sourcing talent, a system that has kept many emerging markets weak through a corrupt hiring system.

"We started this concept of a talent pool, and in this we felt that there were many people in this institution who were well educated, efficient, but because they didn't have the right patronage, they were kind of somewhere buried in the organization because these nationalized banks only function on the basis of patronage, who you knew," he said.

Raza is hopeful that as the MBAs trickle through the system they will introduce a culture of merit in terms of salary increases and bonuses.

"We're paying bonuses for the first time, purely on performance and someone can earn up to 100–200 percent of their salary. Unfortunately we can't give stock options because if we start buying our stock today, the price will shoot through the roof," he said.

Another progressive measure Raza's taking is promoting gender issues and he's proud of an award he's received for promoting female employment and gender equality.

"I have mandated that 10 percent of our branches are going to be managed by women," he said. "This is a command decision. We are hiring women, we are promoting women internally. Now, when I stay 10 percent you're talking about 120 branches, [seven] years ago, there was one branch managed by a woman, so this is a command decision."

He is also an active sports patron and is keen to develop strong branding for the bank, as well as an incentive for sports-mad staff.

Raza also wants to bring younger people into the bank.

"The average age of the decision-makers at National Bank today is 47; the average age of decision makers at National Bank six years ago was 57," he said. "We've reduced it. All these management teams are all new people, except for maybe a handful and all these guys are in their mid-thirties, late-thirties, young Turks. You have to live with what you have and try and improve that and supplement it, MBAs supplement this external hiring, this supplements technology, supplements success. When people see this they feel very proud."

Born in 1950, Raza is only just nearing retirement age. But with his optimism and his obvious love for the bank that he helped rebuild, he's also clearly still having a lot of fun in his job and the opportunities it presents him. Political stability is obviously a huge worry, especially considering the vast business Raza controls, and the effects of Pakistan's ups and downs surely keep him up at night. But sooner or later the government will be divesting its stake in his bank, and if he can hold on until that day, life is certainly bound to become quite interesting indeed.

Once Upon a Time in Beijing

Making sense of the Wild East

> As China's first superstar bank head, the likeable Chairman of
> China Construction Bank Guo Shuqing has dealt a strong hand.

Guo Shuqing is China's first superstar bank leader. He was parachuted into China Construction Bank (CCB) to become its chairman in March 2005, to help get its IPO preparations back on track after the bank's reputation was damaged by the revealing bribery scandal of its former Chairman Zhang Enzhao. That Guo had come from the upper echelons of the Chinese government apparatus meant that his new position at the top of CCB is in fact a sort of *demotion* for Guo, a gracious piece of national service on his part. But fame was his payback, as the CEOs of Wall Street investment banks came calling during the crucial preparations for the listing, and he embraced the international role with ease.

Playing the host is a natural role for the affable Guo. With his easy smile and his good-natured attempts to speak English, which he does much better than many Chinese bankers, Guo does not affect the perched-high-on-a-chair distance that many Chinese leaders

Guo Shuqing
Reproduced by permission of TAB
International

afford, with their leagues of attendants and complex protocols. Instead, he projects an easy, loose-limbed manner.

Born in 1956 in the Inner Mongolia autonomous province that forms the huge crescent-shaped region north of Beijing, he was part of the first generation of young people to rejoin China's universities after the ravages of the Cultural Revolution. Studying philosophy at Nankai University in Tianjin from 1978, he went on to courses in Marxism and Leninism at the Chinese Academy of Social Sciences. While this grounding made him a natural for the political apparatus of the Communist party, his studies continued overseas in 1986 when he spent a year at Oxford's St. Anthony's College as a visiting scholar.

In his career, he was a deputy director of the State Planning Commission's Economic Research Center, showing an early interest in financial planning. He was later a department leader and senior official in the State Commission for Restructuring the Economy from 1988 to 1998, where he had a hand in shaping the direction of the post-Deng march toward a blend of capitalism and socialism that has built China into an economic powerhouse. Heady times, although signs of this outcome were not yet apparent a decade ago in 1998, when the country's banks were steeped in NPLs. At that time, the biggest event on the horizon was the imminent repatriation of Macao to China in 1999, to follow Hong Kong's return on July 1, 1997.

In 1998, Guo was still far away from banking as he took his first real management role as the vice-governor of Guizhou province in the south. Many of the leaders of China's financial services community have been rotated through similar positions, and Liu Mingkang, the chairman of China's regulator the China Banking Regulator Commission (CBRC) was at one point the governor of Fujian province, also in the south of the country.

From 2001, he re-entered national policy as he became the vice governor of the People's Bank of China (PBoC) and director of the State Administration of Foreign Exchange (SAFE), which has recently formed an investment company that has begun investing in Australian banks. In December 2003, he picked up another profile as chairman of the Central Huijin Investment Company, which owns majority shares of the big four Chinese banks. Established in 2003, Central Huijin is the investment arm of the PBoC, administered by the Ministry of Finance.

Under Guo, Central Huijin had been one of the country's four "asset management companies," which oversaw the disposal of the NPLs of the big four state banks. Central Huijin has now been merged into China's sovereign wealth fund China Investment Corporation. The fund has invested in Blackstone Group and Morgan Stanley and manages a US$200 billion fund for China's sovereign investments in overseas institutions, similar to Singapore's Temasek Holdings. The fund represents a small part of China's US$1.4 trillion in foreign reserves.

ENTER GUO

Guo joined CCB in 2005. In September 2004, the bank had just become a joint-stock bank as part of preparations for its IPO, the second of any Chinese bank following the June 2005 listing of the HSBC-invested Bank of Communications that raised US$1.9 billion. There was a lot of pressure for the listing to impress the international marketplace as the pipeline was packed with a dozen other potential listings including what eventually became the US$22 billion granddaddy of them all: the October 2006 listing of Industrial and Commercial Bank of China (ICBC), which would become the world's largest.

To help lend the bank credibility in its IPO, it took a US$3 billion investment from Bank of America (BoA) in September 2005 for a 9 percent stake. Guo has actively managed the relationship with BoA, perhaps more than any Chinese CEO has with his overseas partners or investors. The partnership has proved fruitful. Although a secondary listing in Shanghai in September 2007 has diluted BoA's holding to 8.2 percent, the two banks' relationship has become tightly cemented with more than 20 joint venture operations and partnerships.

On top of this, BoA sold its highly profitable Bank of America (Asia) operations to CCB at the end of 2006 so that CCB is now catching up to ICBC and Bank of China (BOC) in terms of having a Hong Kong subsidiary. ICBC cobbled ICBC (Asia) together out of several smaller Hong Kong banks, as well as the retail banking operations of Fortis Bank, in the early part of the first decade of the twenty-first century; Bank of China operates Hong Kong's second-largest bank, Bank of China (Hong Kong).

Despite the deal-making that he has done with BoA, as well as the celebrated IPO, Guo is best known for the restructuring that he has done at CCB that gave international investors the confidence to invest in it and see its stock price more than quadruple in two years.

"Compared with the international banks, CCB has already established its corporate governance structure and the standard is quite high," said Guo. "We are just operating under the legal framework that has been established."

As the chairman of the bank, Guo and the vice-chairman of the board of directors jointly undertake the role of CEO. With his relative lack of experience in managing a bank, Guo takes a more strategic look at the bank, channeling his many connections into developing the bank's business outlook and future path. He also oversees five committees that sit under the board of directors. That includes committees for strategy development, audit, risk management, nomination and compensation, and related party transactions. Established in 2004, the board tends to be a busy one, prone to holding meetings every month, rather than just at quarterly intervals as it says in the bank's articles of association.

Bringing his bank up to speed has presented three distinct and very serious challenges to Guo. He knows that he must meet the needs of the market, and especially to keep up with the pace of its growth. The operational challenges he needs to address are only exacerbated by the fierce competition he faces every day, not only from the three massive banks that are roughly the same size as his (BOC and Agricultural Bank of China) or larger (ICBC). He will also, in major banking hubs, be seeing more and more foreign competition coming in and taking his clients one by one, at least for certain parts of the business in which they can offer more attractive terms, or have more sophisticated capabilities.

Guo has attacked this problem partially through his many tie-ups with BoA, which include a credit card joint venture, an ATM sharing agreement, a leasing business, a remittance service, and many others. He has also worked on developing innovative services such as a mobile phone ticketing service together with Spring Airlines and an "IPO subscription" product. He has also launched investment products from JPMorgan. Still, the bank has a long way to go before having the types of abilities it will need to keep its most sophisticated clients happy.

NEW DIRECTIONS

Like many bank heads who are very comfortable in their position, Guo speaks frankly about many things, including his personal challenges moving into his new role from his previous positions in government administrations.

"Shifting to be a commercial banker was a big challenge for me, because in the past, I never assumed the role of a chairman or CEO of any big enterprise," Guo said. "I encountered three phases of change: the first is from a government official to a commercial banker, the second is from a regulator to a businessman, and the third is from a spender to an earner. Maybe the last is most difficult because I had to take the market, income, and profit into consideration. If you don't have the market, you don't have the customer, you have nothing."

> **I encountered three phases of change: the first is from a government official to a commercial banker, the second is from a regulator to a businessman, and the third is from a spender to an earner.**

Guo also faces challenges from the structure of the system. There is the internal structure of the bank, but there is also the government and the external environment with such forces as regulation and supervision. Finally, Guo will also suffer a dearth of employee talent. Considering the big gap that he feels yawning between market requirements and employee qualifications, Guo is facing the problems that banks all over the world are facing, which is finding the right people.

But considering the growth that CCB and the Chinese banks are enjoying, the challenge is particularly acute. They truly are suffering a "rich businessman's disease." With more than 10 percent asset growth per year, they are expanding at such a pace that they will very soon be the largest banks in Asia; given recent asset growth trajectories, ICBC is set to become the largest bank in Asia by 2011, with CCB close behind at number two. ICBC had 11 percent asset growth in 2006, CCB 22 percent, and Bank of Communications more than 30 percent asset growth in an economy that is expanding nearly 10 percent per year nationwide and certainly more than that in the cities.

To get there, Guo will need to hire many more staff to keep up with the growth, particularly in the retail banking and risk management departments. The labor market in China is plagued by high turnover rates, and managing training for the revolving door of new staff coming in is a gargantuan task. So few come into the bank with expe-

> If you don't have the market, you don't have the customer, you have nothing.

rience, and the bank draws from the 17 million Chinese who graduate from university each year and enter the work force.

Managing growth is a particular challenge for Guo, as it is for all of China's business leaders, but at least it is a happy problem to have.

"The capital market is highly liquid with ample capital," said Guo. "We do not have a lot of areas to invest. Therefore, we have to further expand our market by innovating our products, and also improving our work processes. The Chinese financial and banking services market is very underdeveloped."

The supply of services is insufficient and yet customer demand for good service is high, he said.

"The authorities may want to slow down the loan growth, but there is still a lot of room for us to develop in the personal banking business," Guo said. "For some small and private enterprises, they want capital badly, but there are only a few channels to get them. If CCB can develop the personal banking business as well as services for small enterprises, we can enjoy high spreads and high margins."

CCB's growth into retail and SME banking means that it is getting away from its core charter as a bank to fund infrastructure projects, as is described in its name.; Guo now describes his bank as 70 percent corporate and 30 percent retail. The bank is now a full commercial bank that needs to survive on its own merit and impress its shareholders with returns, and that means finding them across all industries.

"CCB is also making efforts to transform its image from a specialized infrastructure-focused bank to a comprehensive bank," said Guo. "Over the past ten years, CCB has made a lot of efforts in changing its image and we have achieved a lot."

This is, after all, the bank that had once popularized the slogan "If you want to buy an apartment, you should come to CCB for help" in the 1990s.

"We have the housing mortgage business and it is a good business, and CCB wants to continue to keep its competitive advantage in this area," he said. "On the other hand, financial transactions are under-developed in the Chinese banking industry. Nowadays you seldom see people lining up for anything else, but in banks, you can still see people lining up to do banking transactions. So you can see there is a very large room for improvement."

CULTURAL EVOLUTION

Guo's task of improving the bank is particularly difficult as the market, and his customers, see banks as only taking action if something is to their benefit. Nonetheless, Guo insists that it is for the customers' benefit that he is making these changes, and he has their needs in view. Perhaps this is the greatest cultural change that Guo is bringing to the bank, as it moves away from being a corporate bank that is exposed to the concentration risk that is part of the ups and downs of a small group of related industries, and on to a broader customer diversification.

"Since I came to CCB, I have strongly advocated that we should focus on our customer and we have to improve our work process to better service our clients," said Guo.

Considering his background, Guo has nearly the same feel of the pulse on the street that a recent hire might have.

"For a commercial bank, it is very natural to think that income, profit, and efficiency are the most important," said Guo. "However, as CCB was formerly a state-owned bank, it is quite difficult for people to change their mindsets, and to a certain extent, bureaucracy still exists in CCB. Nowadays, I still believe that changing the mindset and improving the employees' qualities are most important."

But Guo is not yet completely at ease with the pace of improvement in the bank, and he has healthy concerns about the future.

"If we cannot, or if we do not, have this kind of reform, CCB will not have a future," he said.

Although Chinese banks are benefiting from rapid growth, the banks are seen as the country's most underdeveloped industry and are struggling to keep up with the pace of change. In this they are not dissimilar from banks in nearly any country in the world, where the relatively sleepy financial services industry is the supertanker cruising that needs plenty of preparation if it wants to change course. Despite their efforts to improve as fast as they can, their pace seems leisurely compared with that of the cell phone manufacturers, with their ever-shorter product cycles and their need to be able to turn on a dime with zero-defect production if they want to preserve their wafer-thin margins.

If we do not have this kind of reform, CCB will not have a future.

"As new businesses grow, new risks will appear and so will new bad assets," said Guo.

"What we can do is to improve our profitability to cover the bad assets," he said. "If we want to expand our business areas we must take the risks into consideration. We must balance the risks and rewards to make the risks controllable. There are two points we should emphasize. The first is to understand our customers. The second is to improve our market segmentation."

Guo stands by the spirit of motivation instilled in his employees, although he's aware of the serious difficulties that they face adapting to China's changing environment. Everybody—not just Guo—is doing this for the first time. Guo is treading carefully, wary of the many factors outside of his control that may pop up, similar to the U.S. sub-prime mortgage crisis, in the near future.

"The challenge is because of the rapid changes in the market with a lot of contradictions and conflicts this year," said Guo. "For example, for the lending business, some problems that did not surface last year will perhaps surface this year. There may also be changes in the macroeconomic regulation, measures that may come into effect this year. For some industries and some projects, when first initiated, we thought

> **As new businesses grow, new risks will appear and so will new bad assets. What we can do is to improve our profitability to cover the bad assets.**

that it would be a very good project or very good industries to invest in. But as the economy slows down, maybe we will see oversupply areas like steel, cement, car making, and also aluminum. So maybe we will encounter problems in these areas."

MAKING THE MACHINE WORK

Guo has been spending a lot on technology for his bank, and in 2006, he invested US$1.24 billion upgrading the bank's infrastructure.

"We completed a very important project called DCC—Data Consolidation Center," he said. "Compared to the other domestic banks, we are still not the best. There might be one or two banks that are better than us. So we still have a lot to do."

Nearly 40 percent of that investment will be in core banking, while the rest will be in the bank's channels. This includes renovating branches, to bring them from the era of the Cultural Revolution into the new millennium, and buying new ATMs to improve customers' access to their funds. Hopefully this will also help stimulate consumer spending so that China develops a consumer spending-based economy some day to balance its export businesses.

If Guo wants to be the best, he may have a long way to go. According to The Asian Banker's Excellence in Retail Financial Services research program, China Construction Bank ranked sixth in China in terms of its retail banking capabilities. Among it's Big Four peers of ICBC, BOC and ABC, it came in third after ICBC and BOC (ABC didn't even place in the top 15), and behind the best bank in the country, joint stock bank China Merchants Bank, the perennial winner of many of the banking prizes for banks in China.

In terms of The Asian Banker's ranking of the 300 strongest banks in the region—which is judged by a formula that takes factors of scale, balance sheet growth, risk profile, profitability, and asset quality into consideration—the bank fared slightly better, coming in fifth after many of the same banks (the notable exception is ICBC, which placed ninth).

One characteristic of the Chinese banking system specifically, and of China in general, is that it is full of eager learners who scan the horizon to learn from global best practices. They will also keep a lookout for global *worst* practices to avoid repeating mistakes made elsewhere, for example sub-prime mortgages in the U.S. in 2006, credit card NPLs in Hong Kong in 2003 and South Korea in 2004, and cash advances in Taiwan in 2005.

As he looks over his business, Guo is scanning the globe to look for examples he can apply to his bank, or new management concepts he can adapt to CCB. Among the banks he admires globally is HSBC, as well as BoA, the largest single investor in his bank.

As an example, HSBC can be very familiar with the local markets and customers," said Guo. "They show their respect to local cultures and also to the customs. I think in this aspect, we can learn from HSBC."

"Our strategic cooperation partner, Bank of America, is also an excellent bank," he said. "They are very excellent in terms of their service culture and also in the personal banking business. Also the banks from Switzerland are very strong in wealth management and asset management. We can learn from them."

But even as he looks overseas to see what the other banks are doing, Guo's CCB has not yet made any of the steps outside that its larger cousin ICBC has. The larger bank has taken a gigantic investment in South Africa's largest bank, Standard Bank, while Guo has looked no further than Hong Kong, where he did a deal for BoA's small local bank. Among the three listed state-owned banks—ICBC, BOC and CCB— Guo's is not only the smallest but also the most introspective.

But this is more in keeping with Guo's character, as he does not seem keen on using his IPO capital to make hasty investments, preferring to use the funds to strengthen the bank operationally and prepare it for future domestic challenges. Guo is also betting a lot on the bank's partnership with BoA and its many tie-ups and has clearly been drawn into a complex relationship that none of the other Big Four banks have attempted with their overseas partners.

With his combination of forthrightness and skepticism of the future, Guo seems like the prudent manager that investors would want to see at the helm of a major investment in the "wild East," where banking is so new that it feels like it is being done for the first time. Now several years into the job, Guo is finally getting comfortable in his role leading China's number two bank. But that feeling may not last as the bank grows tremendously, apace with a turbo-charged economy, and if he's still around in a couple of years when it becomes the second-biggest bank in the Asia—or the world—it may not seem as comfortable any more. In fact, it may just scare the life out of him.

The Space Cowboy

An industry veteran takes a step into the time machine

What is experienced regional banker K.K. Tan seeing as he takes Thailand's fifth-biggest bank for a ride?

FOR decades the domain of local banks, the Thai financial services industry has finally been cracked open: GE Money has arrived. Once a sleepy territory of bankers who made their living playing golf and arranging corporate loans, everything fell apart in 1997 with the Asian financial crisis. Soon after that, foreign companies like GE Money began buying assets in the kingdom in a big way.

The company has now invested more than US$1 billion in Thailand. For many years Bangkok was the site of one of the company's Asian headquarters, along with Tokyo where its regional CEO sits. The company quickly had its fingers in credit cards, consumer finance, and its own fledgling two-branch GE Money Bank.

But it set its own bank aside under Thailand's single presence policy (which limits a single owner to control a single bank) when it took a massive 25 percent stake in Bank of Ayudhya (BAY) in August

K.K. Tan
Reproduced by permission of
TAB International

> The whole consumer banking proposition is relatively new in Thailand, which makes it very interesting.

2005, a stake it eventually built up to 31 percent by July 2007. The two branches of GE Money Bank were quickly merged with nearly 600 BAY branches.

Tan Kong Khoon, known affectionately as K.K. Tan, was hired away from Standard Chartered Bank in December 2006 to be BAY's first non-Thai CEO, and a new face for the old bank that would integrate an established franchise with modern techniques and global best practices from GE Money.

An affable man with a big smile, Tan comes off as a salesman eager to show off a hot item that has just come into the shop. Born in Singapore, Tan got his start in banking with a tenure at DBS in the 1980s before moving on to Standard Chartered Bank. He eventually rose to become the head of retail banking for the greater China region before being poached away by GE Money. BAY is the third bank in Asia Pacific that GE Money has invested in, along with lenders in the Philippines and Taiwan, typically looking at financial institutions that are strong in areas where it is not and are weak in areas where it is strong.

Now leading Thailand's fifth-largest bank, Tan has his work cut out for him. BAY is still known for its double-digit NPLs, and it is heavily leveraged in the wholesale banking industry with a weak presence in retail banking. But together with GE Money, the mix makes for an interesting formula: BAY has its strength in wholesale banking, GE Money has its strength in back office processes and unsecured lending such as credit cards and personal loans, while Tan's experience straddles both of those spheres.

GE Money is just building up its portfolio of banks in Asia Pacific, with BAY by far the largest. If things work out well, what it learns in Thailand may provide lessons for it to build its portfolio into the retail financial service industry's higher functions such as mortgages and wealth management.

Clearly, GE Money has brought in the right man for the job if what they have in mind is to give BAY a better balance of wholesale banking versus retail banking—to be beefed up no doubt by GE's famous Six Sigma efficiency processes—and one that is more in tune with global best practices.

BETTER INFRASTRUCTURE

"Strategic intent-wise, we aim to be the most aligned universal bank in Thailand," said Tan. "We would very much need a service-led strategy through product innovation, which is a very clear signal, but I don't think we have the low-cost infrastructure today to be able to use pricing as a differentiator. At this point in time in the marketplace, no company has the infrastructure that would enable it to compete on price."

Tan said he hopes to lead more through advanced service offerings rather than simply through stand-alone products, but in order to do it he's going to build stronger IT capabilities in the bank. Until the bank has the capacity to do analytics-backed decisions, rather than those based on the experience of individuals, he won't be satisfied. Tan feels that analytics can help the bank become a performance-oriented organization by showing which customer sector or product stream is showing profitability and where it needs to improve its profitability with better operations.

"There's a lot of work to do around building a better data ware-house, in which we can actually have the information that we need to make good decisions, as well as to do propensity analysis to be able to target the right product streams and service areas to the clients," Tan said. "That's where GE comes in."

With its famous Six Sigma and lean manufacturing techniques, GE Money typically teaches its partners around the region how to improve delivery times, and Tan is hoping that the bank's largest shareholder will do the same at BAY. Credit card and mortgage approval times are obvious areas of improvement for his bank, and GE Money has been able to cut credit card operations at its Hyundai Card joint venture partnership in Korea by one third. In Singapore, it claims to be able to approve personal loans in two hours, even without access to a credit bureau.

Other areas where Tan is seeking help from GE Money are in what he calls "governance discipline," which includes using analytics for risk management, as well as corporate governance issues and a stricter control over compliance.

"Once these foundations are in place, we can actually go out there and chase after the business," said Tan. "In terms of customer segmentation, because we are a universal bank, we actually have a full range of customer segments, which will include corporate banking, SME banking, consumer banking, and last but not least, the treasury and financial institutions business streams."

WOBBLY ENVIRONMENT

Considering the wobbly prospects of the country, which has seen rapid growth as well as the dampening effect of the September 2006 military coup, Tan hedges his growth targets by tying them closely to GDP growth. With this he aims to grow BAY's corporate banking business up to 1.5 times the country's GDP growth, and even more in SME banking. He hopes for four or five times GDP growth for his consumer banking business, but that growth rate will be coming from the low base of only 4.5 million customers in a country of nearly 65 million. At least he has the strong helping hand of a big brother.

"The whole consumer banking proposition is relatively new in Thailand, which makes it very interesting, and at the stage of what I imagine would be extremely explosive growth potential," Tan said. "That's one of the main things that intrigued me in this market. It's green fields, very interesting."

Even beyond retail banking, the partnership has wide potential, and Tan has people at GE he can call.

"GE has a corporate finance group," he said. "Unlike most companies, I would say that GE actually works pretty well across their business lines. Yeah, okay, you can call them silos—they're different business groupings, but they work really well across businesses. If I have a question and want a sounding board at GE corporate finance, I just pick up the phone and make a call. They will listen to me, talk to me, and we'll have an intellectual discussion."

Tan has something similar available with his SME business, and there are ears that will listen at GE Commercial Finance.

But it is clear that retail banking will be the main conversation that he will be having, and mere weeks after taking the job Tan was already presiding over one of the bank's first customer service-oriented rollouts, a domestic money transfer service. The program is very similar to one rolled out at Garanti Bank in Turkey, where GE Money is also a major shareholder.

"The evolution of banks in different countries more or less takes the same route," Tan said. "I've worked in both emerging and developed countries in Asia, and I've been exposed to the operating models in very developed countries like the U.S. as well as Europe. The value of what I can bring is to look at Thailand, the Thai banking market, and see what stage of the evolution they are at, and be able to improve on previous experiences [based on] both the market environment and the challenges that banks face at particular stages in their evolution. I'll try to steer the bank safely through some of the risks of the marketplace, where there is a sudden interest or growth in consumer banking."

Although he knows that he has to give his clients much more sophisticated products than its previous managers ever did, Tan also wants to avoid proliferation of products for their own sake and knows he needs to keep the customer-centric approach in mind from the start of the long, slow road to building a premier retail bank for the country. Given the poor performance of the bank in the past, new ventures will need to have an eye on profitability right from the start and volume will be the key. And now being a part of a demanding corporate culture, he's certain to be looking out for critical mass and his break-even point soon, or he won't bother starting a business. He'll also be on the watch for situations that may expose him to price competition with other banks, many of which have much stronger retail banking operations than he does.

GETTING DOWN TO IT

Only 15 percent of BAY's business is in retail banking, with a 5 percent market share in mortgage lending on top of an 8 percent market share in credit card balance and a 5.6 percent market share of auto loans, Tan said. To build these businesses, Tan will be working on both increasing the number of products that he sells to his existing clients as well as gaining business from clients currently at other banks. One of the areas he'll be focusing on is wealth management, which is an undeveloped market in Thailand, and also one where GE Money doesn't have any particular strength based on its current global portfolio. Here Tan will be on his own, although he knows he can always look to GE Money for back office support in terms of processing power as well as for 100 people brought over from GE Money Bank.

"I am a 'roll up your sleeves' manager, so I am also involved in the wealth management side, sitting in on many of the meetings; they also have me as a resource on that piece of the business," he said.

Despite his eagerness to build a name for himself in Thailand, Tan is acutely aware of the competition that he's facing, and that he will quickly butt heads with some very large Thai banks.

"There are some local players who are very serious about consumer banking, and are making very good inroads into it," he says. "We're not the first, we are probably the fourth or so [in retail banking in Thailand], but this is still the very early stage of the market development and I think there is huge potential for all the banks to reap very good rewards from it. So I do not expect irrational pricing behavior at this time. Not yet."

GE Money is the largest foreign player in Thailand, but it is not the only one. Even though DBS, the largest bank in Southeast Asia and Tan's former employer, has had bad luck in the Land of Smiles, Tan's other *alma mater* Standard Chartered Bank has had a good run. Singapore's UOB has had a presence since it bought Bank of Asia and merged it with its local operations in late 2005. Scotiabank has bought into Thanachart Bank, and China's Industrial and Commercial Bank of China is ready to buy in as well. With so much interest from foreign players, franchise-builders like ANZ, Citibank, and HSBC are surely also not far away. Foreign presences are a concern among Thai banks, in particular for their deep pockets.

"It will be interesting," says Vichit Suraphongchai, the CEO of Siam Commercial Bank, which has the country's largest branch and ATM presence and leads the market in almost every aspect of retail banking. "It's the first time a foreign company has come in to manage a very Thai organization at that size. We are watching. We expect that the competition will be strong from GE. I know they're strong in retail, which again goes face to face with us. In the SME, GE also has the expertise. They could use a lot of new technology in terms of processing, in terms of risk management, product sophistication. I see

> **I am a "roll up your sleeves" manager, so I am also involved in the wealth management side.**

that GE could add value on the risk management part, product diversification, and the processing. Marketing, even if they have very good information on the customer, I would expect that marketing would be quite aggressive as well."

But despite the advantages that Tan and GE Money gain, there will be some challenges, particularly in the cultures of the new and the old. "The culture part is something that I can't predict," adds Suraphongchai. "But I assume that GE must have thought long and hard about that. How do you change the culture of a truly family-run bank?"

The CEO of Kasikornbank, Banthoon Lamsam, has similar predictions for Tan.

"They'll be a tougher competitor of course," he said. "They will bring in new management, but the limitations will be that they still have to access the Thai labor markets, and the HR issue is the real matter in the financial services industry. There are not enough good people to go around, especially in the financial services, because that's where all the best engineering graduates are working."

POINT OF VIEW

But Tan is not unprepared for the complexities of working on an integration exercise that brings together a large Thai bank and a small Thai bank under a large American organization—as well as himself, a mild-mannered regional banker.

"To a certain extent, I'm a neutral outsider," he said. "That adds some value too."

To kick off the cultural melding, a series of cross-cultural training programs were organized.

"What really matters is that the team has been focusing not so much on the differences, but where they can actually get value from each other," said Tan. "That's very reflective of the maturity of the team that I'm working with today. I consider myself extremely privileged to have this level of maturity, where every meeting we sit in people ask us for assistance and even, to an extent, guidance in certain areas. Even to understand a particular customer segmentation that we are particularly strong in, or asking for a clearer understanding or a different approach in terms of how we can tackle certain problems through a process. I think it's that common determination to make this thing work that is making this such a wonderful marriage of two partners— Bank of Ayudhya and GE Money Bank."

In addition to four professionals from GE Money helping out at the senior management level, Tan has 50 or 60 who are helping with the integration. The bank teams have known each other already for a long time because of various joint ventures that they had been working on in the years leading up to the merger.

If he can get his teams integrated efficiently, Tan will be looking at bringing more innovation into the bank along the lines of his ATM remittance service. He is focusing on the customer experience and making processes more efficient so that customers aren't kept waiting through long application procedures, another major strength area of GE's.

Tan already has several layers of innovations in mind.

"Pricing mechanism is something we want to tweak," he said. "Flexibility with payment schedules. Product design itself, different types of features on the asset side—this is all on the loan side. In terms of the wealth management piece, it is so young, at its early stages of development, and there really are a lot of best practices, best in class product streams around the whole region that we can bring home to Thailand to roll out. A whole array of things, the sky's the limit. Especially things like derivative-linked kind of deposit product streams, the market essentially doesn't allow it today but will eventually move towards that direction as it evolves. There's always that evolutionary phase."

Tan is also keen to find areas where he can be creative in catering to specific customer segments. He also wants to bring this thinking into his SME and corporate banking divisions as they also begin to look more closely at segmenting their customer bases and looking along the supply chain clusters.

Of course, he still needs to get past the regulators, as well as the concern that the general public may not be ready yet for the more sophisticated products that he had in mind; if they were, after all, sophisticated players like Standard Chartered Bank in Thailand would have rolled them out already. And on top of this, more prudence is required in light of the sensitivity of the economy, which is no longer pumping along at full steam.

"We are starting to see some weakening of the GDP," Tan said. "That, I believe, is not because of the underlying fundamental weakness in the Thai economy; it has more to do with consumer confidence, which translates into weaker consumer spending and weaker consumer investments."

Although industry is running below capacity and could use investment, a wait-and-see approach to the political situation means that caution is the word of the day, whatever the potential of the country is. While lending margins are being affected, Tan expects that retail banking will shore up weakness on the corporate side.

"By chasing consumer banking we should be able to negate some of the effects of the economic downturn," he said.

STORM CLOUDS ON A SUNNY DAY

Unfortunately, BAY still has a high level of NPLs, and they could creep up if the economy weakens, or if exports are hit too heavily.

"I'm not expecting any major turn-up in NPLs as I'm still very confident that, as seen in the past, Thailand is very resilient to political instability, and it's just a matter of time before we resolve this," Tan said. "I'm very confident of that."

Every day he arrives at his office on the banks of the Chao Phraya River, Tan sees reminders of the last time the country experienced a big shock, but also hints of the good times to come: while the concrete skeleton of a high-rise that was abandoned mid-construction in 1997 rusts on one side of the giant BAY headquarters, a brand new condominium complex for Thailand's new money is going up on the other side. While one represents the despair of the old economy and the other represents the hopes of the current one, across the river itself is a huge patch of dense jungle, completely undeveloped, that represents the potential of development to come. But what does the future hold for any of these three parts of Bangkok, not to mention BAY itself?

For the time being, BAY is well capitalized; Tan will use this to improve the quality of his portfolio and reduce his bad loans, but he will also be investing in the building blocks he'll need to see sustainable growth: better credit risk, stronger corporate governance, and the capacity to understand the bank's data and use that to build stronger revenue streams. In other words, he's keen to spend short term so that he can earn long term.

> **The biggest problem with organic growth is really the fact that on the financials the impact is not as attractive as it would be if it's inorganic growth.**

"The major piece that we have is that there's some data warehousing activities going on right now," Tan said. "We're building the data warehouse. Actually, we are not building it from scratch; we are taking over one of the GE components that we find very useful. So we are taking that on for Bank of Ayudhya. We are also building a customer relationship management platform, which I think is very critical. We're talking about providing financial solutions for customers, be it a loan or a wealth management need—you really need a customer relationship management (CRM) system to be able to do that."

Besides consolidating multiple systems platforms, Tan has to think about the nitty gritty, like training branch staff on the new products, as well as the new consumer banking focus that the bank is going to have, as well as using the new CRM capabilities.

But as far as his capital goes, acquisitions are clearly also not far from his mind. As the foreign head of a largely foreign management team, Tan has a few advantages, considering that he will have none of the cultural inhibitions Thai senior managers have in seeking acquisitions. Being too close to the market, Thai banks often stay their hand when acquisition opportunities arise, usually out of cultural inhibitions that prevent them from acquiring struggling rivals, and they miss opportunities—or block themselves out of them. Here Tan will find he has agility, as long as another foreign bidder doesn't outmaneuver him.

Acquisition obviously has a great appeal over steady, business-as-usual organic growth to the seasoned banker.

"The biggest problem with organic growth is really the fact that on the financials the impact is not as attractive as it would be if it's inorganic growth," he said. "You can capitalize on a lot of things—growth rate and all that—whereas inorganic growth you kind of hit drawbacks. Your cost-to-income ratio will just look crazy, unless you can very quickly break even. For this kind of a business, you need a gestation period to build up your human resources capability and then it grows, so for that period of time—for at least 18 months, 24 months—financials look bad. Investors desert you at this point in time, and if you don't have investors, what business proposition do you have? And that's why I think it's leading to so much inorganic activity in the marketplace today."

Tan's time in Thailand already reminds him of earlier days in his own banking career, especially considering the relatively under-developed level of retail banking in the market. He sees opportunities everywhere.

> Moving from a very developed, highly competitive, almost saturated market environment to one in its emerging phase of development throws up a completely different set of challenges and things to get excited about.

"Moving from a very developed, highly competitive, almost saturated market environment to one in its emerging phase of development throws up a completely different set of challenges and things to get excited about," he said. "Again, it is the sheer size of opportunities that are available, and it's a case of what I would call relatively low hanging fruits that are so within reach that make this market so exciting for someone to want to work here."

Tan sees some similarities to the Singapore he worked in during the 1990s, albeit with the benefit of having had some hard knocks in 1997 and learning some valuable lessons. His work in China was in a developing market as well, although one with much larger scale than that of Thailand's today.

As a former retail banker who has become a CEO, Tan falls into a rare breed inhabited by a few before him, such as Philippe Paillart, who ran DBS in Singapore from 2000 to 2002, Yashiro Masamoto, who ran Shinsei Bank from 2000 to 2005, or Paul Fegan, current CEO of St.George Bank in Australia. The skill is not always valued, as can be seen by how many banks are run by former investment bankers; the case of Citi, with its humongous global retail banking franchise now turned over to a CEO who has no experience running a retail operation, is a case in point.

But, for his new role, Tan feels that he has the skills needed to run the show rather than just a similar business line.

"I think, essentially, it's very similar, and at the end of the day we have the same issues," he said. "Management challenges are always about proper risk control. It's about putting in place not just the rules of compliance and good governance, but it's also that positive mindset as well as motivating people to do their very best."

Chapter 5
The Managers—Engaging Entropy

Two are Better than One

Hedge your bets

Hang Seng Bank's vice-chairman and CEO Raymond Or is leading his bank into its second major market.

ONE of the odd banking relationships in Asia is that between HSBC and Hang Seng Bank (Hang Seng). HSBC invested in the latter in 1965, taking a 51 percent stake that it eventually increased to the 62.14 percent that it owns in the bank today. They are now two of Hong Kong's largest banks, with HSBC carrying roughly 45 percent of the special administrative region's (SAR) assets and Hang Seng a further 10 percent. Both are particularly strong in retail banking, and in many categories they are the SAR's top two banks, and they are clearly each other's strongest competitors.

The banks are both among the strongest not just in Hong Kong but in the entire region: according to The Asian Banker's Excellence in Retail Financial Services Program, the best retail bank in Hong Kong will usually be one or the other (HSBC 2002, 2004, 2006; Hang Seng Bank 2005), and invariably the same goes for the best retail bank in the entire Asia Pacific region award as well (HSBC 2004, Hang Seng

Raymond Or
Reproduced by permission of
Hang Seng Bank

150

2005). In another research study on the region's strongest banks, which is calculated from a formula that looks at factors that describe scale, balance sheet growth, risk profile, profitability, and asset quality, the same is true with Hang Seng established as the region's strongest bank in 2005, HSBC in 2006.

Besides being strong competitors for growth and for excellence, the banks have a curious habit of cross-pollinating each other with talent. Many of HSBC's senior executives have gone from HSBC to Hang Seng, such as Dorothy Sit, Hang Seng's general manager and chief operating officer (and director of Hang Seng China) who had formerly been the head of retail with HSBC. And on the day in May 2005 that Raymond Or crossed over from his job as group general manager of HSBC to Hang Seng to be its vice-chairman and CEO, Hang Seng's vice-chairman and CEO since 1998 Vincent Cheng crossed over to HSBC to replace David Eldon as that bank's first chairman of Chinese origin (and in early 2008 Cheng was appointed executive director of HSBC Holdings).

While it may seem inconceivable that Bank of America may be a majority owner of JPMorgan Chase, or that Singapore's DBS would also own a large part of UOB, somehow the situation has come to rise in ultra-capitalist Hong Kong. Other banks now seem to have taken an interest in the arrangement. Bank of China (Hong Kong), the second-largest bank in the SAR, in late 2007 took a small stake in Bank of East Asia, the fifth largest. Whether it's replicating the HSBC–Hang Seng model remains to be seen, but the investment is curious nonetheless.

It seems like an odd move for Or, who had been with HSBC since 1972, and could have had a larger career in the vast HSBC empire. Although staying at the larger institution would have meant graduating into a realm where senior bankers tend to speak in crisp British accents, and have spent parts of their career in the Middle East, Micronesia, or South America, a place where Hong Kong-born bankers are few in number. But running your own smaller bank is not such a bad consolation prize, even if it means that there are not many other places to go afterward… except maybe back to HSBC.

While at the world's local bank, Or worked in the personnel, securities, and retail banking divisions in the first eight years of his career. In 1980, he joined the corporate banking division as a credit manager, where he worked until 1995, when he became assistant general manger and head of corporate and institutional banking. He started 2000 as general manager before rising to group general manager in the same year. And like many senior businessmen in Hong Kong, Or holds many directorships and other appointed positions.

> HK is probably over-banked. We only got over seven million people. Too many banks. And although we think that there are too many branches, the customers feel that they need more.

A tidy, cheerful man, Or is a younger, more colorful person than his predecessor and has a lot of energy. With his long experience he is the image of the consummate Hong Kong banker with his dense understanding of his competitive market, from the small businesses of Kowloon, to the hungry entrepreneurs looking to set up businesses in China to ride a growth wave and take advantage of potential savings in manufacturing, to the needs of Hong Kong's medium- and high-net worth individuals. That understanding is crucial to surviving in Hong Kong, and if he wants to thrive in one of the world's most competitive banking environments and ultimately be highly profitable despite price wars cutting margins wafer thin, he has to be on top of his figures. There are 23 licensed banks incorporated in Hong Kong as of June 30, 2008.

HOME FIRES BURNING

"I think banking in Hong Kong is very, very competitive," he said. "Hong Kong is probably over-banked. We only got over seven million people. Too many banks. And although we think that there are too many branches, the customers feel that they need more. They want a branch very close to where they live."

Considering the size of the SAR, its economy is relatively susceptible to outside factors besides just regular competition.

"Obviously, banks have to fight for loan growth in this environment; that's not going to help the loan margins," he said. "There's also the uncertainty factors of the threat of bird flu. It's more psychological but psychology does have an adverse impact on consumers' confidence; because they generally feel less confident, then they spend less. This is also reflected in the slowdown of the growth of retail sales."

Competition in the mortgage space shows just how fierce the economy has become, and Or knows that very well from personal experience.

"When I joined as a banker, the mortgage spread went as wide as 450 to 500 basis points. [In 2005], the mortgage spread actually narrowed to something below 50 basis points," he said. "The profitability of mortgage has come down a lot, although it remained a core lending product of retail banks in HK. For Hang Seng yes, I think in terms of our loan portfolio, I think mortgage loans represent a very important component, but not necessarily the profitability."

> **When I joined as a banker, the mortgage spread went as wide as 450 to 500 basis points. [In 2005], the mortgage spread actually narrowed to something below 50 basis points.**

Clearly it's a business any bank in Hong Kong needs to be in, even if it doesn't earn much from it and it ties up resources.

But profitability for banks in Hong Kong is not about traditional banking any more. Or is focusing on keeping his bank's costs down—at one point its cost-to-income ratio was a mere 35 percent—and bulking up on both the vast and growing China business. In Hong Kong Or is focusing, as all forward-thinking bankers would, on the sustainable business of generating fee income rather than interest income, which ebbs and flows with the business cycles.

"Lately, we've realized that it's probably very difficult to continue to rely on deposits and loan advances to maintain your profit growth," Or said. "In the last couple of years, we've focused ourselves on non-fund incomes. It would be the investment and insurance products. On these two areas, the momentum is still there."

Or claims a large market share in the wealth management business, where the bank has built up an impressive supermarket of its own products, and it enjoys a 50 percent market share for guaranteed fund products. It's also an area where he's clearly keeping up with his former employer/current big brother.

But even when he's ahead, Or needs to keep an eye on volatility even in his strongest segments, and the market for these products is susceptible to small interest rate rises as sensitive, fickle Hong Kongers pile out of funds and back into deposits. This is where Or balances his bet with more sophisticated yield-enhanced products, which have more attractive up front commissions. With every twist of the market, Or encourages his team to find products to match the new market sentiment.

> **We behave like a supermarket. A supermarket for wealth management. Every day, we have products out.**

"We behave like a supermarket," he said. "A supermarket for wealth management. Every day, we have products out. Whether you like U.S. dollar, euro, yen go up, go down; we've all kinds of products. Hang Seng's strength is the time to market, which is very quick. We've an investment department that comes out with all kinds of products."

Because Hang Seng has an asset management division that originates the products, it can move more quickly than other banks. Still, it may also be beholden to push its own product at the expense of other, better products for some situations: the bank has a mix of in-house and third-party funds, but favors in-house products.

Besides the sustainability of funds, Or is proud of the bank's insurance capabilities, and he paints a picture by explaining that, "in Hong Kong, if you're talking about new premiums on life policies; Hang Seng is now third in it's market league table. The number one is AIA. AIA has been in the insurance business for 100 years. Hang Seng only probably came into the insurance market less than ten years. The organization that occupies the second position is HSBC, our parent company. If you add HSBC and Hang Seng together, we actually already surpass AIA. Insurance will continue to maintain its momentum. Investment products, it would remain to be our core business for Hang Seng."

SOMETHING OLD, SOMETHING NEW...

One area where Or is using his experience at HSBC is in developing his own bank's private banking business, which he sees as the last hole to fill in his retail banking business. He claims high year-on-year growth from a small base, and he has been putting more resources into the business by recruiting more people to help him tap his own customer base of wealthy entrepreneurs, businessmen, and professionals and offer them more products.

But besides developing a stronger private banking business proposition that takes care of the personal needs of rich clients, Hang Seng needed to look after their business needs as well, as very often rich individuals are business owners. Or has concurrently attacked this side of the equation, aiming at both birds at once. Growth in these areas comes from the fact that when Or arrived at Hang Seng from HSBC he noticed that Heng Seng's commercial banking business for SME clients was not up to what other, smaller banks such as Bank of East Asia and DBS Hong Kong had been achieving.

"We bank more than a million customers on the personal banking side and a lot of these personal banking customers are actually sole proprietors or directors of some of the companies who operate business in HK," said Or. "If the Hang Seng brand is so strong in the personal banking market, there's no reason why we can't capture the SMEs.[8]

Working from the other direction, Or also wants to attract new clients into private banking, figure out which of them are also small business owners, and also offer them services that will help their businesses.

"We've established a number of business banking centers in Hong Kong and we've a lot of relationship managers," Or said. "Our approach to SMEs is that we segment them into two groups: those customers that we think justify some relationship management because they present good opportunities for us, then we'll allocate a relationship manager to look after their business. Then there are those companies that we think probably do not justify appointing a relationship manager. Those we would manage by using credit scoring, behavior scoring."

Or notes that efforts to beef up the market have been successful, and he's seen double-digit loan growth, again from a low base.

In Hong Kong, Or has access to a strong credit bureau, hence the attraction of a fiddly business like SME compared with the broad strokes of large corporate banking. With margins under pressure,

> **Most Hong Kong businessmen, one way or the other, have moved their investments to China, and we'll follow them.**

Or is keen to shift gradually away from the business of doing a few very big deals to doing more medium-sized deals.

"In the past, Hang Seng has lent a lot to big corporates at very fine margins," he said. "The way forward, as I see it, we probably would de-emphasize that. We'll still be in the market because we're a big lender in Hong Kong, but we would de-emphasize our lending activities to big corporates, because the margin is too thin and it just does not justify the capital we deploy for these kinds of activities."

Like the mortgage business, large corporate lending is a business a bank has to be seen in, even if it isn't as profitable as more subtle activities. In Hong Kong, most of Hang Seng's business is with local corporations, seemingly leaving the big international business to other banks like HSBC.

THE OBVIOUS MOVE

Besides growing his private banking and commercial banking businesses, Or is looking eagerly toward China, and in 2007 it already contributed 6.5 percent of group profits. Like all other Hong Kong banks, Hang Seng's strategy in China is that it follows its customers.

"Most Hong Kong businessmen, one way or the other, have moved their investments to China, and we'll follow them," Or said. "Most of the Hong Kong people, businessmen, actually invest in the Pearl River Delta and the Yangtze River Delta, that is, the Guangzhou area and the Shanghai area. Hang Seng would also focus our resources in these two areas."

The bank has 25 outlets in China, and is opening new ones all the time, particularly low-cost sub-branches. It also became a locally incorporated bank in China in May 2007, meaning that it will pay higher taxes as a business but will also be able to apply for new banking licenses and branches.

Besides its own outlets, Hang Seng has an investment in a Chinese bank. In late 2003, it paid US$207 million for a 15.98 percent stake in Industrial Bank, a national joint-stock bank that is based in the southern Fujian Province, together with Singapore's government-linked investment body GIC. Although he wasn't part of the bank when it decided to make the investment, Or is happy with what he inherited as it pays many millions in dividends every year as well as the unrealized gain of US$187 million it made on Industrial Bank's January 2007 IPO.

But the Fujian area is not a part of China where Hang Seng has strengths, and Or will be looking to work more with the bank on areas it has not penetrated yet.

"We have a credit card cooperation with Industrial Bank," he said. "We set up a credit card center for them. We manage the credit card for them and there's an understanding that when regulations permit, we'll convert that credit card business into a joint venture."

Hang Seng will also consider helping the bank in insurance, asset management, or securities.

Or is keen to add personal banking business in China alongside business banking as a focus, and the bank is building a mortgage business in southern China. It is leveraging Hong Kong business clients who are also buying property there, as well as some Chinese who have built a relationship with the Hong Kong bank and prefer it over local lenders. Competing with local banks will be quite difficult for Hang Seng as the Chinese banks have a tight hold on their own clientele, although perhaps Hang Seng has an advantage over other banks that may not even bother to do local retail banking.

"In terms of personal banking business in China, we do not believe we can compete with the local banks in the mass market," Or said. "Our plan is we would behave just like Citibank in HK: we'll concentrate ourselves on the more affluent customer segments. Hang Seng's service culture is very unique, and provided we can implant the Hong Kong service culture through our China network, I believe we'll have very good competitive strengths."

There's plenty of business for all of the banks in China to grow, considering the level of economic expansion the country is seeing, as well as the amazingly undeveloped state that the country's banking services are in, Or said. But clearly, it is the banks that understand the needs of Chinese clients that will succeed in local markets. Or will have to work hard at translating the needs of Hong Kong clients into an understanding of the needs of mainland Chinese clients, even if he doesn't have to translate the language.

SIBLING RIVALRY

Of course, Or is going to go head to head with HSBC in China as well, courting the same Hong Kong clients as well as seeking the high-net-worth individuals that Hang Seng and HSBC and all of the foreign banks will be chasing. But with the vastness of China, Or doesn't see the threat at all.

"If you look at the Hong Kong experience, HSBC in terms of market share is number one, Hang Seng is number two," said Or. "And Hong Kong only has seven-odd million people. Beijing is a bigger market. So if Hong Kong can allow HSBC and Hang Seng to survive at the same time, there's no reason to believe that such a big market as Beijing cannot allow HSBC and Hang Seng to co-exist. Hang Seng competing with HSBC is no different from competing with Bank of East Asia and Standard Chartered Bank. But on the other hand, there are areas where both banks can cooperate, like in the syndicated loans market, we sometimes can do it together. I see it as quite positive."

Or's take on the relationship between the two giants is the same one that is repeated every time it is asked of a Hang Seng banker or someone from HSBC's operations in Hong Kong.

"There's competitive overlap, I think without a doubt," Or said. "The Hong Kong market is so small. Ask my colleagues in Hang Seng, 'who's your keenest competitor in the Hong Kong market?' I can tell you; if you ask this question to ten colleagues and ten of them will tell you HSBC. If you ask the same question to HSBC colleagues, I think probably seven out of ten will say that the keenest competitor for HSBC is Hang Seng."

The difference between this relationship and a regular competitor relationship is that both groups will look at each other's profit announcements much more keenly and measure each other's importance to the group that way. There are differences in the characters of the two banks, and Or notes that because it is a smaller bank some customers find Hang Seng's mood warmer and its service slightly better.

"When I was at HSBC, we also had the same feeling, but on the other hand [clients] perceive HSBC to be more professional, more solid," he said. "So that's the difference."

Of course, one area where the relationship is restrictive is if Hang Seng wants to enter a new market, since HSBC will invariably already be there. Or has talked about Taiwan, although it is a market that Hong Kong banks have traditionally not had much success in.

As for other markets Or is as nervous as a cat, noting that he doesn't want to venture too far from his home turf, and he's not keen to "duplicate" HSBC's presence.

"Hang Seng actually had branches in the U.S. and in London but we sold all those to HSBC," he said. "Those Hang Seng branches were not profitable in those times. It's not easy. In today's financial world, I think unless you have the scale, it's difficult for you to survive."

With his world now focused on Hong Kong and China and a few things in between, Or will certainly have fewer distractions. Although in the grand scheme of things, he is still boxed in as HSBC builds up it operations in Taiwan, Japan, and Korea. But China is large, and HSBC can't be everywhere even in the world's third-largest country; Hang Seng's January 2008 investment in Yantai City Commercial Bank in Shandong province is well off the beaten path, and is certain to let the bank have some of the action in China without brushing against big brother.

Icarus and Daedalus

Fly, but not too close to the sun

Thierry Porté is Shinsei Bank's second leader, looking for growth on the foundation of rebirth that he helped his predecessor lay.

THE story of Shinsei Bank has been one of the most interesting of the past decade in Japan. Shinsei, which means "new life" or "rebirth" in Japanese, was formed from the failed Long-Term Credit Bank of Japan. The bank had a near monopoly on the issuance of long-term debt securities, but it was riddled with bad debt when over-extension of its businesses exposed it to the deflation of the asset-price bubble and caused it to flame out spectacularly at the end of the 1990s.

When no buyer could be found among the other ailing Japanese banks, the bank was sold to an international group led by private equity player Ripplewood Holdings for US$121 billion, with key players being former investment bankers Christopher Flowers and Tim Collins. It was a controversial act, and for the first time in history, a Japanese bank had come under foreign control. The move set a precedent of sorts, and very quickly

Thierry Porté
Reproduced by permission of
Shinsei Bank

two other banks were sold to foreign private equity firms. These banks became Tokyo Star Bank and Aozora Bank.

In the bank's formative years, Shinsei was run by Yashiro Masamoto, who had been an executive at Exxon for 30 years. Yashiro worked at Citibank Japan from 1989 to 1998 and is credited for helping the bank build the only retail banking business of any foreign bank in Japan. Over the years from 2000 to his departure in 2005, one year after the Shinsei Bank's triumphant relisting on the Tokyo Stock Exchange, Yashiro transformed the ailing institution into a much-admired modern bank, while bringing investors spectacular gains.

The internationally-minded Yashiro had brought in an international management team and made significant improvements in the bank's infrastructure. Under Yashiro, the bank gave birth to a smart, young retail banking division. He also kicked off an acquisition program to help Shinsei diversify even further, although some of those new businesses are now proving troublesome for his successor, Thierry Porté (pronounced *por-tay*).

Born in 1957, Porté graduated *magna cum laude* in economics from Harvard in 1978. He also attended an MBA course at Harvard Business School in 1982 on a break from Morgan Stanley, where he worked from 1979 to 2003. The investment bank led him to Japan right after his MBA program concluded, where he ultimately rose to the position of president. Throughout his whole career, and even in his college years, Porté has been close to the primary characters in the Shinsei story, nurturing relationships in a way that is vital when doing business in Japan. Ironically, many of the characters are not Japanese.

TOKYO SKYLINE

"I've been in Japan for over 15 years now," said Porté. "I came here first in 1983. I was running Morgan Stanley's businesses in Japan in the 1990s. I got to know Mr. Tim Collins and Mr. Christopher Flowers who were the two principals behind the takeover of Long-Term Credit Bank. I'd known Collins since 1995 when he first came to Japan to start looking at business here. I happened to be a classmate of Christopher Flowers at Harvard College. From the very early stages when they were looking at the takeover of Long-Term Credit Bank, I was working with them. I also knew Yashiro-san from his days at Citibank in Japan. So when they were successful and took over the bank in March of 2000, I became one of the advisors to the bank. I worked extensively with them on a wide variety of issues. Morgan Stanley was selected as the lead manager for the IPO and the advisor on the IPO process in 2001. I had extensive dealings with Shinsei and Shinsei's senior management and owners as an advisor to them."

Porté was invited into the bank to work alongside Yashiro as Porté was groomed to take over the bank's leadership, leveraging his experience in investment banking, corporate banking, and the institutional banking business that is still his main focus at the bank. Porté became the bank's president and CEO in June 2005.

But even before he took over the top position, Porté was already involved in the acquisition of consumer and commercial finance units APLUS and Showa Leasing. Of these two units, the former is now harming the bank's balance sheet following the November 2006 governmental acts that dropped the maximum interest levels that Japanese consumer finance companies can charge from 29 percent to 20 percent. It could still help the bank gain business in the mid term, but Porté's background is investment banking and he considers the retail banking business and consumer finance still secondary to the institutional businesses he's made his name on.

"Our biggest business is still our institutional banking business," he said. "That is a hybrid of investment banking and commercial banking activity. We have an extensive client list of institutional—and that's both corporate and financial institution clients—with a fairly well diversified business, which is not just commercial lending but also involves a variety of products in which we've established market leadership like securitization, dealing with non-performing loans, like non-recourse financing for real estate, advisory activities, derivatives solutions for customers."

Porté describes consumer and commercial finance as slightly smaller than his institutional business, while retail is small but growing quickly from a small base.

The meticulous Porté is businesslike to a fault, and impresses analysts with his detailed knowledge of his business and his no-nonsense demeanor. He is also known for his thoroughly entrenched Japanese formality, which is seen in the way he refers to Western colleagues as "mister," the side-effect of a long career in Japan. He is clearly proud of his Harvard background, as evidenced in the way he talks about his *alma mater* as well as the many colleagues and advisors that are also connected to Harvard. Equally proud of his training at one of the top Wall Street firms, Porté can also infuriate his competitors with his brusque style and his strong statements, as well as staff that disagree with his policies.

Shinsei under Porté is quite a different place to work than under Yashiro, when the mission was all about putting a new bank on a tight platform under a world-beating brand identity. Many of the foreign managers of the Yashiro era have left as the family atmosphere has given way to a tough management regime that takes no prisoners, tied to Porté's vision of 360-degree performance evaluation and other no-nonsense management school concepts.

The character of the bank is obviously something that Porté thinks very carefully about. The presence of international managers such as himself—as well as the investment by foreign investors like Ripplewood—is still a contentious issue that he has to defend on a regular basis as he defines his bank and his role in it.

A JAPANESE BANK THAT IS NOT A JAPANESE BANK

"First of all, we at Shinsei see ourselves as a Japanese bank," he said. "Ninety-six percent of our staff is Japanese. We're headquartered in Japan. We're listed in Tokyo. I would say that if you look at the work of Ripplewood, I think that they have been the forerunner in this marketplace. They took great risk, they took a long view, and they've done a fabulous job."

Concern about foreign ownership may be one thing, but it would be difficult to deny the improvement that the consortium has brought to the bank.

"Business people and government people tend to judge on the basis of results," he said. "They look at what is done and I think if

you look at the results of Ripplewood in Japan, they're very positive. Not just they made money for their investors, which I think is
very important, but also they helped to advance businesses. They
have shown a long term commitment. I think it will be a very
healthy thing and I think there will be plenty of opportunities for
foreign funds, domestic funds, collaboration of foreign funds and
domestic funds."

> ## We at Shinsei see ourselves as a Japanese bank. Ninety-six percent of our staff is Japanese. We're headquartered in Japan. We're listed in Tokyo.

Institutional banking is the biggest business line at Shinsei. Lending is less of a business for Porté
than it would be at Japan's mega-
banks because of their scale, or
traditional banking businesses of
lending to finance rapid growth in
developing markets all over Asia.
Corporate lending in Japan is, after
all, a tough business in a country full of cash-rich companies that are
turning less and less to banks for their financing.

"The percentage of fee and commission business at Shinsei is a lot
higher than it would be at other Japanese banks," Porté said. "That
fee and commission business comes from all parts; some of it comes
from institutional, some of it comes from retail, some of it comes from
consumer and commercial finance in terms of fees that are collected
from customers."

Shinsei is also looking at global horizons, although more in a
partnership situation than in an extended branch network. It has
taken an investment in Jih Sun Banking Group in Taiwan, and is
partnering with other businesses abroad as well.

"Long-Term Credit Bank had an extensive branch network," Porté
said. "But we don't think that there's much value added that we can
provide by having branches in various global money centers and trying to pursue traditional commercial banking business. The market
really doesn't need us."

Shinsei has greater areas of expertise in businesses such as securitization or non-performing loans or real estate finance, businesses
which the bank would like to expand abroad, Porté said.

"Working in any new markets can be challenging and having good local partners is important," he said.

The bank has worked in Korea with Woori Bank on NPL resolution, and in Germany they have set up a joint venture with WestLB and NordLB for servicing NPLs as well. This business will be extended at Jih Sun in Taiwan as well, where Shinsei is investing up to NT$11.34 billion (US$350 million) for a 32.9 percent stake and the right to appoint the group's chief risk officer and nominate the credit control officer. The bank also has three of the 11 board seats.

Porté has also worked with Mega Holdings' Chiao Tung Bank, now part of Mega Bank, to help them with their retail banking technology. Ironically, relationships such as these are actually leveraging the fame that the bank received in Taiwan from the Chinese translation of *Saving the Sun*, the book written about the Shinsei/Ripplewood story and its 2004 public listing, which confirmed the deal as the most successful private equity deal in history. Porté has also conducted discussions with other Taiwanese businesses for tie-ups, but they did not prove fruitful.

Porté is less interested in China, and he considers the giant neighbor that many of his mega-bank competitors are courting outside his priorities, although the bank has still looked at business possibilities there. There are still small hook-ups, such as a private equity fund with CITIC Group to help Japanese companies build business in China, and Porté hopes that Shinsei's connection with Jih Sun Financial Group could leverage a closer relationship with China.

Shinsei is looking move closely at India than China. Perhaps this is not so unusual, considering the high number of Indian staff who have been employed at Shinsei at one time or another, usually in the IT section but also in the retail banking section of the bank.

"We've developed strong links to India through all the work we've done in technology, transforming our platform, and therefore, we had a very good reception in India," said Porté. "We've made many good friends in the Indian marketplace and we've been reasonably successful in distributing, for example, Indian mutual funds to Japanese investors and we see more potential with that."

In 2007, the bank set up a joint venture in Singapore with UTI International, a 100 percent owned subsidiary of India's UTI Asset Management Company, to conduct investment management and distribution of financial products in the Southeast Asian region.

THE STUNTED GIANT

For the bank's domestic business, Porté is happy with his liabilities business, noting that he's been able to build up a good deposit base through the retail bank that is stable and cheap. But lending is suffering from pressure on spreads to corporate borrowers. There is some growth in loan activity, nonetheless, as some of the customers who had left Shinsei in the early years because of the difficulties of the privatization and the transfer to new ownership began to come back to renew the relationship and to look for the alternatives of "healthy competition." While there had once been 21 major banking groups in Japan and now there are only six, "healthy competition" is not as plentiful as it once was.

"There are customers who would like to have alternative providers and alternative sources of either funding or relationships," Porté said. "The spreads continue to be quite compressed. I think it's an industry-wide phenomenon. You can look at the results of the banks that have been produced."

Porté sees Japan's recovery as not yet fully actualized, and he looks to real estate prices, which are still below their peak in prime districts and have continued to decline outside of the main cities, for an indication. He feels that national prices have at least bottomed out despite the new asset-price polarization between prime and non-prime, and is optimistic that in many ways the country has gained a lot of market wisdom from its harsh post-bubble experiences.

"What's different today than ten years ago is that there are market mechanisms that create, first of all, the ability to assess where the market stands and also create self-correcting mechanisms," he said. "This needs to be better understood by foreign audiences because ten, fifteen years ago, foreigners were not able to buy property. There was no REIT market. Non-recourse lending didn't exist, and securitization didn't exist. But, now we have all of these; we, foreigners are a very important part of the market now, including in real estate. We have a REIT market, the J-REIT market; we have a securitization market, and we now have non-recourse lending. I think that the entire environment is different."

These new instruments create a more transparent market, he said.

"It also enables one to find levels of valuation," Porté said. "It certainly does not mean by definition that it prevents the creation of a bubble, but I think that the circumstances that led to what took place in Japan at the end of the 1980s are not the circumstances we're in today."

> **What's different today than ten years ago is that there are market mechanisms that create, first of all, the ability to assess where the market stands and also create self-correcting mechanisms.**

As he faces the future, Porté is still keen to develop different parts of his business. He has a small securities subsidiary that he is trying to expand, although it does allow the bank to do a certain amount of capital markets business. He's not ready to use it to go into cash equity business because of the infrastructure and investment it requires. It would also pitch him head to head against big players like Nomura and Daiwa.

Insurance is another area that the bank could build up, following on the December 2007 complete deregulation of the bancassurance industry and Shinsei's strong retail brand name. The bank has gone into new niche markets, such as infrastructure finance through a team-up with Macquarie Bank, but Porté's heart is mostly in the businesses that the bank has, and the ones that he knows well.

"The job has not ended yet in terms of what I would call capability building, which is creating the skills, the knowledge, and the judgments in all of our employees at all levels so that we can perform at the highest level possible and also in the process ensure that we create a great place to work," he said. "I think that is still a work in process."

GILDED CAGE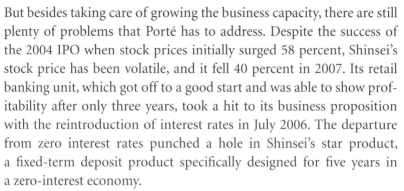

But besides taking care of growing the business capacity, there are still plenty of problems that Porté has to address. Despite the success of the 2004 IPO when stock prices initially surged 58 percent, Shinsei's stock price has been volatile, and it fell 40 percent in 2007. Its retail banking unit, which got off to a good start and was able to show profitability after only three years, took a hit to its business proposition with the reintroduction of interest rates in July 2006. The departure from zero interest rates punched a hole in Shinsei's star product, a fixed-term deposit product specifically designed for five years in a zero-interest economy.

With a big gap where its growth used to be, Shinsei retail began to look like a one-trick pony burdened with a struggling wealth management division. In 2007 it spent money to strengthen its wealth management business, which should see dividends in 2008.

Shinsei had a difficult April 2007 to March 2008 financial year; not only did retail banking suffer, but the bank was harmed by a large position in U.S. residential mortgage-related investments. The complex business environment of the year saw Shinsei restate its full year earnings forecast several times, although when they were announced the bank recorded a profit of ¥60.1 billion, compared with a similar-sized loss a year earlier. But Shinsei still saw its revenue drop in the 2007 financial year, largely attributable to US$157 million in mark downs for exposure to the U.S. residential mortgage market, as well as reserves of US$134 million for the same. As of March 2008, the bank had US$280 million in net exposure to the U.S. residential mortgage market.

The bank's 2004 acquisition of APLUS consumer finance company from UFJ, before it merged with Mitsubishi Tokyo Financial Group in 2006, has been a problem for the bank since the November 2006 rulings that blocked the ability of any consumer finance company to charge high interest rates came into effect. Not only will all consumer lenders in Japan only be able to charge a maximum of 20 percent for personal loans, down from 29 percent before the ruling, they will also have to repay excessively charged interest to clients retroactively. This means that for some accounts the amount of refund has exceeded the principal and any bank that owns or has invested in a consumer finance operation, will need to send in capital to prop up its operations. But despite the troubles in consumer finance in Japan, Porté is keen to stay in the business to see it through and actualize the potential that remains.

The bank's finances are also complicated: it still has the government as a shareholder. This is due to the fact that it has not repaid all of the bailout money that Long-Term Credit Bank of Japan received when it ran into problems, which at one time had represented ¥370 billion in preferred shares owned by the government. Also, because it has not repaid its debt, the bank still needs to hit profit targets or face penalties from the regulator. On top of this, the Ripplewood-led consortium and Christopher Flowers are also still shareholders. Porté will need to keep all of these groups happy in terms of the bank's share price and about the state of the loan repayments.

And the story is getting more complicated still: in late 2007, JC Flowers, the investment group led by Christopher Flowers, bid with a consortium for another stake in Shinsei to provide it with some much-needed capital. It increased the stake in the bank beyond that of the government so that Shinsei would not, in effect, become a government-controlled bank again if the government converts its preferred shares to voting shares, as it was entitled to after March 2008.

Shinsei's future is looking somewhat grimmer than it has in past years, all from events such as a drop in stock price, the unforeseen effect of an interest rate hike, and problems in the U.S. sub-prime market. Shinsei is also facing problems of scale; it may benefit to an extent from corporates' comparison shopping for loans in a tighter market with fewer players, but it also needs scale quite badly if it wants to take them on. The same can be said for Aozora Bank and Tokyo Star Bank. There has been speculation for quite some time that the three banks would do well to join forces or merge; how that is possible with strong personalities like Porté running Shinsei, with its complex ownership, is difficult to see, especially taking into account the well-moneyed minds running the other two banks. But if it ever happens, it would make for another interesting book. Call it *Selling the Suns*.

Fighting for the Gold

Hana is hoping to get into South Korea's medal round

Deals are getting harder and harder for one of South Korea's acquisition kings, Kim Seung-yu, chairman of Hana Financial Group.

WHILE many international investors have long considered Hana Financial Group (Hana) a key Korean institution to hold a stake in, recent events make Hana look more like a player that's gotten stuck in a bit of a growth rut, a voracious mankiller turned perennial bridesmaid. Together with consortium partners, Hana has been a bidder for both Korea Exchange Bank (KEB), practically the last significant bank available for purchase in the Korean market, and LG Card, the country's largest credit card player; it achieved neither.

Had it achieved either—or both—it would have become the largest bank in Korea by assets, the proud possessor of a strong overseas branch network, and an undefeatable card player, although still relatively weak in retail banking next to strong players like Kookmin and Shinhan. The KEB stake, which has been attached to both Kookmin Bank and HSBC, may come around for sale again,

Kim Seung-yu
Reproduced by permission of
TAB International

but Hana seems confined to organic growth and modest acquisitions for now. Ultimately, it looks set to become an acquisition target.

But it wasn't always like this, and the bank has come a long way. Hana was founded in 1971 as Korean Investment Finance Corporation, the first of a new wave of now-major banks that include Shinhan Financial Group, the country's third-largest, and KorAm Bank (now Citibank Korea), which both sprung up in the 1980s. Before the 1997 Asia financial crisis, it had grown, but was still only the country's fourteenth-largest bank by assets.

During the difficult years following the financial crisis, Hana actually grew significantly by acquisition. It took on several smaller banks, both via government mandate and through opportunistic expansion, before it bought Seoul Bank from the government in 2002. (Until the acquisition, Seoul Bank had been run by Kang Chung-won, now CEO of Kookmin Bank.) Because the bank had started off as an investment bank and had a very market-oriented and performance-driven culture, it was less exposed to the corporate lending that so harshly affected the other banks that were driven out of business or were nationalized—many of them under the Woori banner flown by Korea's second-largest lender, which is still government owned.

Considering its relatively clean history, Hana sits close to other banks that were less strongly affected by the crisis such as Kookmin Bank, which had its largest exposure to retail banking, and Shinhan Financial Group, which was mainly a bank for SMEs in the years that led up to the crisis. Both banks seized opportunities at the same time as well and acquired weakened players that helped them to increase their asset sizes dramatically.

Perhaps this is one reason Hana, like Shinhan and Kookmin, has become such a favorite among international investors.

"Our shareholders are very much diversified among foreign institutions and Korean institutions," said Kim Seung-yu, the company's chairman since it became a financial holding company in 2005. "So that's why from the beginning, it was with joint ventures with foreign partners such as Goldman Sachs, Bankers Trust, and International Finance Corporation. And that's why only CEOs of companies were included among the board members from the beginning. The rest of them are outside directors. So that's why we try to keep transparency, corporate governance, and financial statements. We are the first ones to issue quarterly reports back in 1973. We reported to our shareholders where our company was listed on the Korean stock exchange in 1972. From the beginning we issued quarterly reports to our shareholders."

Kim is clearly used to talking about the bank and his numbers after so many meetings with investors, and he is comfortable doing it without referring to any information packs or PowerPoint slides. With a distinctive charm, he also has a good ability to connect with foreigners that many of his generation lack.

As Kim's bank has grown by acquisition, it has had to become a commercial lender with a full array of risk management capabilities for credit risk and lending. After the 1997 crisis set in, the bank tapped Allied Irish Bank to help develop credit analysis and risk management systems with criteria that were not being used in the Korean banking industry at the time.

Through its late-1990s acquisition trail, the bank drew on its expertise as an investment bank.

"We are very much acquainted with M&A, because we are an adviser for M&A in the past, so that is why we are proactively approaching other players," said Kim. Having joined the company with its 1971 launch, only six years after he graduated from college, Kim was thus also among the 150 staff that were with Hana before it became a commercial bank and blossomed into a lender with 1,200 staff in 1996, and then over ten times that amount a decade later.

THE BIRTH OF A DEALMAKER

"I was not familiar with investment banking activities in the beginning, but I was the general manager of the securities and underwriting division, so that's where I learned how the market is going and how to make the deals with others," Kim said. "I made so many deals with others. I acquired one of the local banks and two of the commercial banks, and also contacted with many others, but several of them were afraid to finalize our talks."

Kim may have been an astute dealmaker, but as the stakes get higher, the bank seems to be losing its touch with the recent hiccups in its attempts to take KEB and LG Card. Then again, Kim is working in a tighter market with fewer, more powerful players than he had been in the eighties and nineties.

With his experience, Kim has earned a reputation as the godfather of the Korean banking scene.

"I'm the oldest bank CEO in Korea," he said. "When I assumed my job I was the youngest, back in 1997, and I am the oldest. Well, it is about time, I should retire, but we do have some sort of dream to be a leading financial group in Korea, which means we should continue our tradition of asset management, insurance, so (I could) maybe work on those areas, not daily operations."

> I'm the oldest bank CEO in Korea. When I assumed my job back in 1997, I was the youngest.

Acquiring banks and other assets, Kim has developed the technique of looking deep into a deal to try to understand what it will bring his company.

"A very simple way is [to understand a deal is by analyzing] how to improve our synergy effect, in case we merge with others," said Kim. "What is our weakness? How can we strengthen our weakness through a merger? That's why I start through analysis, of ours and theirs, and their strengths are going to be reflected in the price. Their weakness I should deduct from their price. I try to understand their side so that I can negotiate with them. So we try to be very tough. We try to finish within several months; we are not going to take a long time. But several times we have talked with government officials, it is very tough, because they are not concerned with the value of the acquisition, because they are [state] employees," said Kim, well known for his straight talking, another trait that has endeared him to overseas investors.

But having taken the acquisition path, Kim has to live with what the bank has become, and having converted from an investment bank into a commercial bank, there is no turning back. With such dramatic changes over the years, Kim's mind has already integrated the two businesses and found them to run on the same principles.

"There are no boundaries between commercial banking and investment banking these days," said Kim. "There is much consideration about market change, rather than long-term growth. I think we need the economies of scale, so that's why we try to apply strategy for the M&A as it grows. Well, up until now, the most difficult thing is how to integrate corporate culture. Other things like IT integration are a matter of time, but for corporate culture, we must really endeavour to integrate."

Having gone through so many acquisitions, Kim feels that conducting the integration exercise earlier is better, clearly a reference to the long, careful merger process that Shinhan planned out for its acquisition of the much older, weaker Chohung Bank which it bought in 2003. For Hana, he insists that the core culture is ex-Hana Bank and the small core of people who defined it in its formative years, even though they are now vastly outnumbered by the huge number of staff that came on with the Seoul Bank acquisition in 2002. Tellingly, the bank divides its culture between its many components, and among the senior management, 40 percent are from Hana, and 35 percent each from Seoul Bank and Boram Bank, which Hana acquired in 1999.

> **Other things like IT integration are a matter of time, but for corporate culture we must really endeavour to integrate.**

GETTING GRANULAR

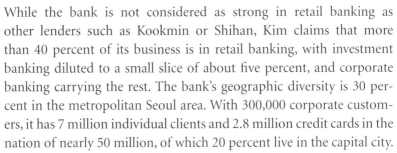

While the bank is not considered as strong in retail banking as other lenders such as Kookmin or Shihan, Kim claims that more than 40 percent of its business is in retail banking, with investment banking diluted to a small slice of about five percent, and corporate banking carrying the rest. The bank's geographic diversity is 30 percent in the metropolitan Seoul area. With 300,000 corporate customers, it has 7 million individual clients and 2.8 million credit cards in the nation of nearly 50 million, of which 20 percent live in the capital city.

Because of its early start in investment banking, Kim and his bank have now grown close with some of Korea's richest businessmen and entrepreneurs, making it a strong niche player in wealth management.

"Well, basically, we are very strong in high-net-worth individuals because of our background as a commercial paper dealer, so we are going to maintain our customer base," said Kim. "But we are also going to try to expand our credit card business, which is middle market. I guess we are strongest among Korean banks for high-net-worth individuals, even [more than] bigger-sized banks like Kookmin or Woori, but we should expand and strengthen the middle market, so we can expand cross-selling for credit cards or insurance."

Hana has kept the acquisition trail warm in recent years, beefing up many of the areas where it is not yet strong. With the current trends in banking in Korea, it will certainly need to if it wants to grow: low interest rates mean that depositors have begun moving their money into funds, securities, and insurance, often disintermediating the banks, which have had to fight for deposits at attractive interest rates, crushing their lending margins.

The bank bought into Daehan Investment Trust and Securities Company as a way to improve its fund management capabilities. In May 2007, the group also bought out its shareholder Allianz from a 50:50 insurance joint venture that the two set up, which had only managed to take a very small market share. The deal was in some way a tit-for-tat arrangement since stakeholder Allianz had done the reverse in buying out Hana from the duo's asset management joint venture in 2005. But Hana has not given up on the business and is still hoping to build up its insurance capabilities, possibly with more acquisitions.

In another type of tit-for-tat, Hana sold the 50 percent insurance stake it bought from Allianz to HSBC for US$56 million, showing that Byzantine deal-making is still in Kim's blood. With HSBC's ambitions in South Korea, speculation is high over whether Hana is indeed a takeover target for the world's local bank, vulnerable to pressure to grow beyond the role it seems to have been confined to by selling out to a major international player that it is philosophically close to. But Kim isn't telling.

Although he's been flip-flopping somewhat in his acquisition strategy in Korea by wavering between Allianz and HSBC, acquiring new businesses is becoming more interesting for Kim now that Hana is a financial group and can fold them easily under its umbrella. The financial holding structure was created so that businesses under the financial holding company can, for the most part, share data and cross-sell more effectively; regular banks are not allowed to share data with other businesses in the same organization. So far, in Korea, only Hana, Woori, and Shinhan have formed financial holding companies, while Kookmin, Citi Korea, and Standard Chartered Bank are seeking the status.

Despite the bank's flirtation with foreign institutions, the entrance of global banks in the Korean market as players rather than investors has somewhat shaken the unflappable Kim, especially with their potential to leverage global networks and resources, which Hana is a long way from developing. They also have intense global customer bases and data from such long histories.

"The problem is the expertise and the network, which we don't have like Citibank," said Kim.

At 30 percent fee-based income, Kim is unhappy that the bank also doesn't have as large a fee-based income as the typical foreign bank would have through investment banking activity and specialized products such as derivatives.

"Foreign banks like Citi, they can utilize the global customer base, so for example in case of issuing rate swap they take the affluent customer base and they can match and produce new types of products, which we can't," Kim said.

But even if he is wary of local players, he still knows how to keep them at bay. In order to compete with Citi Korea and its CEO Ha Yung-ku, Kim is keeping in close contact with his customers to find out their needs, and is working on reducing red tape and creating faster, more efficient procedures.

"So that's why our brand managers, our relationship managers, call me through my mobile phone at any time, and we can decide when they visit our customers," said the very hands-on Kim. "If they cannot decide at that place, they can call me up and solve the problem. That kind of practice cannot be afforded by Citibank, so we try to move fast and make fast decisions and have closer contact with customers."

MEET HANA

Despite Kim's grumblings about foreign companies' competitive advantages in Korea, the bank is actually taking steps to internationalize. In late 2007, the group took a majority stake in Bank Bintang Manunggal, a small bank in Indonesia, perhaps testing global waters for something more substantial. Indonesia was also the location of the largest banking stake by a Korean financial institution, namely Kookmin's stake in Bank Internasional Indonesia with Temasek Holdings. It has also been active in Shenyang in China across the Yellow Sea where Kim notes that, "There are many Korean companies doing business."

The step is part of a distinctive long-term policy.

"In the long run, we want to be one of the leading financial institutions in East Asia," he said. "Because there are so many Korean companies doing business in China, especially in Shandong Province—there about 5,800 Korean companies doing business in Shandong Province —so that is why we acquired one of the joint venture banks in Qingdao in January 2004. In Shenyang there are more than 1,000 companies, so we are going to follow our customers first, and then we can expand our business to retail in those areas like Shandong Province because the employees of Korean corporations will have their needs. So we are going to expand in several years."

As a bank that has not missed a dividend in 34 years, Hana keeps a close relationship with investors, often consulting them on acquisitions. The bank is good to its supporters, and in turn the bank has had their support. But it will be interesting to see if they will be put to the test in the event that Kim—and Hana—fail to grow at the rates that satisfy them.

Certainly Kim, with his confident tone and over three decades of experience in a smart, relatively young bank, is a good representative to take them there. Experienced and bold, and with the gravitas of someone who's been a part of the wars for several decades, he has a full understanding of every business that the bank touches. Numbers are at his easy command, and his mind is as sharp as a tack as he scans the horizon and considers how to get what he needs to fill out the bank even more and protect it from takeover. It's not time to retire just yet.

The Long Road

Out with the bad, in with the good

Bank of Beijing President Yan Xiaoyan has spent nearly a decade bringing her bank's bad loan levels down from 30 percent, and has now launched a successful IPO.

Iɴ the years leading up to the 2008 Olympics, Beijing should be a very good place to be a banker. But if you're a medium-sized city commercial bank like Bank of Beijing, you also have competition from some of the other banks in town, which happen to be among the largest in Asia. Of course, it also doesn't help that the government is breathing down your neck to hold off providing too much financing in order to keep the economy from overheating.

Founded in 1996 out of 90 credit cooperatives, Bank of Beijing has grown so much in just over one decade of operation that it now has US$28.8 billion in assets and ranks as the 106th-largest bank in Asia Pacific according to the Asian Banker's list of the region's 300 biggest banks. Among the country's 114 city commercial banks, only Bank of Shanghai is larger.

The bank changed its name in 2005 from Beijing City Commercial Bank to Bank of Beijing, following the trend started by Bank of Shanghai, Bank of Nanjing, and Bank of Ningbo to become "of" banks. Ironically, the name is quickly becoming somewhat of a liability as the bank now operates outside Beijing, with branches in Tienjin and Shanghai since 2006. Perhaps another name change is in order as it spreads its wings to further corners of the country, or even overseas, although the world has plenty of "of" banks that haven't seen the need to be restricted to their place of geographic origin—Bank of America and Royal Bank of Scotland both operate outside of America and Scotland respectively, and the list goes on.

Yan Xiaoyan (*yan schau yan*) is the president of the Bank of Beijing, a woman who is unusually modest about her bank's accomplishments and its prospects, talking just as easily about the bank's difficulties as she does about its many significant successes. In September 2007, for example, she led the bank to its initial public offering on the Shanghai Stock Exchange that raised US$2 billion. Considering that the subscription was 125 times oversold, more than any other bank in the recent China bank-listing spree, it may be considered one of the more successful of its era. Clearly, the Olympic halo effect is turning into a gold medal for the bank.

The listing came just two years after Yan sold a 19.9 percent stake in the bank to ING Group of the Netherlands. The bank also sold a 5 percent stake to the International Finance Corporation (IFC), the private sector investment arm of the World Bank. The Bank of Beijing investment is thus the IFC's sixth investment in China after Bank of Shanghai, Industrial Bank, China Minsheng Bank, Nanjing City Commercial Bank, and Xi'an City Commercial Bank.

A BAD START

The route that Yan has taken to get the bank to its current level has been a long and arduous one.

"The Bank of Beijing has been a very active market player in recent years," she said. "We have been established for 11 years, but for the past seven or eight years, we have channeled much of our energy and resources into solving the bank's historical problems."

When the bank was established from a clutch of credit cooperatives, it took on a massive NPL burden that accounted for 30 percent of its loans.

"It took us nearly a decade to write off these bad loans," said Yan. "Because of this predicament, in our first ten years we did not do much to enhance our business standing. We started a strategic investment partnership with ING and IFC in 2005, which has done much to make up for lost time in this respect. But, the legacy of Bank of Beijing's historical burdens runs deep and its residual effects cannot be underestimated."

Yan has been with the bank since it was founded, her first position after graduation from China's South Western University of Finance and Economics with a master's degree in money and banking. She starting off at the bank as its vice-president, and then became its president in 2001 when her predecessor retired.

"Bank of Beijing's senior management has remained very stable, and under its direction, our development and operations have remained stable too," said Yan. "We have effectively written off the NPLs. On the back of our management team, we now see a lot of good opportunities to develop ourselves as a business."

> **Bank of Beijing's senior management has remained very stable, and under its direction, our development and operations have remained stable too.**

The bank has been able to reduce its NPLs to a tenth of their highest level, and Yan said the bank had 3.4 percent NPLs at the end of 2007 after four straight years of NPL reduction exercises.

The bank's business model is not dissimilar from other banks in the capital city, and Yan focuses on corporate loans, SME banking, and retail banking. But its strengths are still in SME lending, where it has a "30–40 percent market share" in its market, and in medical insurance, where Yan said the bank is a leader with five to six million customers. The bank is also innovative in some regards, opening "Women's Bank," a bank marketed solely toward female clients, especially women entrepreneurs, with relatively sophisticated wealth management offerings and a lifestyle element.

Banking in China is a challenging game, with banks struggling to come up with their own responses to the difficult modernization exercise that the whole country is going through. Even as China's manufacturing sector is making leaps and bounds in terms of sophistication, banking is, in general, not making the same advances, and Bank of Beijing has been caught up in the modernization process along with all of China's banks.

The lender currently faces strong challenges of its own, particularly in corporate governance, which Yan describes as, "an ongoing challenge for city commercial banks."

"Business transition is also a major hurdle, particularly in areas such as retail," she said. "IT is another big one. Every bank wants to set up a sound, comprehensive IT system to provide better customer service. City commercial banks are closely related to retail customers and SMEs, so if we do risk management well, we can provide better service. This is an important city commercial bank advantage."

With SMEs in China typically underserved, the role of the city commercial banks in developing that side of the economy is highly valuable.

FUNDING

Scale is another problem. It may be Beijing's fourth-biggest bank, but overall it is the country's sixteenth-biggest bank. This naturally affects its cost of funds, although Yan finds that funding costs are relatively low.

"Toward the beginning of our establishment, we had about 80 percent current deposits and 20 percent fixed deposits," said Yan. "We made a lot of profit from this arrangement, but are gradually shifting the liquidity risk and adjusting our deposit ratio. Now, we have about 50 percent current deposits and 50 percent fixed deposits. This ratio is relatively high and we still face liquidity risk. Nevertheless, in profit terms, we maintain relatively low funding costs."

The bank is active on the interbank market for about 40 percent of its activity, both in terms of lending and borrowing.

"Since our establishment, we have always paid a great deal of attention to the interbank lending market," Yan said. "In this respect, we have consistently ranked among China's top ten city commercial banks by transaction volume."

When the interbank system was created, large state-owned banks stayed away, leaving the market very much to the smaller banks.

Bank of Beijing has used the opportunity to become one of the top ten commercial banks in the interbank market. With the huge amount of deposits it has been able to rake in, the bank has also seen its assets increase rapidly, growing ten times in ten years, with most of the growth happening from 2003 to 2007. But despite her success in the interbank market, Yan's business started to be affected by the large state-owned banks, which began to pay much more attention to the business as they began entering the market in force.

Being based in Beijing, the bank is able to catch some of the trade flows between China and other markets. Yan explains her bank's position in the extremely large, complex domestic market by saying that "although there are four state-owned banks and a growing number of foreign banks flowing into China, there is still enormous market potential left to be tapped. There are a lot of businesses that have not yet been developed, among them investment and automobile-focused businesses. In our home market, Bank of Beijing is ranked fourth among Chinese banks, but we still have lots of opportunity and room to develop. We set up a new Tianjin branch, spearheading our geographic expansion drive. We believe the Binhai area in northeast China is potentially very lucrative and one open to financial innovation."

BEYOND BEIJING

Yan has her eyes on all parts of China. She opened her branch in nearby Tianjin in November 2006, and already considers it a great success with assets of RMB4 billion (US$562 million) in its first six months of operation. The Shanghai branch opened exactly one year later, putting Yan in the enviable position of being headquartered in Beijing, near the seat of government, but with a foot in the door in the commercial capital of the country, Shanghai. She is also finally putting herself on the same footing as some of the biggest banks in the country, albeit on a much smaller scale—ICBC has hundreds of branches in Beijing and Shanghai. But on a peer level, it is the only city commercial bank to be in both of China's most important cities, one step ahead of Bank of Shanghai.

"I still think the Shanghai market has lots of potential. We are confident in this respect," she said.

Even more ambitiously she is seeking opportunities in south China along the Pearl River Delta

I still think the Shanghai market has lots of potential. We are confident in this respect.

in cities such as Shenzhen and Guangzhou, which are powered by industry that has spilled over from Hong Kong. As the first part of China opened up to experiments in capitalism by Deng Xiaoping in 1979, it is the new ideological center of modern industrial China, and an important frontier for her to crack. But closer to home she is also looking at China's industrial northeast. Despite being the home of many of China's rusting state-owned enterprises, cities such as Dalian and Qingdao in the Bohai region beyond Tianjin offer opportunities, as well as the massive city Shenyang in the northeast with its huge catchment area. But here she will run into a fresh competitor, China Bohai Bank, a new bank set up with help from Standard Chartered Bank.

Yan needs to bring more than her distribution network into her strategy if she hopes to catch up to China's leading banks and build a brand that will attract the new generation of Chinese clients.

"Apart from the setup of new branches through a strategy of geographic expansion, we are also thinking of ways to expand our business through innovation," said Yan. "We only issued debit cards before. Now we are entering into the credit card arena and further plan to enter the fund and wealth management business. Bank of Beijing is well positioned in other areas. Based in the nation's capital, we are facing out toward the rest of China and I think that there is much potential for us to develop in the foreign currency area."

For financing this growth, Yan has funds from her IPO to draw on, and she points out that her capital adequacy ratio is at 12.87 percent, well beyond the 8 percent threshold prescribed by the regulator, the China Banking Regulatory Commission. There is also capital from IFC and ING, which can also help the bank develop capabilities and innovate. With services ranging from insurance to wholesale banking and retail banking, an interesting prospect is its

ING Direct Internet-based bank, which could help the Bank of Beijing expand well beyond its physical footprint by increasing its presence on the Internet by penetrating far-flung pockets of retail savings.

With the Olympics coming in August 2008, Yan and her bank will be at the center of the world for two weeks. It will be interesting to see how she faces the post-games hangover, when real estate prices and construction rates begin to normalize. Staring down a slowdown in the U.S., 2008 is set to be a tumultuous year for her, and for China's banks as well. But with her operational issues getting sorted out, Yan can start looking ahead to introducing her Beijing bank to the rest of China.

Chapter 6
The Niche Builders—Catching Cookie Crumbs

The Keys to the Kingdom

How to unlock part of US$14 trillion in consumer savings (part 2)

While Sony Bank and eBANK offer radically different business models, both are trying to shake up Japan's banking establishment.

IN the heyday of the dot-com era, commercial banks all over the world became enthralled with the new technology of the Internet and began closing expensive branches, hoping that the action would force customers to get used to using virtual channels heavily. Unfortunately, the move was vastly premature, and it only succeeded in driving clients to smaller, more personal institutions that were happy to meet their customers face-to-face.

Internet penetration is not as high as many in business would hope, and even today most banks in Asia cannot speak of more than 30 percent of their clients actively doing their banking online. Normally, 30 percent might not seem so bad, but when the definition of "active" often means that they log in to their online banking portal once a *month*, it's hard to be very impressed.

Matsuo Taiichi, eBANK
Reproduced by permission of
TAB International

Ishii Shigeru, Sony Bank
Reproduced by permission of
TAB International

Certainly, the online proposition is still appealing, and no bank can be without an Internet-banking facility. But instead of limiting channels, banks are now thinking more in terms of broadly offering all channels to clients as a way to demonstrate their sophistication and flexibility. Banks like OCBC in Singapore and China Merchants Bank in China have been particularly forward in this regard.

> **We have to support good infrastructure for the public. It's very important. It means it must be stable and at the same time very price competitive.**

But other banks have been persistent in trying to understand the Internet in terms of its role in the future of banking. Egg, an online-only bank in the U.K., has been working on this proposition for years, but it has floundered, and in late 2007, Citigroup finally acquired it.

ING Direct started a wave of Internet-only direct banks that offered interest rates that were higher than those offered by brick-and-mortar banks. Typically offering only a few simple services, the direct banks have been a way for banks with regular branch banking operations to diversify their sources of low-cost deposits. Citibank and HSBC have launched their own versions, with the latter making use of the channel in high-tech markets in Asia like Korea and Taiwan where it has low penetration. They are often branding exercises for more established institutions as they leverage a well-known brand name and bring it into cyberspace in markets where it makes sense to do so. As stand-alone businesses they probably have less to offer the company in terms of bottom line profits, especially since they may very well cannibalize existing customers as established depositors shift funds from their regular accounts to their direct account to earn more interest.

HOW THEY DO IT IN JAPAN

There is still a case for the Internet as a channel for certain niche markets in the world of financial services, and one of them is transaction banking for online payments. Bill Gates has boasted that banks are dinosaurs, and if he can get a piece of the transaction, the banks will be history, seemingly without thinking much about deposits and loans. Much is made of how PayPal stole a march on the U.S. banks by developing the payment mode for online shopping, especially for those who didn't want to—or couldn't—use credit cards to make online purchases.

In Japan, where PayPal didn't exist until May 2007, eBANK and Japan Net Bank have taken up the gauntlet and thrust themselves into the business, the former with venture capital and the latter with the backing of big money from Sumitomo Mitsui Banking Corporation (SMBC). They did this by showing verve and commitment, but also by being in the right place at the right time. Sony Bank is also an Internet-only bank, but it does not focus on payments for online transactions and functions more like a traditional bank, albeit a tech-savvy one.

Helped along by Japan's zero-interest environment, as well as the take-up of the Internet, the banks have found interest among the huge segment of affluent urban Japanese that were at once attracted by the banks' higher interest rates. They also valued practical transaction services it offered to bored office workers fiddling with their 3G cell phones on their early morning and late evening commutes.

Another regulatory twist, unique to Japan, has helped make the online bank truly virtual—account-opening does not require any face-to-face meeting for identity verification and account-openers can mail in photocopies of their documents or send in image captures of their ID cards. Out of regulatory loopholes, entire industries are born.

The appeal of Internet-only banking is great—besides the appearance of PayPal in 2007, others are coming, with ING Direct opening its operations in 2008. Bank of Tokyo-Mitsubishi UFJ and telecommunications provider KDDI are also planning to launch an Internet-only bank together.

THE BITE OF THE UNDERDOG: eBANK

eBANK is a true renegade institution in a country where banking is run by tight networks of old school blue bloods who graduated from the same elite universities. Matsuo Taiichi is a cheerful, affable entrepreneur, who is proud of the broad range of experience he has been able to gather in Japan and overseas, even as he disdains the chummy banking networks he has been a part of for so many years and strives to create a new model for the future of banking in Japan. Starting his bank in 2000, and then racing neck and neck to get ahead of the very similar Japan Net Bank, Matsuo has not had the backing of a major bank or conglomerate to help his bank along, which also means he has been able to retain personal control.

Long before the Internet, Matsuo joined Long-Term Credit Bank of Japan, the predecessor to the current Shinsei Bank, in the early 1970s and embarked on the typically Japanese generalist journey of learning the workings of different divisions and understanding various government and private institutions. He started as a loan officer for the chemical and oil business before moving into various parts of the business such as securities and foreign exchange. He worked for a time in the U.K. as a loan manager, and he also managed investment banking as the director of LTCB International, a securities company in the City. From 1985 to 1987, he was the head of sales for Eurobonds.

He also claims to have been the largest options trader in the City when the bank started handling futures, options, and derivatives. When Long-Term Credit Bank of Japan entered the securities business in 1978, Matsuo was sent to build the business, spending some time at Nomura Securities to learn about deal making in Japanese government bonds. In the latter part of his career, Matsuo worked as a government liaison officer for ten years, contacting various ministries and the government agencies that worked with local governments. Having been seconded into the Ministry of Economy Trade and Industry (METI) where he worked in the planning division for special government banks, he picked up an understanding of how these institutions were financed, but also about the difficulty that institutions, such as SMEs outside of the mainstream, had in securing financing. It was from here that he made his move to open his own bank.

Although Matsuo was building profitable new businesses within Long-Term Credit Bank of Japan, such as helping municipalities buy city land for urban development projects, he asked to be taken out of

> I started to learn every area of the Internet, I started a homepage. I made a new server, CPU, hard disk. I learned Linux.

the lending business when a credit crunch required him to go to clients that he had built good relationships with and ask for funds.

In the dark days of 1998, when bankers survived by their wits, Matsuo latched onto a new growth industry: the Internet.

"I started to learn every area of the Internet," he said. "I started a homepage. I made a new server, CPU, hard disk. I learned Linux."

He was 51 years old at the time, not too old to learn something completely new, but no longer young either. Besides learning the language of this new technology, he also had to learn how to use it to build a business. Working with Itochu Corporation and a young organization called Kabu.com—now a major online brokerage that is being bought by Bank of Tokyo-Mitsubishi UFJ—overseeing a new Internet-based company, the seeds of the idea to develop an online bank were formed.

Disagreements with Itochu's main bank, Deutsche, which seemed to have concerns that Itochu was trying to outmaneuver it in financial services, led Matsuo to strike out on his own. He toyed with the idea of forming a securities company, but when he saw that would really need to collect deposits in order to survive, he formed eBANK in January 2000 and took the role of president. The bank went live later the same year after receiving money from Japanese investors that left Matsuo with a majority stake.

"They were very kind," he said. "If they had kept a majority at that time, I'd lose the passion. They were very generous."

Matsuo seems to rue the fact that he did not have the backing of a large corporation to help him get started like Japan Net Bank with SMBC and Sony Bank with Sony Corporation. But he credits the extensive relationships he has with government agencies for helping him get off the ground with a banking license.

As an entrepreneur, Matsuo has a surprisingly uncapitalistic bent. With transaction banking as his main activity, the keen thinker is still eager to find a model that allows him to offer remittances free of charge, the cost of business borne by other parts of the bank. On the other hand, it could also be a plea to attract the Internet everyman to his offering, which could potentially give him one of Japan's powerful databases of consumer information: names, addresses, online shopping habits, and banking activity.

"We should be more fair, and at the same time, profit making is not so important," he said. "We have to support good infrastructure for the public. It's very important. It means it must be stable and at the same time very price competitive."

Considering the importance of banking to social infrastructure, Matsuo is concerned about providing a stable business to everybody, and he likens his business to other forms of infrastructure like highways, subways, and the electric grid. Considering his majority ownership of the company, a relaxed attitude toward profitability is easy enough to have. His ideas about helping society by bringing financial infrastructure to the common people come off as sounding closer to those of the head of a Sri Lankan family-run consortium hoping to pull the country up by its bootstraps than a maverick Japanese banker trying to turn the system on its head, but are refreshing nonetheless.

There are social inroads to be made, even in a prosperous country like Japan, where fringe dwellers are often kept at arm's length. Having observed how difficult it was for SMEs to secure financing in his METI days, Matsuo was certainly interested to see that so many of the smallest and youngest start-up operations coming up had found a new home and source of distribution on the Internet. Although he has not been interested in building a loan portfolio of any sort, he clearly saw the benefit of working with them, often one-person operations, to grow their businesses. His model was to offer payment services as a sort of Internet-based cash management system for online SMEs as a fee-based business. Matsuo is bringing retail clients together with online businesses for sales, the fees of which will eventually be borne by the business so that consumers can feel that they are getting a "free" service. He sees himself as a facilitator of a new economy that is outside the conventional one fuelled by large institutions such as the country's mega banks, or the foreign banks that are participants in the global economy.

But this is not the only area where Matsuo has turned the model on its head. While he provides certain transaction services—convenient Internet- and cell phone-based methods of sending person to person payments, or paying for horse-racing bets—eBANK does not engage in traditional banking services like lending. He will do neither mortgages nor consumer loans, and certainly not corporate loans. To keep itself going, the bank collects fees from the payment services it provides, collecting a very thin margin. It uses the float it collects and keeps within the virtual walls of the bank to engage in the volatile business of buying and trading equities, bonds, and investment tools, essentially functioning as a giant consumer-backed hedge fund. Anything is possible on the Internet, especially in Japan.

Matsuo relies on his human resources to keep the whole thing oiled and moving smoothly as he focuses on retail payments and treasury investment.

"One side is the retail area and must be supported by advanced technology," he said. "I believe that I can control the mass market with advanced systems. It must be most competitive, very high performance. On the other side, I collect very good brains, skills, and talented people. I expect that group to go into the investment banking area. Those areas are very important. My image of the future of eBANK is that those two areas must be combined, so it's very important."

Besides its lack of any kind of branch network, the physical size of the company keeps Matsuo nimble.

"I think many big banks would like to do this kind of business, but unfortunately they already have large staff pools or are big organizations," he said. "We are very lucky because we have just started and then we can concentrate on those two areas. We don't have any other areas."

Unfortunately, the model doesn't always work, and eBANK's profitability has been volatile, especially in light of the subprime crisis affecting banks with high risk appetites that had been heavy investors in CDOs and other sophisticated investment instruments linked to the U.S. sub-prime market. It has not shown many profitable quarters during its existence.

But all of this would be incidental to Matsuo, who has faith in his model as part of a process that is as much evolution as it is revolution. And besides this, the number of clients has continued to grow well beyond any of the other Japanese Internet-only banks, while it also has a high deposit ratio per client.

"When I started this business I thought that technology, the Internet, will make a complete revolution," he said. "It means that common sense must be changed. The banking industry started from the eighteenth century. That business model must be adjusted to the new century. I thought about this model. Many bankers think about using new technology for their business. It means that they don't want to change their business style, just use new technology especially to cut the cost."

> **The banking industry started from the eighteenth century. That business model must be adjusted to the new century.**

Matsuo goes so far as to predict that other U.S. Internet-only banks in the picture will fail if they don't change their business models.

Like PayPal, Matsuo's bank got started as a method of facilitating online auctions, although here the similarities end—eBANK, while it has a banking license, does not have as many customers as PayPal, which doesn't need a license. PayPal already had 10 million subscribers at the time that eBANK first opened its virtual doors, and is now already a global payment powerhouse.

On top of his plan to engage the Internet, Matsuo has many other missions, among them to turn the cell phone into a personal bank. It is an idea that he seems to consider one of his own, even though banks all over Asia have been engaging the channel on one level or another. Most banks in Sri Lanka and some banks in Malaysia, for example, have low-tech versions of the service, while Koreans are fully plugged in with a top-of-the-line version. But Matsuo is still hoping that eBANK can be the player that takes the model regional, and the bank has set up an office in Hong Kong to explore the possibilities in Greater China, while there is also some interest from banks in India. Again, Matsuo is thinking of how to out-do PayPal, which has finally popped up in Japan.

"We are close to many candidates who do the same business outside Japan, mainly banking and at the same time telecommunications," he said. "My dream is I'd like to make eBANK Singapore, eBANK Hong Kong, eBANK Philippines, or eBANK China. And when people open accounts in their country and they take along their cell phone when they travel in Asia, they won't need any local money."

Matsuo's bank has also received permission to open a representative office in the U.S., which it will set up in San Francisco.

Matsuo even mentions ideas about turning the cell phone into a travel document like a passport, but is vague on details of a technology that might still be years away. But considering how often he mentions his close connections to government officials, maybe he knows something that most others don't. Much can change in a decade, or even just five years, especially on the Internet.

Matsuo is betting that his model will be as compelling to others around the region as it is to his Japanese clients.

"In the last two years, many Japanese buy a lot of things through cell phones," he said. "I think it will be a very good new fashion among Asians because Asians are quite familiar with cell phones. A big difference between eBANK and PayPal is that they don't want to go into the cell phone market, but eBANK is very keen to turn the cell phone into a personal bank."

But not all of Matsuo's dreams have come true just yet.

"At the first stage, at the beginning of 2000, I thought that cards must be installed to the cell phone of the user especially since technology is rapidly changing," he said. "I'd like to omit the stage of issuing a physical card. In five years it's nonsense because the cell phone has a card function. Unfortunately, this kind of infrastructure didn't happen, and I have to start issuing [real] cards."

The bank has issued a debit card, a product that is still a relative novelty in Japan, and one that is surprisingly low-tech for a bank like eBANK. Other Internet-only banks, such as the well-connected Sony Bank, have beaten eBANK to the draw here, and began issuing credit cards through its parent corporation in late 2006. Mega-banks such as SMBC and Mizuho are working on enabling credit card payments on their cell phones.

Matsuo keeps his bank going with a skeleton crew of 140, of which 50 are technical staff who keep the bank running and also dream up new technologies. The bank has developed a way to send money as an email attachment, as well as a way to use a cell phone's built-in camera to capture identity card information for account opening services, in addition to other nifty applications.

IT'S A SONY... BANK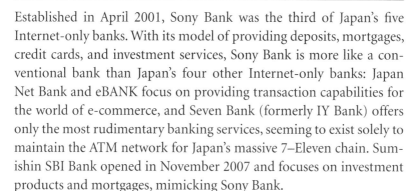

Established in April 2001, Sony Bank was the third of Japan's five Internet-only banks. With its model of providing deposits, mortgages, credit cards, and investment services, Sony Bank is more like a conventional bank than Japan's four other Internet-only banks: Japan Net Bank and eBANK focus on providing transaction capabilities for the world of e-commerce, and Seven Bank (formerly IY Bank) offers only the most rudimentary banking services, seeming to exist solely to maintain the ATM network for Japan's massive 7–Eleven chain. Sumishin SBI Bank opened in November 2007 and focuses on investment products and mortgages, mimicking Sony Bank.

Seven Bank seemed, for a while, to be the most profitable of the three, earning fee income by providing third-party services for nearly all of Japan's banks. It was even able to sell its story to the markets, managing a successful February 2008 IPO at a time when global markets were gloomy. But that model may soon be challenged by Sony Bank's highly elastic, scalable proposition that is not based on the expansion of a physical ATM network but by the awareness of the general public of its services (eBANK and Japan Net Bank have yet to show sustained profitability).

Compared with eBANK's do-it-yourself ethic, Sony Bank is very much a corporate animal, as its name would suggest. The bank is 12 percent owned by Japanese mega-bank SMBC (which also owns 57 percent of Japan Net Bank) and 88 percent owned by Sony Financial Holdings, which was established in April 2004 and saw a successful IPO in October 2007. But whatever its ownership, its fate is inextricably linked with Sony Corporation, a fact that makes its world-weary president Ishii Shigeru the model of patience.

According to Ishii (pronounced *ee-shee-ee*), Sony had long been keen to deliver innovation to Japan's massive base of habitual savers, and the huge, fabled US$13 trillion savings base that they represent. By servicing the need for personalized products that Japan's financial institutions have tradition-ally neglected through their focus on corporate lending, Sony Bank stands to make a mark, at least until the big boys gain the public's trust.

"We thought Japanese financial institutions do not provide enough service for households," said Ishii. "That's why Sony decided to intro-duce new services into the financial services area. Sony already had some financial services like life insurance and casualty insurance, also introducing innovation in life insurance; it is very familiar with finan-cial services. [In 2000] Sony thought it had to leverage Internet ser-vices into the financial area. Most financial transactions are just data. Information technology treats data very effectively. If Sony uses the Internet, it can use it to leverage all these services."

Unfortunately, because of banking secrecy laws, the bank is not allowed to access the huge database of customer information in Sony's many other divisions and Sony Bank has to fend for itself in one of the key ways that membership in a huge conglomerate could be of key benefit.

Ishii, who had begun his career at Yamaichi Securities, joined Sony in 1998 to head an unspecified Internet business—the same year, ironically, that Matsuo made a move from Long-Term Credit Bank of Japan to get to work on the Internet projects that led to eBANK. Sony held a series of high level meetings, and then several years passed. As with the germination of the eBANK project, the strategic planning for Sony Bank included debates about whether the new Internet-based unit would be a securities company or a brokerage. Here Ishii again discovered something that Matsuo also learned when he was inducted into the club that is banking in Japan.

When the bank set out to build up its businesses it researched other Internet-only institutions around the world that had failed, trying to understand what had brought them down. It looked at the settlement business, such as the one that eBANK and Japan Net Bank engage in, but concluded that transaction costs were already low and Japanese consumers would not pay for the service. There was also no assurance that volumes would be big enough to balance the thin margins.

"Our strategy was to establish our base with our asset management business, like selling mutual funds to get the deposits, and so on," he said.

This was very conventional, but also very sensible as Ishii attributes the bank's first push into profitability to its asset management business.

Sony initially found it difficult to get a banking license, so it sought a guarantee. SMBC provided the avenue into banking when it became a shareholder, and the mega-bank also provided access to an ATM network, the largest among the conventional Japanese banks (only Seven Bank, the Internet-based "ATM bank," has a larger network). JPMorgan Chase also became a shareholder for a time, and with it came know-how for the bank's essential wealth management capabilities.

"We have the system that was sponsored originally by JPMorgan," said Ishii. "JPMorgan developed that system in the United States to support private banking, and we combined the system with our own system, which we call an "advice engine." So people can analyze their portfolios by that computer system. Also we introduced some risk management figures called "risk grade" so that people can calculate their risk product by product. They can calculate their risk based on their portfolios."

The system is used by 10–20 percent of the bank's clients.

But whatever the ownership, it is clear that Sony calls the shots, from whether the bank will build new businesses or whether Sony will give access to its credit card operations to the bank or not. Ishii would surely envy Matsuo the autonomy to make decisions, as well as the hold he has on the entrepreneurial spirit in a new industry in a huge organization that has a very strong consensus culture that is part of the slow, harmonious process of business progress in Japan. Perhaps now that the bank has been decoupled somewhat by the stock market listing Ishii will get some breathing room, but it is unlikely that as long as the bank carries the name Sony that Ishii's corporate masters will be very far.

"Basically, the IPO was initiated by Sony's headquarters because they have to reshape their current business," Ishii said. "They tried to focus on core businesses. At that time they decided that the financial business and some other retail business would not be the core business anymore. They decided to let those companies go public."

The sedate Ishii is just as low profile in the way he runs his bank, with pull marketing rather than hard push selling.

"That is the feature of our business and people believe us because of our attitude," he said. "We do not force our customers to buy anything. Customers choose our products based on their judgment. We focus on very narrow lines, because we focus on some very knowledgeable people regarding finance, and also the Internet."

Ishii is keen to preserve his soft-sell formula, which he sees as the best for wealth management, and wants to keep his infrastructure as simple as possible to the extent that he won't consider recruiting a sales force.

"If we had a sales force, we would push the people into channels, so we try to avoid that," he said. "We leave our customers to do as they want."

Ironically, the former stockbroker comes off as less aggressive than your average, sleepy loans officer watching the day go by from the window of his office on a rural street. But he is also confident in his system and the ever-increasing profitability of the institution he leads.

One result of Ishii's soft-sell strategy is that Sony Bank is the respected choice of Japan's savvier active investors. Ishii characterizes his average client as largely thirty-something urban men, the most active of which may move their money every day. The bank has tried to attract female clients—the fabled army of Mrs. Watanabe day traders—with a pink-colored mirror site that had cute characters, but it was not a success, and Ishii's practical heart is clearly not into the vagaries of mass marketing.

Ishii values the spirit of innovation that is part of the Sony culture, and he wants to bring a service culture to his institutions, but also "to enrich the image of Sony in the area of financial services."

In terms of performance, the bank so far has been overshadowed within the financial group by Sony Life, the largest revenue contributor and the longer-established institution, which was founded in 1981. Sony Bank sells insurance products from the parent organization within its walls, but it is a limited type of insurance that it can manage without a sales force—and also, until recently, by regulations. In addition there is some work with Sony Finance International, a subsidiary of Sony that does some business in credit cards and some non-banking activities. But it has also recently branded with some Sony businesses, and the company also engages in businesses with SMBC.

The bank has slowly been getting into more and more regular banking activities. It started mortgage loans in 2002, the only big ticket borrowings Japanese take from banks, and is slowly breaking into credit cards as well through the relationship with Sony Financial International. Getting into the credit card business is not an easy task for Ishii, who is running a bank that doesn't have the marketing power of powerhouse global banks like Citi that can crank up the volume needed to make the product profitable. As a result, the bank is more likely running whatever businesses it has as a marketing and branding exercise than a real business with its focus on P&L.

"It is based on a step-by-step procedure because we do not have enough resources at this moment," Ishii said. "First we want to establish our business in some finance asset management area. Then we move to settlement, and also credit card might be part of some settlement business. We could go to the next step like credit card business, and also some securities transaction."

In 2007, the bank opened its own securities affiliate called Sony Securities.

Clearly, being on a short leash with the parent organization, the bank needs to think long and hard about the profitability of a project before it engages in anything, as well as the strength of its brand. Others, such as Egg, have failed for not following these rules.

"Originally we checked Egg Bank and also some other Internet banks, but we found out that most of the Internet banks failed," Ishii said. "They are very costly. They provide very high interest rates and I think [at one time] Egg Bank almost worked as a credit card company."

Ishii is realistic about the customer demographic that he is working with, and the situation among the retail banking market in Japan is certainly quite unique in the world.

"Even with low interest rates, people put their money into their bank deposits," said Ishii. "That's the reality of the Japanese people. Even though they complain that the interest rate is so low, once they use an ATM [and pay the ATM charges] they wipe out their interest earnings—if they deposit ¥1 million, the interest is, say, ¥100 or so. But still they put their money into the bank."

Ishii is certainly hoping he can convince more people of the benefits of the higher interest rates he offers, but the model is sure to be affected by any interest hikes to come. Japan is no longer at zero interest rates, but hope is fading for the types of interest rates any time soon that the big commercial banks—Sony Bank's main rivals—will need to be really profitable again.

"We had a very hard period because once the interest rate goes up we follow the market level," Ishii said. "We declared from the beginning that we move our customers very close to the market. We provide a 24-hour foreign exchange rate to our customers. Now we have to provide the market level interest rate to our customers."

WHO'S ON FIRST?

Many predict that there will be a time when Japanese banks will once again have real interest rates to play with, allowing them to finally *function* as banks once again. Until that day comes, however, they will need to wring their profitability out of a few poor businesses, including fee-based businesses such as payments. While the volumes are so huge that there will probably be enough for everyone to survive, it may be difficult for many to really prosper.

And perhaps more of them will be innovators and entrepreneurs like Ishii and Matsuo, coming up with smart ideas and trying them out. Both of these leaders, in their own ways, are shaping their institutions, even as the undercurrents of the industry shape them. With time, the models will prove themselves. But with fierce competition over a small slice of a difficult pie, the circumstances will certainly make them mean as hell.

Slim, Trim, and Hungry

How to make a man out of Mack

> *Simon Cooper, HSBC's President and CEO for South Korea, is sitting inside a bank at a crossroads.*

WHILE there are plenty of markets where the world's local bank has a large presence... Korea isn't one of them. Operating 11 branches, the bank has twice missed out on opportunities to grow by acquisition. There was Seoul Bank in 2002, which was lost to Hana Bank, and Korea First Bank in 2005, which went at the last minute to Standard Chartered Bank. In 2007, it struck an accord for Korea Exchange Bank (KEB) with the latter bank's embattled owner, Lone Star Holdings, but the deal looks tenuous given the arcane complexities surrounding the case—KEB is being held ransom by a court case about the exact circumstances of Lone Star's purchase of Korea's sixth-largest bank. If it gets KEB, HSBC will grow larger than Standard Chartered Bank, Korea's seventh-largest lender, and Citi, the country's eighth-biggest financial institution; but the odds are against it, and it looks like a strike-out in Korea for the world's local bank.

Simon Cooper
Reproduced by permission of
TAB International

To work around the fear that the bank would never be able to buy into a serious branch network, HSBC South Korea became the second Asian unit of the world's local bank, after Taiwan, to launch HSBC Direct. As an Internet-only branchless bank, the Direct offering provides HSBC with a way of collecting deposits and reaching out beyond Seoul via the information superhighway.

It is also slick marketing, an art that HSBC has mastered. After all, its brand name has a life of its own beyond the bank's narrow branch reach. It is also something innovative from the sleepy outpost operation that plays second fiddle to the massive HSBC operations in China across the Yellow Sea. HSBC in China has the largest branch network among the foreign banks and multiple investments, not to mention the work that Hang Seng Bank—which HSBC is a 62 percent owner of—is doing in that market. HSBC Korea, in contrast, doesn't even offer the famous HSBC credit card.

And yet, things are starting to warm up. Against the expectations of many observers, HSBC's deal for KEB may yet yield results of one sort or another, and the election of a new president in 2008 may at least break the stalemate. President-elect Lee Myung-bak has even hired HSBC's former chairman David Eldon as an advisor.

But if the HSBC deal really doesn't work out, then at least something may happen with Hana Bank. To hedge its bet on KEB, HSBC bought a 50 percent stake in Hana Financial Group's very small insurance operation for US$56 million in late 2007. Hana Life Insurance ranks twenty-first out of 22 Korean life insurers in terms of the amount of premiums it takes in, but at least it's something. And besides that, it is interesting that Hana would choose to sell to HSBC just half a year after Allianz exited the business, which it had set up with Hana as a joint venture.

HSBC is managed in Korea by its President and CEO Simon Cooper, who took over the position in March 2006, after his predecessor Rick Pudner went off to the United Arab Emirates to head Emirates Bank, a rapidly expanding Dubai-based bank.

RATIONAL EXUBERANCE

Cooper's background is in investment banking, having spent the early years of his career doing mergers and acquisitions, equity capital markets, structured debt, and leveraged debt transactions, a path which took him to the bank's home turf of Hong Kong. He went to Thailand in 2000 to run the group's wholesale bank there, eventually becoming the deputy CEO of the country business. He was also at the bank's Singapore office for two years in the wholesale bank, seemingly taking "emerging market country CEO courses" as so many

> **I was given a presentation when I arrived, saying Korea is a developing market. If this is developing—my God! It's well developed, but still with tremendous potential for growth.**

other mid-career HSBC international managers do in the city state before taking up the post in Korea.

"I'm tremendously impressed by the dynamism that is Korea," Cooper said about his new home. "Just the development that has come on in the last few years. You look around and it's a very developed country. I was given a presentation when I arrived, saying Korea is a developing market. If this is developing—my God! It's well developed, but still with tremendous potential for growth."

In Korea, Cooper handles corporate and investment banking, commercial banking, and retail banking. With the bank's large global network, the immediate fit is with Korean corporates that have regional or global aspirations.

"When I talk to Korean customers, they're always asking about China, Vietnam, maybe even Brazil or Mexico," he said. Cash-rich Korean companies are venturing outside of Korea, with their eyes squarely on markets in Southeast Asia that have very little Korean bank presence—for the moment.

"They're all interested in either investing in those countries, or trading with those countries," said Cooper. "From HSBC's perspective, we're able to offer tremendous bias in terms of doing business in countries where we're the largest or one of the largest banks or foreign banks."

Another factor is the bank's strength in Hong Kong and China. While it may be a minnow in Korea, Qingdao is only a short boat journey across the Yellow Sea from the port town of Inchon, not far from Seoul, or a 70-minute flight.

> **When I talk to Korean customers, they're always asking about China, Vietnam, maybe even Brazil or Mexico.**

"Korea's external FDI [foreign direct investment] in China [in 2006] was about forty percent of the total," Cooper said. "Hence, China is a very important trading partner and investing partner with Korea, and we have forty offices in China, we have invested in Bank of Communications and Bank of Shanghai. We're very well positioned to assist Korean customers as they develop opportunities there." With local incorporation for HSBC in China, the pace of its expansion there will only pick up.

As competitors in those areas, Cooper notes that HSBC is starting to see Korean banks opening offices in China, but none of them have the 140 years of history that HSBC has in the Middle Kingdom. Unfortunately, Cooper has none of these advantages in Korea itself, where he's quite solidly outnumbered by other foreign banks, as well as local players. This would change if HSBC ever acquired KEB, which is significantly bigger than Koram Bank, acquired by Citi in 2005, or Korea First Bank, acquired by Standard Chartered Bank in 2005. Unfortunately, KEB's overseas branch network—which would be a boon in creating a regional champion if the bank could be merged with a Korean bank like Kookmin or Woori—will overlap with HSBC's branches around the region. HSBC could even look at another lender—Hana Bank, for example, which already includes Seoul Bank, which HSBC passed on in 2002. But then it would have to face Hana Financial Group's wily chairman Kim Seung-yu, who would seriously test the bank's aversion to over-paying.

But the bank still has its strengths, which are mainly intangibles such as quality and service as well as regional strengths such as trade finance and cash management.

"I think our differentiator is on the corporate side, the global and regional footprint, the quality of the people, and of course the products that we are able to offer here," said Cooper. "Likewise for the retail business, our competitive advantage is not going to be having a branch on everybody's corner high street. It's going to be offering better wealth management products, looking at the higher-end market, where we've been successful in growing our Premier [wealth management] business. Customers are clearly attracted by the HSBC brand. It's a very powerful brand globally, and a very powerful brand still in Korea."

Even if Korea weren't Asia's fourth-largest economy, the challenges of the sophisticated market's regulatory regime means that establishing a local presence is a must for any serious bank doing business in Asia. As Mike Smith, the former CEO of HSBC's Asia Pacific operations explained while he was still with the bank, "somewhere like Japan or Korea, it is very restrictive on what you are allowed to do unless you are onshore, unless you actually have a presence onshore. And it's incredibly important that the compliance is understood and adhered to." In Japan, the bank has an even smaller branch presence than in Korea, but it is opening wealth management centers in 2008 and aims to have 50 branches there by 2017; an acquisition would go a long way there too.

The two countries actually are a big hole in the bank's Asian presence, considering that it beefed up its presence in Taiwan in 2007, being paid to take over the ailing Chinese Bank. It is also seemingly as bullish on Vietnam as it is on China, and its Malaysia franchise is faring very well indeed. It will need to fill these holes, as the group is facing pressure from investors to focus more on its core strength as a bank that specializes in Asia, and to stop flirting with markets it doesn't understand: low-end services like U.S. sub-prime mortgage loans and high-end businesses like investment banking.

With his HSBC Direct proposition, Cooper is keen to emphasize the tech-savviness of Koreans and their openness to mobile- and Internet banking technologies. He feels that the consolidation that is taking place in the industry places an excessive emphasis on bricks and mortar. He would certainly be able to do much more as the country's fifth-largest bank: more branches, more staff, and more experience in the country. Senior bankers at HSBC have already expressed regret that the bank wasn't bigger in such an important market.

ROADBLOCKS TEMPORARY?

"Korea—it was unfortunate," said Smith of the bank's failure to acquire a bank in Korea while he was with the bank, reflecting the mood of

HSBC's senior management. "In Korea I felt we were a long way down the track there in terms of missing the deal. StanChart beat us to that one. That was just one of those things."

Smith now runs ANZ in Australia, which is rivaling Standard Chartered Bank as the Asia Pacific region's most aggressive acquirer in emerging markets—but probably not Korea.

While Cooper has denied that he was sent to Korea with a mandate to shop for acquisitions, a natural part of the HSBC mantra goes something like, "if something comes along, then we'll obviously look at it." Another mantra is, "HSBC gets hundreds of ideas across its desk on a daily basis." But Cooper would obviously be pleased if the KEB deal did blossom, and in its anxiousness to market its progress in Korea HSBC even went against its tradition of being hush-hush about deals underway by putting out a press release stating that it was in talks with Lone Star over KEB.

"Our view of the Korean economy is very positive, and it's an economy we want to invest more in," Cooper said. "We would be interested in a few more branches. We would be interested in growing our existing business. We are supporters of the economy. I think the Korean ambition to be a North Asian financial hub is an admirable one, and we'd like to support the economy and business."

But where it is not growing its branches, the bank has quickly been building up its staff strength, from 400 people in 2003 to over 2,000 in 2007, most of whom have gone into the retail banking side of the business. Many of them have their offices at Cooper's downtown headquarters across the street from the Shinhan Financial Group headquarters on the downtown traffic circle that rings the historic Nandaemun gate, recently destroyed by an arsonist's match. While Cooper cannot break down his profits by business, in 2005 the bank earned a respectable US$100 million, which makes it a profitable operation branch by branch and a decent contributor to the bank's bottom line.

But the size issue is certainly going to come back to haunt the bank before too long. This is an issue not only in Korea, but also in Japan where the bank is starting to feel badly under-represented.

"Are there other markets we could do better in," Smith asked himself when he was still CEO of HSBC's Asia Pacific operations.

"Yes, and I think an obvious one is Japan. I think that it would be nice to be able to do more in Japan. I think Korea as well; there is more opportunity. So there are a number of countries where I think we could do more."

HSBC is at a crossroads. The bank could remain a small niche player in Korea, like it is in the Philippines, Indonesia, Malaysia, and Sri Lanka, and the bank won't suffer too terribly. But being top-heavy in Asia with massive China and Hong Kong operations is not an ideal situation either, especially with pressure from shareholders to make use of inroads its made in developing markets; in other words, be more like Standard Chartered Bank. Cooper still has some work ahead of him.

One in Ten Thousand

Sitting pretty in the Philippines

As a niche player heavily focused on treasury, Alberto Villarosa is leading his bank to a new zone.

WITH the 2007 merger of Banco de Oro and Equitable PCI Bank that formed a new number two bank in the Philippines, wedged somewhere between the sleepy giant of Metropolitan Bank and Trust (MetroBank) and the wily Bank of the Philippine Islands (BPI), "mergers and acquisitions" are the words that are on everyone's lips (such as those of bankers at Philippine National Bank and Allied Bank, for example). But looking around, there are not many strong banks left to buy that aren't already part of one of the three families that hold court in the Philippines.

Security Bank was the first private and Filipino-controlled bank of the post-World War II period. It is most famous for being the holder of the Philippines' Diners Club franchise,

Alberto Villarosa
Reproduced by permission of
Security Bank

which it launched in the 1970s as the country's first credit card. It got its license to convert from a savings bank to a fully-licensed commercial bank in 1994, and quickly launched an IPO in 1995. While it has a broad range of services that span retail banking, middle-market, corporate and investment banking, it is best known for its focus on certain profitable niches.

"We believe that within our particular niche we can be the market leader in that particular middle market and mid-size niche of the market," said Alberto Villarosa, the bank's president and CEO. "It's almost like, if it is an airline, we're

> We arm ourselves with 737s and we don't go for the Airbus 380s. We don't go for the long-haul market.

on a regional carrier, we arm ourselves with 737s and we don't go for the Airbus 380s. We don't go for the long-haul market."

Villarosa began his career in banking at CityTrust in the Philippines, a unit of Citigroup, running an investment banking segment, which was composed of asset management, treasury, and corporate finance. When Bank of the Philippine Islands (BPI) bought the unit from Citigroup in 1996, Villarosa went over to that bank where he rose to the position of executive vice president and treasurer. He left the bank in November 2002 to join Security Bank as the chief operating officer, with the view of becoming the chief executive officer when the standing CEO retired at the end of the following year. Villarosa started as the bank's new CEO on the first day of 2004.

While Security Bank is a family-run bank, 48 percent owned by the Dy family, it also has large shareholders in the Social Security System private pension fund. An active Singapore-based fund manager also bought 5 percent of the bank in 2003 when its stock was undervalued at 17 pesos, which Villarosa describes as "a 50 percent discount to book."

The stock has been strong ever since, at one point hitting 76 pesos in 2007 on stellar performance figures that are more typical of much bigger banks. Its profits have nearly quadrupled in the past three years, and for the 2007 financial year it declared US$60 million in net income. It had 22 percent return on equity, the highest among banks listed on the Philippine Stock Exchange at the time, and 2.0 percent return on assets, with its 25 percent loan growth. The bank has a staff of 1,800 people and three major operating subsidiaries including a credit card subsidiary, an investment house, and a stock brokerage house.

SPREAD THE WEIGHT

Like any good leader, Villarosa doesn't try to do everything himself and he gives a lot of credit to his staff for helping the bank get to where it needs to be. But this requires a certain amount of finesse.

"All through my various assignments in Citibank, CitiTrust, it was basically not so much the management of the technical skills *per se*, or performing the technical skills, but more the management of the people," he said. "Basically, that was a question of making sure that you managed your people well for them to deliver the results. Let's say it's a strategic management skill plus a complement with the people management skill. That basically has been what I would call the aces that I have."

On his staff, Villarosa has bankers from all across the international banking sector, since he didn't pillage BPI for talent when he left. Instead, his CFO is ex-Standard Chartered, as is his corporate bank head. Others came from HSBC and Citibank, while his consumer banking people came from a local bank, UnionBank of the Philippines.

"To strengthen our investment banking franchise we have been talking to some returning Filipinos from abroad," Villarosa said. "I think there's been a significant change in the brand image of the bank, not just from the customer standpoint, which is obviously the most important standpoint, but also in terms of being able to attract raw materials for our organization."

Villarosa had a mandate to push the bank into high gear and he was given very aggressive financial targets in terms of compounded growth in earnings that were almost double the historical growth earnings of the bank, normally quite difficult to pull off, but in a developing market much more is possible with growth rates than in a developed market.

The bank has a very aggressive treasury unit, and treasury activities account for nearly half of the bank's earnings, with the balance coming from corporate banking and consumer banking.

"Our consumer banking, which is basically sort of our baby, is quickly coming up the curve in terms of contributing a more significant portion to the revenue base of the bank," Villarosa said. "When we did the three-year plan, and we articulated what we call our first priorities, we went back to the basics and said we are going to focus on the customers. We organized accordingly the various businesses to put its proper focus on the customer. We used to be a product-driven organization. Now we basically focus on market natures."

This has given the bank a stronger focus on salespeople as a result, and Villarosa hired more of them after he joined the bank in order to build a consumer franchise. Industry wisdom says that retail banking will be the growth driver of the industry going forward, fuelled by remittances from the overseas workers who account for 20–40 percent of the growth of various parts of that business.

"We believe that the rich market niche will be in the consumer banking side," Villarosa said. "We reorganized accordingly to put a proper focus across the consumer and basically made strategic niches within the overall consumer market. We can't be a BPI. We have 114 branches versus 900 [BPI outlets], so we had to focus on specific market niches within the consumer market."

HAPPY GO LUCKY

But just as he can't be BPI, Villarosa doesn't *want* to be like his former employer, and he feels his retail banking strategy is much more fine-tuned and close to the pulse of his clients.

"BPI, Philippine Savings Bank, and a lot of consumer lending institutions go into consumer lending as a product, so it's a product driven strategy," he said. "We are a consumer driven organization. We will lend to Mr. De la Cruz basically to prevent Mr. De la Cruz from getting his mortgage, his car, whatever his credit requirements from MetroBank or from BPI or from any other bank. The minute he does it, the next thing to go will be his current account, his savings account. It is still going to be based on relationship. At least in the first two to three years, we figured that we have enough relationships that will enable us to launch an honest-to-goodness consumer lending program based on the clients that we already have, which is the same strategy on a credit card. The cross-sell has a lot of room to grow. By cross-selling to our existing customer base we can grow our card base more than a 100 percent."

Villarosa is chiefly looking at high net-worth individuals, as any good ex-Citibanker would, primarily in the Filipino-Chinese community that the bank is already very close to. Of course, this comes easier when the bank already has a strong brand presence via the Diners Card and the strong loyalty of those very affluent long-term customers. The bank also issues a MasterCard of its own and has over 125,000 cardholders. In his card portfolio, Villarosa claims that his average spend per card is almost double the industry average, surely attributable to the Diners factor.

Leveraging its treasury capabilities, the bank is looking to boost its capacity to offer wealthy clients wealth management products and treasury products, emphasizing quality much more than they had in the past.

"Where before we were basically focused just on plain vanilla deposits—current accounts and time deposits—we now offer them an array of treasury products which, by the way, in the last surveys, positioned Security Bank amongst the leading providers of domestic funding products and foreign exchange products," Villarosa said.

Clearly he takes great pride in the revamp of offerings that the bank has for its most valuable clients, and in doing so he looks a shade like the slick international banker who speaks of putting the client first, offering customer centricity, and focusing on service excellence. But these are also important for the 30 percent of his income that is fee-based, which is more constant than interest income.

For now, however, the bank's capital markets business is not contributing much to that fee income, but this is a factor of the market.

"The capital market, like for instance the securitization market in the Philippines, still hasn't taken off," he said. "There are still some regulations and basically because of the general liquidity in the system, the big names are still carried on the balance sheets of the banks. There's a dearth in loans. We believe that over the short time there will be a migration especially of the capital market-ready firms into the capital market."

In investment banking the bank has done better, and it has very rapidly picked up a fixed income distribution business that Villarosa can already brag about.

"For 2005, small or mid-size as we are on the balance sheet versus the big boys, we were the number one fixed income trading participant in the Fixed Income Exchange of the Philippines," he said.

> **Small or mid-size as we are on the balance sheet versus the big boys, we were the number one fixed income trading participant in the Fixed Income Exchange.**

Villarosa distributes securities and trust funds that look after the investor market. Most are invested in Philippine assets in either local or foreign currency. Villarosa wants to make sure that the bank develops a core base of investors so that he has someone to sell to when the private sector starts coming into the capital market.

"My philosophy of investment banking is investor driven," he said. "With all due respect to the corporate originators and deal structurers, if you don't have a strong distribution you will be held hostage in terms of corporate finance deals by somebody who has a large distribution."

STAY SMALL, THINK BIG

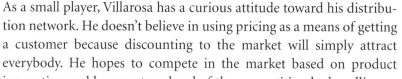

As a small player, Villarosa has a curious attitude toward his distribution network. He doesn't believe in using pricing as a means of getting a customer because discounting to the market will simply attract everybody. He hopes to compete in the market based on product innovation and be one step ahead of the competition by bundling or unbundling products.

"We did that with our cash management system, which was the first Internet-based cash management system in the country," he said.

"If you are a corporate treasurer you may be playing golf, and you can still authorize a transaction. You don't have to go back to the office to authorize a transaction. We launched the first cardless ATM. On the fixed income side, there are some proprietary products involving bundling and unbundling just to make sure that if you are an investor, if you want monthly or every 45 days' interest, we'll structure a product for you."

> The lack of size works to the advantage in terms of creativity because you have to be faster, otherwise you're dead; eight out of ten times we can bring a product to market faster than the bigger-sized banks.

Villarosa's identity is so clearly in his niche that it seems at times difficult to believe that he had previously worked in the culture of sprawling banks such as Citibank, or BPI—which was the second-largest bank in the Philippines at the time he worked there. Or perhaps entering a niche bank is simply a way for a banker who is a crack business head to be able to run an entire bank.

"We want to be a bank of value rather than size," he said. "We're not going to chase total assets *per se*. It makes sense to put it on the balance sheet from an economic standpoint. If the corporate customer is better served via the capital markets, we're not going to lose sleep because the loan is not in our balance sheet."

Villarosa doesn't seem to need much sleep to begin with.

"Everyday what wakes me up at three o'clock in the morning is [the question of] how to beat [the competition]," he said.

Villarosa has confidence in his team that, despite their small size, they have the agility and creativity to build products that can be priced competitively without the advantage of scale.

"The lack of size works to the advantage in terms of creativity because you have to be faster, otherwise you're dead," he said. "Secondly, because of our medium size versus competition, I'd say eight out of ten times we can bring a product to market faster than the bigger-sized banks."

Outmaneuvering the big competitors is also a game of Villarosa's, and he allows the bigger banks and the global players to fight for the top corporate clients while he seeks out the middle-market, SME, and Filipino-Chinese clients. The bank is on more of a level playing field when it comes to derivatives trading, where Security Bank is one of three in the Philippines that has been granted a license.

With a very high capital adequacy ratio (CAR) of more than 20 percent, Security Bank seems like it should go out and buy something the way the Philippines' other high-CAR bank, China Banking Corporation, did in 2007 when it bought Manila Bank. But Villarosa is careful here as well and has rainy days in mind.

"I don't want to bring my capital adequacy to 12–15 range and then find out later that I have to go knocking on the door that I need more capital because the loan market is picking up," he said.

Villarosa is also a CEO who keeps his shareholders in mind with strong dividends, and under the watchful eye of his shareholders he keeps his corporate governance practices a top priority, always with an eye on shareholder and stakeholder value. And, of course, his treasured ROE is a good sign that he's keeping up.

With his profitability and strong growth, Villarosa is keen to grow his market share and become a more substantial player. He's hoping to have 6 percent market share by 2011, up from 3 percent in 2006, as long as there are no surprises with capital requirements coming from the regulator of the Basel Committee.

In the end, his growth strategy will all boil down to the talent that he is able to attract. He may be able to find some smart Filipino bankers to come back home to sit at his right hand, the way Teresita "Tessie" Sy did in convincing Nestor Tan to come back to the Philippines from London to help her run Banco De Oro and to manage the biggest merger that the Philippines has ever seen.

But then again, he may not be able to find his Nestor Tan.

"The entire banking industry has a problem," he said. "I was chairman last year of the Bankers Association Committee on Education. One of the issues that was a total industry issue was we're not getting our fair share of good graduates into the banking industry. They thought that banking is boring—accounting, money... It's an industry-wide issue and therefore the association is trying to do something about it, not to mention losing out to the business process outsourcing operations and the call centers. We've been able to succeed. We're not where I would like to be, yet, in terms of the brand image; but as far as the prime educational institutions are concerned, name recall is already there. And to that extent, I'm decently happy."

And "decently happy" is a good way to describe Villarosa, who seems to be thoroughly enjoying the challenges thrown his way by the industry, not to mention the success that he has seen. He's coy about the future, being careful and taking out his insurance as well, and he's quiet about the eventual knock on the door from an interested bank. Until that day comes, as long as he keeps running on that treadmill, he'll stay trim and tidy.

From the Inside Out

How to unlock part of US$14 trillion in consumer savings (part 3)

Standard Chartered is boosting its Japan operations with its tireless CEO Mark Devadason.

WHILE they have direct access to the largest market in Asia, foreign banks in Japan have not really met their destinies yet. The important exception is a very persistent Citibank, which has been in the country since 1902, stepping up its presence in the 1970s. It has recently incorporated as a Japanese company, purchased the country's third-largest brokerage, and launched into aggressive branch expansion.

Standard Chartered Bank (StanChart) may also have been present in the country for over a hundred years, as it has been in most countries in Asia and the Middle East, but with only one branch in Japan it doesn't have much to show for it—yet.

Mark Devadason
Reproduced by permission of
Standard Chartered Bank

But appearances can be deceiving, and the Japanese chapter of the region's most aggressive acquirer has less in common with what is going on with the parent organization in other countries as what major regional and global banks like ANZ, UBS, JPMorgan Chase, and Pictet et Cie are doing: building a niche presence.

What we do here in Japan is very much tied in to what we do in the UK, Australia, and the U.S.

The country's CEO and head of corporate banking is Mark Devadason, who arrived in Japan in 2003. Unfortunately for him, that was also the time when the country's mega-banks were going through the toughest patches of their reconstruction processes and weren't thinking of building relationships with global banks.

"That was really the bottom of the bottom," said Devadason. "So I came to Japan actually not so clear as to how tough the situation was. But I came with a mandate: Japan is the largest economy in Asia, it had been kind of off the [StanChart] radar, but the proposition I had been told to look at was to figure out how we could become more relevant [to the group]. How could we better look at this opportunity, to make better use of the network, because we have a 127-year history, but it wasn't contributing enough to the group at the time."

The general reputation that StanChart has is that of an "emerging markets bank," but this tag wouldn't necessarily apply to Devadason's operations in Japan, or to the group's major operations in developed markets. Considering the fact that its largest operations are in Hong Kong and South Korea, hardly emerging markets, and the bank's wholesale operations have a presence in the U.S. as well, there are plenty of bridges to build between East and West to make sure that the twain shall meet.

"Where we can add most value for OECD large multinationals, reflecting our corporate banking network philosophy, is the referral process into the Asia, Africa, and the Middle East regions," he said. "In that sense what we do here in Japan is very much tied in to what we do in the UK, Australia, and the U.S. So it's different from India and China and Indonesia where we have large, embedded domestic strategies, which will be local retail, SME and middle market. That is not so much what we are doing here."

BIGGER AND BETTER

Before arriving on Japanese shores, Devadason had looked after off-shore banking as the bank's group offshore head looking after Asia and the Middle East, even before the group launched its private banking business in 2007. He brought with him knowledge of consumer and corporate banking.

Since Devadason has been running the business, he's seen his head count more than double from 110 in 2003 to over 230 at the end of 2007. He's also clearly managed to keep the attention of the people in headquarters as they invest in the business.

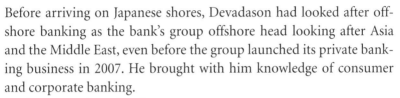

While we are in competition with the Japanese banks, they are also one of my biggest customer segments.

"Our wholesale banking customer base has doubled since I have been here," he said. "We have significantly increased the seniority of the wholesale relationship managers. As we grow in Asia, we have become more confident that we can add value to Japanese corporates as they invest in Asia, the Middle East, and Africa. So we really increased the number of target customers. We are not talking about thousands, we are talking about Japan's biggest multinationals."

From his single branch opposite the Imperial Palace in Otemachi, the district that hosts the head offices of all of Japan's largest banks, Devadason is slowly stealing some of the clients from Japan's mega-banks' backyard as they diversify out of lumbering Japan to tap that fast-moving Asia that is StanChart's playground.

Devadason runs a financial institutions business alongside the corporate banking business.

"While we are in competition with the Japanese banks, they are also one of my biggest customer segments," he said. "We do a lot of work with the mega-banks, supporting them on the other side of trade and

FX transactions. It is a very important part of our business because, in many cases, we are in the markets that they are not. Over the last ten years, in many cases, they have shrunk or withdrawn, and so we have been providing them with services to help their customers. A good example, which I was directly involved in, was working with Sumitomo Mitsui Banking Corporation after they closed their operations in India, now we are basically business partners in India. We have a Japan desk in India, and any of their customers that want business support in India we can provide through StanChart. So it's a classic case of working with our customers."

One of Devadason's fastest-growing businesses is his global markets business, where he has increased the complexity of his product range.

> **The margins here are somewhat tighter than in Hong Kong or Singapore, but my volumes are bigger than Singapore and Hong Kong combined. So this is not a small market, you'd be quite surprised at the volume.**

"Part of my head-count growth has been associated with growing our global markets business, specifically with financial institutions customers, the Japanese regional banks whose customer base is primarily SME," he said. "They are all doing trade. They have needs in terms of international trade and FX flows, which is where we can step in. So the key areas of growth have been sub-custody, supply chain finance, global markets, derivatives, FX, the whole range."

But among these, it is the sub-custody business where Devadason might get some extra notice from headquarters, and where he's seeing the biggest benefit of playing to a niche in a complex, difficult market.

"We have the biggest volumes of Standard Chartered globally in Japan, in our sub-custody business," he said. "The margins here are somewhat tighter than in Hong Kong or Singapore, but my volumes are bigger than Singapore and Hong Kong combined. So this is not a small market, you'd be quite surprised at the volume. It is a very, very exciting market if you can find your niche, and what I am saying is that we have been quite comfortable over the last couple of years developing these areas where we can operate without going into every aspect of the market. And it makes sense."

With so many cash-rich corporations limiting their bank borrowing, smaller banks don't find the lending business very rich in Japan with the main relationships in a declining business sewn up by the mega-banks. Even mid-sized banks with established deposit-taking capabilities like Shinsei Bank don't do it much. Accordingly, lending is one business that StanChart does not look at much in the country, and the bank has made a conscious decision to focus on other businesses.

Devadason's business growth is being driven by his wholesale banking business, and he claims to have strong ROE even though his businesses are still small compared to StanChart overall. Devadason is building up capabilities to cover what his clients will be asking for, and has made sure that the bank has added Japan desks in StanChart's operations in Thailand, Singapore, China, and India, where people look after the local subsidiaries of his Japanese customers.

ENTERING ORBIT

On the consumer banking side, the bank is aiming at even smaller niches, but ones that are potentially just as profitable. Devadason estimates the market to be worth US$200 billion in Japan, and while the country's banking industry as a whole is only seeing modest growth rates of 2–5 percent, he sees the fastest growth within the industry in the business of mutual funds, deposits, REITs, and foreign exchange. Here the growth rate is more like 15–25 percent, closer to the levels that StanChart is used to in its other businesses, or as Devadason calls it "emerging market dynamics in an established OECD market."

Having studied his market, Devadason has found a startlingly underserved segment at the doorstep of his bustling wholesale banking business.

"We estimate 20 million high-net-worth households within two hours of this office," Devadason said. "Now think about Hong Kong: only eight million people, and of those, how many are high net worth? Not so many. Maybe one million. Standard Chartered's biggest business growth opportunity is to learn and understand how to look after those 20 million customers. What we found is that a lot of banks, including foreign banks, are chasing the private banking market, which is typically US$3 million and above. But you can argue that it's only 10,000 or 20,000 households. But at the US$200,000 level and above there are four million households in the Tokyo area."

> We estimate 20 million high-net-worth households within two hours of this office.

Although the 20,000 will have much more money than the 20 million, it's difficult to ignore a medium-strength market that is 1,000 times bigger than a full-strength one. StanChart, with its young private bank, still looks at private banking more of an obligation—the unavoidable extension of its wealth management specialty—with wealth management the more established division and showing better profitability. All this has only become more the case with StanChart's late 2007 acquisition of American Express Bank, which gives the bank more capabilities in product building and distribution. Now with the unit in Japan, Devadason is hoping to find the profitable segment of professionals that fall between mass retail and mega-rich. And while he knows that he won't be able to pry anyone away from their local bank, where relationships are long-standing, he knows that he has something to offer the curious and the dissatisfied.

Devadason is also hoping to get in on the demographic of the retiring baby boomers and their retirement packages, which is estimated to be US$680 billion coming due to three million households between 2007 and 2010, with payouts averaging US$200,000. Recipients will need to find an effective way to make this money last through their old age in expensive Japan and some will look to the banks. Devadason hopes to be there with something to offer them. Of course, so do all of Japan's other banks, including the mega-banks, and plenty of thought has been going into beefing up branches, prettifying them, making them more friendly, and more geared toward the investor with one last, big windfall.

> **These people cannot live off the yen-denominated earnings, they will have to use that money more efficiently.**

Like the other banks, StanChart in Japan has beefed up its branch facilities for the affluent.

"These people cannot live off the yen-denominated earnings, they will have to use that money more efficiently," Devadason said. "The aging population means people live longer, so the proposition is that we believe these people need to have more products, more options, more ability to work their money and so that they can actually live off of it. You cannot live off of 0.1 percent. So that's why we have chosen this business proposition. If you have been to some of the banks' retail banking propositions here, you see people sitting in chairs asleep during their lunchtime because they are queuing up to make a payment, but all they are doing is a transaction."

In its single branch, Devadason is at play with a seminar space with a screen and seating for 100 where he presides over jazz nights, wine tastings, charity fund raisers, and financial services seminars. Even the paintings that hang on the walls come from local galleries and are changed every month, showing Devadason's handle on the business and his love for detail.

COST CONTROL

So far the bank's engagement with retail clients has not been completely straightforward.

"We made mistakes and we learnt some lessons," he said. "We thought that we could advertise a lot more and that didn't really work. In the first six or seven months we had a great start and after that it slowed down for a while. So we thought, what's the issue? We found that great account managers are much better at attracting new customers and building the business than just advertising. We've learned."

Devadason claims that priority banking hit its breakeven point after two years, but this is largely because he has kept his costs low. He has so far managed to run his operations from a single, scalable branch, stretching his client reach far outside of the city. He notes specifically that "with one large branch in Tokyo, you can do a lot more than one branch in another city in Asia," a sentiment shared by Sunil Kaul, president at Citi Japan. Less than 200 yards from Devadason's branch is Tokyo Station, where account managers can hop on a train and be in distant parts of Japan in only a few hours, speaking to a whole new niche.

But at some point soon he's going to have to think about building new branches, especially with rival Citibank causing such a commotion over its expensive new branch expansion policy. Devadason will have to decide how big his niche is really going to be, or how many of those 20,000 households he can realistically grab without causing his cost base to spiral out of control. And while rents may have been coming down in Japan for the past decade, this has not been so in prime downtown locations in city centers.

"The question now is how do we scale it up," Devadason said. "I think that having the right sales force is key and we are now developing a view about where we should be—should we be in Osaka or Nagoya or Yokohama—or should we focus more on Tokyo?"

The products that the bank sells are both in-house and third-party products, although it plans to be originating more ideas for special styles of deposit products that will be based on group best practices and experience. But doing business in Japan means following a unique set of regulations, and Devadason hopes to do his best to shake the system up here.

"There's a complication to this market," he said. "We can't just sell foreign-originated products. They have to be registered here. The process is very cumbersome and very expensive so we tend to have to work with the scale providers such as insurance and asset management companies. That's one of the issues that we face. What we are trying to do is simplify the pricing tariffs because this is a complicated market. I have said that we want to disrupt this market."

One of the ways Devadason wants to do something unconventional, for example, is waiving the punishment fees that are unique to Japan for his top customers, such as one percent for foreign exchange on top of the exchange commission.

"We have changed our unit trust tariffs toward greater transparency," he said. "We're saying this is what it is, it is a simple fee. It's 1 percent, that's it. We want to make that side of things fairly clear. We want the customers to do more things with us. And our experience is that the business model is where we want it."

GONE SHOPPING

But despite its high organic growth, Standard Chartered Bank is a highly acquisitive bank in Asia. It has in recent years acquired banks in Pakistan, Taiwan, and Korea, on top of its purchase of American Express Bank. If the business goes well in Japan, the bank could make a move. There are plenty of good banking prospects available, and Citibank has shown that it is possible to get regulatory approval to buy something big in the country. Besides some of the smaller regional banks that are struggling, the bank could yet strike a deal with the prickly characters that run one or more of the private equity troika of Shinsei Bank, Aozora Bank, or Tokyo Star Bank, which were all failed banks at the turn of the century that have been turned around by foreign money and international management teams.

"What we need to think about is do we actually scale up through buying another bank," Devadason said. "Do we buy portfolios from other banks? Or do we do partnerships with other banks that need us in the region? We've made this investment, we started in 2003 at a pretty tough time in the market, and we have belief that this market will come around. I'm happy with it."

Certainly, there is the precedent of Standard Chartered Korea, which in 2004 ran a tight operation out of only two branches, but has quickly swollen to become the group's second-biggest operation globally with the acquisition of Korea First Bank; it is now the seventh-biggest bank by assets in Korea.

If Standard Chartered wanted to invest heavily in East Asia—big in Hong Kong, big in Korea, big in Taiwan—then Japan is the next piece of that puzzle. On the face of it, Devadason's previous posting in a regional role would indicate that his posting in a one-branch operation—albeit a lucrative one-branch operation—is clearly not his style. Growth by acquisition is clearly something that Devadason has firmly in mind.

But even as he keeps his eyes open and works on his mandate, it is abundantly clear that StanChart Japan is not the creature it was in 2003 and has grown with (slightly) headier times. Since Japan is a creature of scale, tapping a sliver of that beast is good business indeed.

Mark Devadason was appointed as president and CEO of Standard Chartered Bank's Thailand operations in February 2008. Although he no longer manages the bank's Japan operations, the situations he describes in this chapter are still valid.

Chapter 7
The Emissaries—Fighting the New Fight

National, International, National, International...

Nothing is permanent except change

> *Ha Yung-ku has had a wild ride managing two of Korea's largest banks: KorAm Bank and Citi Korea.*

KOREA is a tough market. Besides the phenomenon of overzealous government regulators breathing down the necks of foreign private equity players with criminal investigations, allegations of slush funds, worries over credit card bubbles, accusations of aggressive sales tactics, and other nasty surprises, there's always trade unions and the threat of strikes to worry about.

For Citigroup, Korea has at least been relatively straightforward. They were the first foreign bank to enter Korea in 1967 and ran their own operations, focusing on organic growth and niche markets. Then they found a bank called KorAm that they liked, and they got to work. In early 2004, the world's largest bank by market capitalization (at the time) tussled with banks like Standard Chartered Bank over the purchase of a 36.6 percent stake held by The Carlyle Group, the private equity firm that had run the bank from 2000 to 2004; it was

Ha Yung-ku
Reproduced by permission of
Citibank Korea

the largest equity investment deal the hugely successful group had ever put together. At the same time, Citigroup also put out a tender offer for the remaining shares, getting the requisite 80 percent needed to delist the operations from the Seoul Stock Exchange and merge its existing operations with its new acquisitions—branches, ATMs, unions, and all.

KorAm, founded in 1983 as a joint venture between large Korean conglomerates and Bank of America, had specialized in SMEs rather than corporations and was thus not brought to the brink of ruin like so many other Korean banks in the 1997 financial crisis. But it was in a tight place nonetheless when a huge loan to Daewoo soured.

A wily operator on both sides of the story has been Ha Yung-ku, known affectionately by staff and friends as Y.K. Having graduated from Seoul National University in 1976, Ha earned an MBA at the Kellogg School of Northwestern University in the U.S. in 1981. He joined Citibank in Korea that year, eventually rising to the level of country business manager for Citibank's global consumer bank.

In May 2001, Ha joined Carlyle's KorAm Bank to be its chairman and CEO and see it through its restructuring, while Carlyle thought about how long it would hold the investment and to whom it would ultimately sell the institution. So in November 2004, when the US$3 billion merger with Citigroup's local operations was completed, Ha found himself in the unusual situation of rejoining old colleagues, those who had stayed under the Citi umbrella, as their new CEO.

The acquisition got off to a troubled start. With an 18-day strike, the longest ever at a financial institution, the bank suffered a huge loss of deposits that it has never truly recovered from. As a result of its shrunken deposit base, and the trend in Korea among depositors of moving funds out of banks and to brokerages and insurance companies, Citigroup Korea has tended to focus on fee businesses. It leverages the parent company's product development strengths for foreign exchange, cash management, and trade finance services, as well as credit card and wealth management services.

Besides hooking up with a new branch network and a broader distribution for its wealth management products, the acquisition has given Citigroup a new tap into corporate Korea and the large *chaebol* companies, as well as some financial institutions business. On the consumer side, Citi gained 223 KorAm branches on top of its existing 15 branches, allowing the group to have better access outside of the metropolitan Seoul area.

A NEW START

Citigroup had bravely decided to ditch the KorAm name in favor of the Citi brand, testing the sentimentality of Koreans in seeing the KorAm brand fade away and replaced by a well-known global giant's. Ironically, it also paved the way for Standard Chartered Bank to do the same a year later when it acquired Korea First Bank.

> **Globality means not only the global network, but also the secure set like the risk management, control, compliance, and sales process.**

"Of course in the case of cards, legacy KorAm had more than 3 million cards," Ha said, explaining the strength of the initial deal. "In the case of the number of accounts, also like 4 million accounts, and the number of corporate customers, 35,000 corporate customers. So after this was combined, it was a combination of the large distribution network plus a large number of customer base of legacy KorAm, plus the globality of Citi; globality means not only the global network, but also the secure set like the risk management, control, compliance, and sales process."

Unions are strong in Korea, and nearly all of the country's banks are hit by strikes from time to time. Any merger will be fraught with difficulties, as the unions jostle for bargaining positions with new owners, and Citigroup's acquisition of KorAm proved, if anything, to be even more contentious. But Ha still sees that the two banks had plenty in common as they set down the merger path.

"If you look at the history of legacy KorAm, it started as a joint venture bank," he said. "The U.S. bank and the local big corporate names, and then a kind of American bank culture is embedded in the legacy KorAm, so of course the culture is not the same."

But the unions would not see this international marriage as anything particularly romantic, and KorAm's union has decried discriminating policies against former KorAm staff at the new Citibank Korea. They resorted to harsh whistle-blowing tactics by accusing the American bank of overcharging clients on their mortgages. The merger should have gone better: KorAm was a much younger institution than most of the other banks in Korea, which would have deeply entrenched cultures.

Unforeseen difficulties made the integration take much longer than initially expected by anyone, and it took nearly two years to bring the two banks' IT systems together after the acquisition. At least it now has its integration exercises behind it, although this doesn't always mean Citigroup is now realizing full economies of scale.

Compliance with local regulations have left the merger a less than complete operation because data processing cannot by insourced to Citigroup's data centers in Singapore, leaving the bank no choice but to use its old KorAm-era facilities to do the work in-country. More integrated, less cost-effective.

"On the technology side, we are investing a lot of money," Ha said, explaining the intricacies of folding the bank he ran for three years into a global infrastructure. "Once it is regionalized, of course savings might be there, but on the other hand the response time and customer satisfaction may be not as strong as the other banks that have data centers in Korea, so there are pros and cons."

Ha has managed to straddle the various pressures of integrating the steely, no-nonsense Citigroup culture with the steely no-nonsense business culture of Korea. But then again, managing ambitious growth targets has always been a goal of both the Korean people in general and Citigroup specifically, so perhaps in the end there are more similarities than differences between the two groups, not even mentioning the "American" culture present in the legacy KorAm bank.

The staff of the bank is mostly Korean, with only about 40 of the bank's 5,000 staff non-Koreans. Ha expects the culture of the bank to remain Korean as well, and doesn't see many new foreign staff joining the bank.

KOREA CITI, CITI KOREA

Being a global bank that is strongly associated with the U.S., Ha is having to market Citibank to a different type of customer than the sort that was initially attracted to KorAm. Indeed, in the first year of operation, the bank did see depositors taking their money out of the bank, to the net benefit of its competitors, and it had to raise its deposit rates to keep them interested.

> We cannot say we like this type of customer or this type of customer, because we provide a very comprehensive product line.

Meanwhile, its corporate loan levels also slackened as integrations continued and Citigroup prudently initiated credit checks on KorAm corporate borrowers. For the Korean public, Citi's big appeal comes from sophisticated wealth management products, although even here the bank has strong local competitors like Hana Bank.

But Ha does feel that Citigroup in Korea still retains some universal appeal, and he markets banking services to all segments.

"We cannot say we like this type of customer or this type of customer, because we provide a very comprehensive product line," he said. "For example, the Citiblue retail banking and the consumer finance and the credit card get a wide range of customer spectrum, and the investment products attract a certain category of customers. We define the different customers by different product lines."

The bank has products for large corporates down to small and medium enterprises, he said.

When Ha looks at his business, he sees over half of it coming from net interest income, with the rest as fee income, although the latter is more likely to rise in the future than the former. Much of it is a factor of the bank's branch exposure. Where the bank is the fifth-largest in Korea, it will also come in fifth or sixth in most of its products. Ha feels that the bank is closer to the top in terms of investment products and wealth management, where it has an 11 percent market share, and corporate foreign exchange.

Ha looks to trade, foreign exchange, and derivatives as his growth areas.

"Also the SME segment, in terms of the customer bases," said Ha of the segment that had been one of KorAm's specialties. Overall, the consumer side of the business will grow, he said. In his loan portfolio, half of his book is corporate loans while most of the other half is mortgages. He sees credit cards as 8 percent of his total assets.

BUILDING ON THE BASICS

Ha is hoping to increase the number of medium-sized businesses that use Citi as their main bank. In an export economy such as Korea, its international networks give it plenty of leverage, although it faces competition from Korea Exchange Bank and Standard Chartered Bank, as well as the gigantic Shinhan Bank, which is also SME-focused. But certainly, cost-effective access to sophisticated international networks is something that KorAm could not have managed as well on its own before the acquisition as it can now that it has thrown its lot in with Citigroup.

> The credit card is turning around, turned around in a sense, and I expect also the whole market has got the experience of the down cycle of the credit card business.

One of the areas that Ha will focus on growing in his retail banking portfolio is the credit card. With the shocks of the 2004 credit card crisis behind him, Ha is ready to give it another strong push, but not too strong as over-aggressiveness in Korea has led to vicious spirals in the past that could be easily repeated.

"The credit card is turning around, turned around in a sense, and I expect also the whole market has got the experience of the down cycle of the credit card business," he said. The country has a new consumer credit bureau that Ha and Citigroup Korea actively participate in.

"Still a way to go, but it's a good start," he said.

With the trends in Korea of funds disintermediation as money flows out of the banking system and into other businesses such as insurance and securities, Ha is facing challenges running a traditional bank that takes in deposits and gives out loans. Banks in Korea have been trying to staunch the flow by organizing themselves as financial holding companies—the country now has three among its top ten banking groups—and Citigroup Korea is considering the structure, as is the country's largest, Kookmin Bank, and Standard Chartered Korea.

Now that Ha has laid the integration groundwork, he will need to keep a sharp eye on expansion. He's hinted at new business networks and a broader branch network. Another acquisition may be in the works. Standard Chartered Bank, after all, did not stop at the Korea First Bank acquisition and bought Yeahreum Mutual Savings Bank in January 2008. Wth a new CEO in New York to get used to, along with the cost pressures that headquarters is facing with new investors bringing cash on board and asking lots of questions, Ha may soon have a wide series of new challenges ahead.

The Bold New Banker

Cracking frontiers is hungry work

Sebastian Paredes is taking his emerging markets experience at Citibank and translating it into progress at Indonesia's Bank Danamon.

ONE of Asia's largest countries, and the world's most populous Muslim nation, Indonesia is a complex market. With 130 banks fighting for their share of the pie, it is also one of the most over-banked markets in Asia. Add to this the fact that several foreign banks invested in many of Indonesia's banks, some of them as parts of consortiums, and it becomes more complex still.

One of the hardest-hit markets during the Asia financial crisis of 1997, Indonesia is only now considered recovered from the after-effects that saw the number of banks reduced from more than 300 down to about 130. The country's economy is still largely commodities-based, and banks are heavy corporate lenders with the retail banking market still under-developed, the Islamic finance market woefully so.

One of the only foreign-born banking heads in the culturally-diverse archipelago, Sebastian Paredes arrived at Bank Danamon (Danamon) on the first of March, 2005, becoming the bank's president director in May of the same year. Taking up the position was a bit of a risk for the 44-year-old,

Sebastian Paredes
Reproduced by permission of
Bank Danamon

as he was turning his back on an 18-year career at Citigroup, which saw the ambitious young banker become the country head of Ecuador three years after joining the company there. He had been a country or business head in Ecuador, Turkey, and South Africa, and when he left the group was the head of Citi's 11-country South and Sub-Saharan Africa group. But in this regard, he joins a worthy cohort of CEOs that dot the Asia Pacific region who also once worked under the red umbrella and now work for someone else.

"The reason I left Citigroup to join Danamon is because clearly the story of Danamon is an extraordinary story and the vision that our group wants to have throughout Asia is a vision of entrepreneurship," said Paredes. "It's a vision of ambitious expansion and it's a vision that centers on the customer and the power of its people. Danamon is at a fundamental part of the beginning of that vision, and when the board approached me and asked me to join this group, I came here and saw what Danamon was all about and their aspirations in Indonesia. I thought that this could really be a significant uniqueness in a bank that is highly differentiated from the rest—that I could make a difference."

Established in 1956, Danamon became the first privately-held foreign exchange bank in Indonesia in 1976. It was listed in 1989. Danamon was one of the banks that had become insolvent as a result of the Asia financial crisis in 1997 and was placed under the supervision of the Indonesian Bank Restructuring Agency (IBRA) like many other Indonesian banks. IBRA folded the legacy Danamon in with eight other banks in 2000. In 2003, Asia Finance Indonesia, a consortium that includes Singapore's Temasek Holdings and Deutsche Bank, bought a majority stake in the bank from IBRA. Indonesia's fifth-largest bank by assets, Danamon is in a size tier of its own that is roughly half the size of each of the next three larger banks in the next size tier up. It is roughly a third of the country's largest, the government-held Bank Mandiri, in the top tier. Meanwhile, it is significantly larger than the banks that come after it: Bank Internasional Indonesia, Bank Niaga, and Panin Bank.

With Temasek as an investor, the head of the group's financial institutions investment wing Francis Rozario brought in a new management team that steered the bank toward the mass market, making fundamental acquisitions into the consumer finance business and introduced a new risk management structure.

"The bank that you see today has transformed dramatically since 2003," said Paredes. It will also compete heavily with two of the banks in the tier above it, which are also strong in consumer segments, Bank Rakyat Indonesia and Bank Central Asia.

Temasek's investment in Danamon is somewhat controversial, as it is one of a clutch of banks in Indonesia that Singapore's Temasek government-linked investment firm has a direct or indirect investment in—the others are Bank Internasional Indonesia, DBS, and Standard Chartered Bank; and through the latter's roles in a consortium that owns Permata Bank, it has indirect access to one more Indonesian lender. Complicated rulings made by Bank Indonesia, the country's central bank, have established a "single presence policy," which requires an investor in Indonesia's banks to limit their investment to a single bank. For Temasek, the ruling applies most concretely to Bank Danamon and Bank Internasional Indonesia (BII), where it is recognized as having a controlling stake, leaving the investor three options: reduce the investment below the 25 percent level that is considered a "controlling interest," put the banks under a financial holding company structure, or merge the two. After giving early indications that it would merge the two, in early 2008, Temasek decided that it would divest its holdings in BII to keep it simple and focus only on Danamon.

> It's very unique. There are very few banks in the world that can say they are in the micro-lending business and the high-end corporate institutional business.

SETTING OUT

Temasek's investment and compliance concerns aside, Paredes points out that he is an employee of Danamon, one of 30,000, and managing that one bank is his main priority. Through his background at

Citigroup, with its sophisticated universal banking model that covers nearly any aspect of financial services, Paredes is pleased to be at the wheel of a similarly diverse enterprise, which he—in typical Citi fashion—describes in terms of its customer-centric focus.

> **Are we there yet? Of course not. The road is long and the road is harsh, but we have aspirations and believe we will get there eventually.**

"It's very unique," said Paredes. "There are very few banks in the world that can say they are in the micro-lending business and the high-end corporate institutional business, and Danamon is all about that."

The enthusiastic Paredes was also attracted to the value of entrepreneurship that he sees in the institutions, and the staff decision-making culture that he's been trying to define and refine.

"We can be small, but we aspire to have probably the best global standards in our bank," Paredes said. "Are we there yet? Of course not. The road is long and the road is harsh, but we have those aspirations and believe we will get there eventually."

Continuing the work that Temasek and Rozario put in when they bought the bank in 2003, Paredes is hoping to build a significant business that reaches out to all stakeholders inside and outside the bank and form a significant business that puts the customer in all business segments at the center of the transaction; again, all of them very Citi concepts.

One of the businesses that the bank is succeeding in is its consumer finance unit for financing motorcycles and cars. Danamon is the second-largest bank in Indonesia in the motorcycle finance business, where it has quickly achieved a 12 percent market share and finances over half a million motorcycles a year. Paredes is aggressive about building up the new business and is spending heavily, but he is strategic in his focus.

"We are already focused on addressing and protecting our net interest margin and growing it in good and bad times, so we will continue investing in high margin business," he said about Adira, the bank's motorcycle and car financing company that also forms its microfinance network. "In less than 18 months we have opened 750 branches for our mass market, we have hired almost 7,000 people in the mass market, and in less than one year we have been able to obtain critical mass to turn this business into a profitable business, a business that after 18 months represents about 10 percent of our total loan book; it's a massive transformation."

The bank is aggressively tackling Indonesia's subprime area, a business that has practically been owned by Bank Rakyat Indonesia (BRI), Indonesia's fourth-largest lender by assets, after over 100 years of development. Paredes has spoken at investor conferences about the massive potential that exists in Indonesia for microfinance and he's investing heavily in the business for Danamon. While microfinance is generally linked to not-for-profit models like that of Grameen Bank, Indonesian banks like BRI have commercial models and Danamon is throwing its hat into the ring.

"We went through a very profound analysis of the opportunities in this segment and with the help of McKinsey and different consultants, we came up with a model that showed that we could enter this market creating a unique value proposition and obtaining critical mass that will drive the growth of Danamon," said Paredes.

Through Adira, 25 percent of Paredes's loan book is in sub-prime for microfinance, but he hopes to boost that to over half since the margins are better than in conventional lending, albeit more labor-intensive. To aid the development of the business, the bank is rolling out fingerprint-enabled biometric technology to speed up processing of savings and loans to individuals who cannot read or write. It is marketing to them through places of high turnover business such as produce and meat markets, where the bank competes heavily with BRI, which has over 30 percent of its loan portfolio in microfinance. Rural banks are also competitors for the business, although they represent a highly fragmented, localized front.

"Our model is community-based; it's one-on-one selling, person-to-person selling," said Paredes of the bank's resources in deploying the service. "It's unique technology recognizing the profile of the customer in deploying the technology, thumbprint technology rather than documentation and so forth. We know the customers personally, we know who they are, what they do, where their families are, where they live, their business, we know everything personally."

The business targets the country's 42 million self-employed workers who may not have collateral or a tax file number or a credit history, but run sustainable businesses and have the ability to repay loans that they may take to expand their businesses. Danamon's loans average US$2,200, but loans may actually range from US$2,500 to US$56,000. The business is very labor-intensive, and requires a huge management commitment, but margins are fat and the potential market is huge. The existing market is estimated to be growing at 20 percent per year.

WHAT'S ON THE CARDS?

Being an ex-Citibanker, Paredes is also interested in credit cards, and it is a part of his customer-centric relationship. Paredes hired "one of the top talents in the region," an ex-Standard Chartered banker named Suba, to run his cards business and help him reach a goal of quadrupling his card base from 250,000 in 2005 to 1 million in 2008, by which time he expects his revolving portfolio to represent 10 percent of his receivables book. In Indonesia, Danamon has taken over the local American Express portfolio as that company converts the portfolios of several countries around the region—Malaysia, the Philippines, Indonesia—from its proprietary cards business to its bank-partnering Global Network Systems business.

While Paredes has both the microfinance and sub-prime business, he is branding it differently than the credit card business as it is largely for different markets. He is also pushing hard with bancassurance proposals, among them insurance for the many motorcycles the bank helps finance a year.

Naturally, with a heavy emphasis on mass retail and its many segments, Paredes has to think of what's going to hit his business the most.

"Clearly right now since the fuel increase, all there is going to be is a very important glitch in this rate of growth, because interest rates are going up, NPLs are going up, and the consumer is going to be affected," he said. "But we believe that Indonesia in the next five years has the potential of selling up to eight million motorcycles a year and if we maintain 12 percent market share, I think we can do the numbers."

Unfortunately, with his focus on lending to the mass market, he has not built up a significant fee-based business, and fees only represent 20 percent of the total operating profit of the bank.

Because it is Indonesia, Paredes is able to see fat margins of 9 percent in his business still—although margins can pass 20 percent in his microfinance business—but he's hit by the reduced volume of lending due to the effect of higher fuel prices and inflation. The bank has built infrastructure for high growth that is not being utilized despite the cost of putting it in. But the bank is constantly pursuing new customers despite the macroeconomic setbacks it gets from one source or another.

With his aggressive growth plan, naturally channels are a key area of focus for Paredes.

"We are focusing on distribution," he said. "First, we closed 54 non-productive branches. With that closure we funded the hiring of 600 salespeople in the current branches. We have revamped our product suite. We have invested substantial amounts in sales training courses and we are investing money and awarding loyalty programs, things that we have not done in the past."

Focusing on branches also includes changing their look and the feel, as well as cutting into his cost base by reducing unique transaction costs through technology to automate the bank and complete his end-to-end processes before he makes his businesses scalable.

With the massive amount of changes that have happened to the bank over the past 10 years—nationalization, consolidation with eight other banks, and a sale to a foreign investor—having a foreign president director running the show is not out of sorts for the bank that has seen almost everything. With an ambitious plan to take on an industry leader in microfinance, the bank is entering a high-growth arena that is not yet its own, but in which it wants to be an able player.

Now that Paredes and his team are delving into the jungles to offer products, the bank is building its own character as an Indonesian lender to the common people. While it is not the first to do so, clearly

Danamon is another one of the banks around the region that is tying its lot to the man on the street, at least in terms of organic growth into relatively open business areas.

With his good humor and optimism, not to mention his youth in an exhausting business that is pushing out into Indonesia's frontiers, Paredes is the perfect antidote to the old school leadership that specialized in backroom deals that were built so high up into the sky that they caused vast destruction when they crashed to earth. And with concerns about the uncertainty a union with BII would cause now out of the way, Paredes's energy and optimism will continue to help him find direction in a bold new bank.

Inch by Inch

What's a smart bank in a tough market to do?

Under its internationally-trained managing director and CEO Rajendra Theagarajah, Hatton National Bank is hoping to become a regional name.

WHILE it is still quite a way from being Sri Lanka's largest privately held bank, Hatton National Bank (HNB) has long been known as a progressive institution that is interested in innovation and sophisticated, progressive banking activities in the conflict-troubled nation. Founded in 1888 as Hatton Bank to cater to the needs of investors and laborers in Ceylon's tea plantations, it took its current name in 1970 when it made its first major acquisition: two local branches of Grindlays Bank.

Since that era, the bank has been steadily gaining assets, branches, staff, and expertise through the acquisition of foreign banks' Sri Lankan businesses as they gradually exited the troubled country. In 1974, it acquired Mercantile Bank of India's branches, and in 1989, it did a similar deal with Emirates Bank. This was followed in 1996 with the purchase of Banque Indosuez's Colombo branch, and in 2002, the Sri Lankan branches of Habib Bank A.G. Zurich.

Rajendra Theagarajah
Reproduced by permission of
TAB International

Rajendra Theagarajah, the bank's managing director and CEO, joined the bank with the Banque Indosuez purchase, where he had been the French lender's deputy country manager. Theagarajah started his career at PricewaterhouseCoopers in Sri Lanka, before going off to Europe to study for an MBA. He joined Chase Manhattan Bank, working in global custody, treasury, and operations in the Europe, Middle East, and the North Africa region before returning to Sri Lanka in 1992 to work for Banque Indosuez.

As HNB's head since January 2005, Theagarajah describes the bank's development from a sleepy player into the country's fourth-largest bank by saying that, "it's grown very much organically for the first 78 years, then you see a combination of organic and inorganic. The retail portfolio is very much an organic growth evolution into semi-urban and rural Sri Lanka, but the corporate and institutional book has developed very much inorganically."

With the most recent purchase in 2002 of Habib Bank's Sri Lankan branches, the bank got a mid-cap commercial portfolio and good corporate and financial institutions accounts and assets, all of which complemented the retail bank.

"And today, the focus to continue will still be organically wherever possible within Sri Lanka," he said. "And as opportunities come, we will make use of inorganic growth, as long as there is incremental plus."

The bank is relatively diversified, with 40 percent of its business in the corporate space, and 60 percent SMEs and retail. Theagarajah prefers to see the large percentage of his business in retail and SME in order to get diversification, but also because ratings under Basel II make retail banking attractive to the bank as a strategic business from the regulator standpoint. But supporting SME is also a national statement as the country's government has put its weight behind developing its small businesses.

As a sophisticated local player, HNB also fits into a unique slot in terms of the type of fee-based services it has access to.

"We feel as a national bank we have a role and opportunity there that some of the bigger foreign players may not want to venture into," said Theagarajah. "And secondly, certain specific areas such as residential mortgages, real estate, and others, come into the upper end of consumer financing that makes it interesting as long as one understands the risk associated and takes the right infrastructural protections. It is interesting—there is a good yield, a good balance."

SMALL BUSINESS IS BIG BUSINESS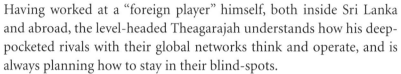

Having worked at a "foreign player" himself, both inside Sri Lanka and abroad, the level-headed Theagarajah understands how his deep-pocketed rivals with their global networks think and operate, and is always planning how to stay in their blind-spots.

For Theagarajah and HNB, SME is the sector with the fastest growth, although the challenge is always how to define SME—the lower end blends with retail, and the top end blends with corporates as large SMEs are often considered small corporates. But for Theagarajah, "the conscious attempt has been made to segmentize and to use the right tools to harness that potential."

Despite SME being one of the bank's specialties, the sector is a challenge in Sri Lanka, and the bank has developed risk management dashboards and other projects with the International Finance Corporation, the private sector finance arm of the World Bank that finances and provides advice for companies in developing markets. Theagarajah is trying to bring professionalism to the bank in terms of resource allocation, systems, capital, and talent. He's also working on changing the mindset of the businesses to help them move to the next level of sophistication as they shift from asset-based lending to cash flow-based lending. This, of course, is a scary move for these businesses since it means reconciling a need for formalized audited accounts. Adventures in business such as these practically require a leap of faith in Sri Lanka, where everyone is shy of bookkeeping, and tax dodging is a national sport.

Clearly, a great deal of education is required, and Theagarajah will need to find out how to, "get them to appreciate the need for reflecting [business] activity in terms of numbers so that lending could be based on numbers rather than bricks-and-mortar assets," he said. "And convincing them of the challenges of better disclosure, which eventually will be a win-win situation for them as they have a requirement for asset-based security, because traditionally Sri Lanka has been a very much asset-backed lending environment, and we are slowly and steadily getting away into cash flow lending."

With the maturation process among his business clients, there comes confidence-building, an especially precious commodity in Sri Lanka. But Theagarajah is not cowed by the challenges of the country and is keeping a cool head, his demeanor measured and nonplussed.

"It is a level playing field here, open to anybody—it is a question of who dares wins," he said of the country's competitive environment. "We currently have 29 licensed banks in Sri Lanka, of which 18 are licensed commercial banks. If you look at 29 banks, you would say for a small economy of 28 billion dollar GDP, it is disproportionately large. But again if you look at the skewedness, the distribution, and the role these people play, you then question if it is large."

> **It is a level playing field here, open to anybody—it is a question of who dares, wins.**

With the emphasis in Sri Lanka on the area immediately around Colombo, where there is access to good infrastructure, Theagarajah is concerned about how wealth creation is being polarized. Banks are trying to use their distribution networks to distribute capital outside of Colombo if they can. A larger number of banks building niches in rural areas may keep too much of the country's wealth from flowing into a handful of Colombo-based lenders.

The bank is working on building its retail banking network to cast a bigger social net, and it is focusing on increasing its capacity in remittances, big business in a country with nearly 20 percent of its citizens working overseas and sending money home and a business where any bank will want to be a big player. A business that requires high volumes to be profitable, remittances also bring much-needed funds into the country and the banks. Theagarajah feels the bank has the second-biggest market share in Sri Lanka for money transfers after the government-owned Bank of Ceylon, the largest bank in the country. He hopes to use remitted funds to add value to the bank and its clients by cross-selling services. But as large as any player is, there is always room to grow, especially in a small market of 20 million.

Nonetheless, he is still hoping to see a greater regimen of consolidation among the country's 29 banks, where there will be opportunities to create synergy and scale.

"There is certainly room for scaling up in developing a few larger banks to compete very effec-

> **When you look at our big neighbor, one needs to look at large banks to even compete with small- to medium-sized Indian banks, which are much larger than most of us.**

tively and go out of Sri Lanka," he said. "Especially when you look at our big neighbor, one needs to look at large banks to even compete with small- to medium-sized Indian banks, which are much larger than most of us."

SPREADING WINGS

And with the bank's history of acquisition, deals are not far from his mind either.

"We will look at other parts of South Asia and certainly Southeast Asia, and that process has already commenced whether it is commercial banking or corporate finance or investment banking, where we believe we have the capability," says Theagarajah.

Having settled on an overseas strategy, Theagarajah is excited about his avenues into India after two years of intense lobbying, and his aim to attack the market through niche services. Theagarajah has signed a memorandum of understanding with City Bank of India to create a joint venture operation that focuses on capital raising and advisory services in the south of India. As one of the oldest private sector banks in India with a history of over 100 years, Theagarajah is very positive about his new partner and is already thinking of how he can broaden the relationship.

Bangladesh is another market where the bank hopes to do work, following the trail of local competitor Commercial Bank, which already has eight branches in the country. The avenue into those markets will definitely be through acquisition of a local player, since "forming a branch and scaling up over another 20 years does not make any sense," he said.

Breaking into a new market means looking at all channels, whether they be accessing local ATM networks or tapping the potential of palmtop banking by PDAs, which require nearly no staff, but are completely mobile.

"You look at a billion people, and then you see what everybody else is following," Theagarajah said.

Yet he is pragmatic and knows he doesn't stand a chance unless he gets his angle right.

> **People who have wealth in Sri Lanka don't have wealth managers, they go to Singapore for that service.**

"And then look at yourself and see what you do with an asset book of 2.5 to 3 billion dollars," he said. "And you compete with a typical competitor from Europe or the U.S., which would have a balance sheet in excess of a hundred billion dollars, what do you do? So, you don't go and knock against what they are trying to do. And you see the differentiator. So you look and see what target they look at, and where is the gap? And if there is something you could do, which even the big Indian boys would not do, and are you comfortable in doing that, and then are you able to find a partner or partners who are willing to perhaps share their networks with your expertise, and you bring in a proposition that makes sense."

On top of the other businesses it is pursuing, the bank is trying to break into new segments of retail banking in Sri Lanka, namely wealth management. While foreign banks have typically owned that space, Theagarajah is keen to become the strong local player in the segment.

"Wealth management is still very new to Sri Lanka, or people who have wealth in Sri Lanka don't have wealth managers, and they go to Singapore," he said. "There is always room for a good strong bank with a strong proposition, and the important thing is the continuity and commitment for long term."

TECHNOLOGY ENABLERS

Theagarajah's specialty is in technology, and he is most comfortable when he is talking about the bank's IT tools and gadgets, particularly in how they interact with the tools and gadgets of society at large.

"And the other area I think, locally, certainly from my bank, we feel the opportunity to grow further is to harness not on bricks and mortars but to use more technology-oriented solutions to bring down the cost and drive volumes," he said. "I look at my own bank. I am probably hitting at two million to 2.5 million customers with a 20 million population. I think I can go to five. I don't need to replicate infrastructure. I need to look at marginal costs."

The bank has invested in Internet banking, SMS, and Internet-enabled phone banking available in three languages anywhere in the world that is GPRS-enabled.

> **Why not have one savings account for every handset? For every guy who has a mobile, you have a relationship.**

"That has a tremendous proposition, especially to our Sri Lankan diaspora, mainly of Tamil origin," said Theagarajah. "If you look at people in Scandinavia, Switzerland, there are people who don't speak good English, who are fearful of going to a typical Internet site because it's in English, or a kiosk; but if you give them something in their own language, and they can access from overseas. All you need is a GPRS connection."

Theagarajah sees the cell phone as a way to win new business. With banks in Sri Lanka short on funds, the two ways of gaining them would either be from other banks, or to find the potential clients out there who are not saving or not banking. The cell phone is everywhere and as infrastructure goes, wireless has the potential to be as useful for banks in developing countries as roads and bridges. Theagarajah is hoping to reach out more to the villages, to bring "top class banking at affordable prices into their localities," as an alternative to local loan sharks and unregulated finance companies. When he sees that nearly half of the people in the country have mobile handsets, he asks "why not have one savings account for every handset? For every guy who has a mobile, you have a relationship. That's where we feel we can start to acquire."

Theagarajah is hoping to leverage not just the cell phone, but also ATMs and POS terminals to reach out to new clients with the bank's low-cost suite of solutions for basic needs.

"The basic thing is a simple savings account, which could be perhaps linked to a small microfinance loan," he said. "ATM is used to leverage everything else, so that the branch is not cluttered. And one thing which is also happening in this market is that certain people like us— I have 3,500 POS terminals in my network—are even looking at harnessing the point of sale (POS) infrastructure beyond pure merchant enquiring. Today, the POS terminal is there just for a credit card to be swiped, that's it. But we see far more opportunities from that same infrastructure in terms of utility payments, loan recoveries, deposits, if it is correctly programmed."

The sedate bank head speaks excitedly about the possibilities offered by this sort of innovation, although he does note that HSBC is doing something similar for its own upscale client set as well. But as a local bank, Theagarajah knows that he can go deeper into the local economy.

SRI LANKA MATURING

Besides his passion for distribution, technology, and innovation, Theagarajah hasn't forgotten the big corporates, and one thing that he feels passionate about is seeing how the bank can make a difference helping local companies. As they stake their claim in the globalization process and the sophistication of their financing changes, a greater deal of trust is needed. And as the mindset of industry changes, and Sri Lankan companies get used to the idea that they can take advantage of sourcing and production in markets such as China and Madagascar, Theagarajah is keen to work at understanding these maturing Sri Lankan companies and take them to another level of development.

"That's a challenge for a few of us," he said. "But I think it should eventually work, because once these guys go global, the diversity in terms of political and country risk becomes manageable and they become more sought after. So, I think we have a strategy to follow some of these big players."

Theagarajah is also seeing commodity exporters, like tea and spice growers, changing as they get smarter about branding and marketing, and take distribution into their own hands.

"This is where we feel our investment banking, corporate finance expertise can come in to convince some of these private family-owned businesses to give up part of their ownership and go and get public listing," said Theagarajah. "Or [they could] get into convertibles, private placements so you have an opportunity to harness those balance sheets, restructure them, and open new windows other than traditional bank financing for them to grow. So we have an important role."

Clearly, the investment banking needs of Sri Lankan companies are not big enough to attract the likes of Merrill Lynch or JPMorgan Chase—although Theagarajah also has competition from Citi, HSBC, and Deutsche Bank, which have offices in Colombo not far from his. But for tea brands that are being sold "from Istanbul to Hanoi to Seoul in any supermarket," clearly there is big business for banks with sophisticated means to help these companies fulfill their potentials.

"Sri Lanka to date has only two companies which have gone out the global depositary receipt (GDR) route," Theagarajah said. "One is the AAA rated corporate John Keells Group, and other one is us. We are the only bank which went out in 2005 into Luxemburg, and that was 10 years after the first company went in. And we have 300 companies listed in the Colombo Stock Exchange. So, you can see the gap and the opportunities for people to professionalize and go out there."

Theagarajah is now hoping to take the pain of issuing its GDRs to leverage its experience in a way that will pay off in the next five years. He counts on the experience of ten years of financing syndicated deals as well as equity through some very tough times in the country, having done deals of up to US$100 million. The bank has also launched a joint venture investment bank with DFCC, the Development Finance Corporation of Ceylon, and it is hoping this expertise and professionalism means that it can look forward to a bright future, even as the country faces continued violence and almost 20 percent inflation.

Clearly, the challenges that lie before it are troubling, especially considering the large number of financial institutions in such a small country. But with more than 6 percent GDP growth in Sri Lanka in 2007, there may just be enough for everyone in spite of the troubles the country is experiencing. Then there is also the chance that a positive outcome with the rebels up north could allow growth to go well beyond that and catch up to what is going on in India, although not many in Sri Lanka see that as a possibility in the near term.

As it diversifies overseas, the bank will become even less and less a local bank and more of a regional player with several specialist areas. And with an internationally-trained CEO who dreams big, HNB may quickly start to become a more recognizable name in overseas markets beyond South Asia as well.

Index